FORD MADOX FORD'S
LITERARY CONTACTS

International
Ford Madox Ford
Studies
Volume 6

General Editor
Max Saunders, King's College London

For information about the Ford Madox Ford Society,
please see the website at:
www.rialto.com/fordmadoxford_society

Or contact:
max.saunders@kcl.ac.uk
or:
Dr Sara Haslam S.J.Haslam@open.ac.uk
Department of Literature, Open University,
Walton Hall, Milton Keynes, MK7 6AA, UK

IFMFS is a peer-reviewed annual series. Guidelines for contrib¬utors, including a full list of abbreviations of Ford's titles and related works, can be found by following the links on the Society's website. Abbreviations used in this volume are listed from p. 265.

Ford Madox Ford's Literary Contacts

Edited by

Paul Skinner

Rodopi

Amsterdam - New York, NY 2007

The Ford Madox Ford Society

Cover illustration: Ford Madox Ford with Ezra Pound; Rapallo, Italy 1932
© Estate of Janice Biala, New York, NY, 2007

Title page illustration: Ford c.1915, pen and ink drawing.
© Alfred Cohen, 2000

Ford Madox Ford, 'To Petronella at Sea', 'Books for Exchange. II', and
quotations from unpublished letters, © Michael Schmidt 2007

The paper on which this book is printed meets the requirements of "ISO
9706: 1994, Information and documentation - Paper for documents -
Requirements for permanence".

ISBN-13: 978-90-420-2248-5
©Editions Rodopi B.V., Amsterdam - New York, NY 2007
Printed in The Netherlands

[I]t is only by exactitude of expression between man and man that honesty and decency in human contacts can be attained to.

(Ford, 'France, 1915 (continued)',
Outlook, 35 (8 May 1915), 599-600.)

Art, you know, is a contagious thing – or rather a thing of contacts.

(Ford to Stella Bowen, early September 1918)

After all, kindness of personal contacts & tentativeness in framing judgements are the real essentials of life – at any rate for me [. . . .]

(Ford to Bowen, 18 Sept. 1918)

The history of the fifty years of contacts with the Great in letters that I have been telling in these vignettes divides itself sharply, like All Gaul, into three parts. Each runs for some time contemporaneously with the others; they never mingle.

(Ford, *Mightier Than the Sword*, 1938)

CONTENTS

GENERAL EDITOR'S PREFACE

Max Saunders

Ford Madox Ford has as often been a subject of controversy as a candidate for literary canonization. He was, nonetheless, a major presence in early twentieth-century literature, and he has remained a significant figure in the history of modern English and American literature for over a century. Throughout that time he has been written about – not just by critics, but often by leading novelists and poets, such as Graham Greene, Robert Lowell, William Carlos Williams, Gore Vidal, A. S. Byatt, and Julian Barnes. His two acknowledged masterpieces have remained in print since the 1940s. *The Good Soldier* now regularly figures in studies of Modernism and on syllabuses. *Parade's End* has been increasingly recognized as comparably important. It was described by Malcolm Bradbury as 'a central Modernist novel of the 1920s, in which it is exemplary'; and by Samuel Hynes as 'the greatest war novel ever written by an Englishman'.

During the last decade or so, there has been a striking resurgence of interest in Ford and in the multifarious aspects of his work. As befits such an internationalist phenomenon as Ford himself, this critical attention has been markedly international, manifesting itself not only in the United Kingdom and the U. S. A., but in Continental Europe and elsewhere. Many of his works have not only been republished in their original language, but also translated into more than a dozen others.

The founding of the International Ford Madox Ford Studies series reflects this increasing interest in Ford's writing and the wider understanding of his role in literary history. Each volume is normally based upon a particular theme or issue, and relates aspects of Ford's work, life, and contacts, to broader concerns of his time. Previous volumes have focused on ideas of Modernity, History, the City, and Englishness.

This sixth volume represents part of an ambitious project initiated by the Ford Madox Ford Society to reappraise Ford's situation in literary history. Future volumes are planned on his responses to cultural transformations, and on his activities as an editor working to transform modern writing. The present volume, originating from a creative suggestion by its editor, Paul Skinner, explores Ford's literary imbrication from another point of view, considering his 'literary contacts' with other writers. Such 'contacts' include some of the many writers Ford knew personally, from Turgenev to Graham Greene. But, as Skinner put it in his invitation to contributors, 'literary contact' is also a matter of 'influence', 'understood here as including figures influencing Ford, and also those influenced by him. The volume is based on the premise that "major" writers don't just build on the work of other "major" writers, that influence (positive or negative) sometimes comes from the peripheral characters and that, for instance, the major modernists often took off from less well-known or less-successful artists, either reaching beyond or over them, even frankly stealing things that hadn't been made the most of. Ford's relations with writers such as James, Conrad, Crane, Pound, and Rhys have been well-studied. Rather than sustained revaluations of such contacts, this volume covers the less obvious but nonetheless revealing figures'.

Two short but revealing pieces are published here for the first time. One, by Ford himself, is an early manuscript discussing the importance to him of Turgenev, in ways which also elaborate the meanings of 'literary contacts'. The other is a biographical sketch of Ford and Violet Hunt, written by the novelist and autobiographer Marie Belloc Lowndes (the sister of Hilaire Belloc).

As Skinner says in the Introduction, the number of writers Ford discusses is immense. A single volume of this scale could not possibly cover them all. Separate volumes could be devoted to Ford's reading of the Classics, his contacts with the Pre-Raphaelites, German literature, French Literature, the Imagists, or American writers of the 1920s and 1930s; and indeed the Society hopes to examine such areas in future publications.

The list could easily be extended, and doubtless readers will compile their own groupings of significant contacts and networks of writers and other artists with whose work Ford interacts. I was struck to see that (with the exception of my own essay) contributors had not opted for the more prominent contenders, such as those to whom Ford devoted chapters of *Mightier Than the Sword* (*Portraits from Life* in the U. S. A.) – Hardy, Wells, Lawrence, Galsworthy, Hudson, Dreiser. But it is often the less-expected contacts detailed here that place his achievements in a new perspective, and a new light. What such thoughts, and books such as this one, bring home, is how much exciting work there still remains to be done on Ford's voracious reading, prolific critical writing, and profound deployments in intertextuality, as well as on his ever-deepening literary legacy. All in all, it helps us to gauge the extent to which Ford was truly 'a writer's writer' or 'a novelist's novelist'.

The series is published in association with the Ford Madox Ford Society. Forthcoming and projected volumes will be announced on the Society's website, together with details of whom to contact with suggestions about future volumes or contributions. The address is: www.rialto.com/fordmadoxford_society

INTRODUCTION

Paul Skinner

Ford Madox Ford's complicated inheritance from his upbringing amidst 'the hothouse atmosphere of Pre-Raphaelism'[1] included a characteristically ambivalent attitude towards groups and movements. Both fascinated and repelled by the 'tremendous quarrels' which characterised Pre-Raphaelite interrelations, while also noting the mutual support and artistic solidarity, Ford remarked that 'any sort of union for an aesthetic or for an intellectual purpose seems to be almost an impossibility' (*MI* 25). They did things differently in France, naturally – and it remained Ford's conviction that '[i]t is only by movements that literature can be carried forward…'.[2]

Ford was at or near the centre of several distinct groupings during his lifetime. At the close of the nineteenth-century and the opening of the twentieth, he was a member of H. G. Wells' 'ring of foreign conspirators plotting against British letters'.[3] The *English Review* circle overlapped with the literary-political complexities of both Imagism and Vorticism, launching distinguished literary careers, seminal anecdotes and personal mythologies. After the First World War, the *transatlantic review* was a brief but lastingly significant feature of literary Paris, while, in the 1930s, in the United States, there were other, smaller groupings, not least 'Les Amis de William Carlos Williams', as Christopher MacGowan recounts in his essay for this volume.

And what of Ford's contacts with the unaligned, those novelists, poets and essayists not customarily associated with any group or movement or who might seem to transcend them? Sometimes it seems as though he must have been at least acquainted with them all. Yet there are marked absences, oddities and silences. Among the major modernists, Ford maintained a close, if sometimes fractious, friendship with Ezra Pound for thirty years. He knew and got on well with Joyce; knew and did not get on so well with Wyndham Lewis. Of Yeats, Woolf and Eliot, there has seemed, thus far, little to say in relation to Ford. And, while we have had several excellent studies of Ford's literary relations with Pound, James, Conrad, Joyce, Crane and

others, many more names suggest themselves, people with whom Ford
was closely acquainted, or who crop up repeatedly in his writings, or
who write about him. Some have been attended to in the pages that
follow. Dozens of others await, and surely deserve, similar attention.
Though 'major' writers may dominate a period in literary history's
retrospective gaze, and serve, perhaps, as landmarks, similar to those
principles which are "'like a skeleton map of a country – you know
whether you're going east or north'",[4] true knowledge of that country
requires a wider and deeper ranging.

Ford's dealings with some writers will never be known. There is
an enlightening moment in an interview with Janice Biala, when she is
asked about Ford's daily reading. She says: 'He didn't have time for
that kind of reading. He was always reading books that other writers
had sent him or manuscripts. When he was writing *The March of
Literature* he reread everything he wrote about'.[5] For those not
acquainted with this work, it contains nearly 900 pages and deals with
world literature from the classic Greek and Latin authors to the early
twentieth century: many hundreds of books in many languages. He
'reread everything he wrote about'. It is, in its way, a remarkable
testament to a man in his mid-sixties, often in ill-health, who
remained, always, rather more than a little 'mad about writing'.[6]

Ford's sense of collaboration and community weathered more
than the storms which assailed him as editor. Strikingly, even in his
efforts to reject or shake off some elements of his bulky inheritance,
that sense remains strong, rendered highly visible in the knots and
clusters that his attention shapes. There are the Victorian figures
whom he frequently sees and presents *as* figures: Ruskin, Carlyle,
Holman Hunt, or 'the gentleman who built the Crystal Palace' (*MI*
xiii). He gets swiftly into his stride when recalling what, as boys, he
and his friends tried to read of those familiar names, Swinburne,
Tennyson, Browning and Pope (Pope's sins, clearly, sufficing to
catapult him forward into the company of the Victorian great). 'We
couldn't read any of them – we simply and physically couldn't sit
down with them in the hand for long enough to master more than a
few lines'.[7] Just as briskly does he dispose of the poets of the 1890s,
'– Dowson, Johnson, Davidson, and the rest – struck us as just
nuisances' (*CP1* 23). These are conscious stratagems. Ford wants and
needs to outdistance those Victorian giants, those Great Figures who
blotted out the light and sucked the air from the world. He needs also
to convey how the revered Victorian poets left those younger readers

with the impression that poetry must be 'boring and pretentious' (*CP1* 22) – because he wants a poetry, and a language, capable of embracing and articulating the prosaic facts of crowded modern cities, their lights and noise and cafés and traffic. None of it diverts us from the recognition of how much Ford loves to name writers, to list them, to revel in them, not merely as a critical strategy but for the joy of it. Notwithstanding his ability to register and articulate subtle discriminations among the works of individual writers, Ford is drawn irresistibly to the plural, the multiple, the lavish. In his short book on *The English Novel*, barely 30,000 words long, he manages to name (or clearly allude to) upwards of one hundred and sixty writers, plus Bach and a handful of painters.

For many readers, Ford remains the author of *The Good Soldier* and perhaps the four volumes – or three! – that make up *Parade's End*. Yet serious claims have been made for many of his other books, including the memoirs, *It Was the Nightingale* and *Return to Yesterday*; the autobiographical fiction *No Enemy*; his trilogy called, in the omnibus editions, *England and the English*; and the extraordinary, unclassifiable late works, *Provence* and *Great Trade Route*. These are remarkably varied works but again, one feature common to almost all of them is precisely that they *swarm* with writers, writers known personally or writers read, in such a manner as to call into question that very boundary so confidently drawn between 'known' and 'read'. Ford did indeed feel a strong and direct contact with the writers whom he admired. There is a real sense of a horizontal plane across which they are ranged and on which they might, at any time, be encountered. Richard Aldington recalled Ford keeping his (Aldington's) father amused with tales of his meetings with literary figures. Then Ford embarked on the tale of his encounter with Byron: 'I saw my father stiffen'.[8] Aldington presents this simply as an instance of Ford telling tall stories to a credulous listener. Yet there is something else here, something in the vividness of feeling, the vividness of *telling*, that breaches the walls constructed around such processes, a glimpse too of what enabled Ford to remain the kind of reader of other people's books that he desired for his own.

(1) Predecessors

The essays that follow are arranged, for the most part, in chronological order and are divided into three sections, roughly 'predecessors', 'contemporaries and confrères', and 'successors'. The earliest

'contacts' here are nineteenth-century ones, precursors but not, by any
means, obvious 'influences': George Borrow, Anthony Trollope,
George Eliot, Ivan Turgenev. Though not by design, this quartet offers
a wonderful mapping of the kinds of relationship that Ford had with
his predecessors and the ways in which they developed.

D. H. Lawrence told Jessie Chambers that Borrow 'had mingled
autobiography and fiction so inextricably in *Lavengro* that the most
astute critics could not be sure where the one ended and the other
began'.[9] Curiously, since it seemed to become almost obligatory for
many years to say something similar of Ford, Ford himself had doubts
about the wisdom of Borrow's playing fast and loose with the facts, as
Helen Southworth discusses in the course of a wide-ranging analysis
of the two writers, which also considers the ways in which Borrow's
ideas about nationality, and the relationship between the city and the
countryside, may have helped to shape Ford's own.

When he weighed together George Eliot and Anthony Trollope
in *The Critical Attitude*, Ford set against an Eliot who had become
'inflated by the idea of the writer as prophet' the novels ('hardly
constructed at all') of Trollope ('never remarkably engrossing') who
was, however, 'content to observe and record'.[10] Fifteen years later,
one of the sins of 'Trollopism' had become 'the author's comments'
but, perhaps more revealingly, while Ford was clearly delighted by
John Rodker's remarking that *The Good Soldier* was 'the finest
French novel in the English language', Trollope, Ford believed,
'would have been mildly disgusted'.[11] Monica C. Lewis examines
Ford's   ambivalent and evolving view of Trollope and the
preoccupations that they shared, particularly those of *character*, with
its pleasingly fluid meanings, and the construction and analysis of the
figure of the English gentleman. Sara Haslam reviews Ford's dealings
with George Eliot, focusing on the relatively few instances of his
critical attention to Eliot's work – and placing them in revealing
context – to ask whether Eliot did indeed influence Ford's approach to
writing, and just what part the figure of Henry James played in
constructing Ford's view of her. James was one of the recent writers
whom Ford saw as having truly advanced the art of the novel, along
with Conrad, Flaubert and Turgenev. Max Saunders draws on a
previously unpublished Fordian manuscript as a point of departure for
his scrutiny of the Ford-Turgenev relationship and a close
consideration of what 'literary contact' actually comprised for Ford.

Through a careful reading of Ford's critical responses to Turgenev, he charts the evolution of the Russian's exemplary role for him.

(2) Contemporaries and Confrères

Ford never forgot the phrase that his father applied to him, 'the patient but extremely stupid donkey' (*MI* xi), nor the apparent favouring of his younger brother, Oliver, who later produced volumes about England, France and New York, as well as a dozen novels. It is the relationship between the two brothers *as writers* that here engages Joseph Wiesenfarth's attention. Querying why Ford's writings about the same places have survived and Oliver's almost completely disappeared, Wiesenfarth points up the significant differences between them, and particularly considers the role of 'work' in the making of both the cities that attracted Ford and the books he wrote about them.

Ford's friendship with the Garnett family also went back to his childhood and when, in 1898, Ford was living with his wife Elsie at Limpsfield, close to the home of Constance and Edward Garnett, it was Edward that brought Joseph Conrad to meet him. Here too Ford met David Soskice, the Russian political exile who subsequently married Ford's sister Juliet. Ford's later relationship with Edward Garnett is the subject of Helen Smith's essay. Partly territorial, partly a matter of literary predilection, this is an intriguing, not always salutary, story of Garnett attempting to make Joseph Conrad in a Slavic image while Ford tugs him towards the French, a battle complicated in part by the Pole's fierce dislike of all things Russian. David Soskice, who later became involved in the financing and administration of Ford's *English Review*, is the main focus of Anat Vernitski's essay, which also looks more broadly at the history of Russian revolutionary exiles in early twentieth century Britain. She examines Ford's responses to them, and the Russian references in several of his books, particularly the 1912 satire, *The New Humpty-Dumpty*, written as 'Daniel Chaucer'.

In the immediate pre-war period, two of Ford's preoccupations were the launching and editing of the *English Review* (1908-9) and his affair with Violet Hunt, which involved a long sojourn in Giessen in a doomed attempt to secure a 'German divorce'. Marie Belloc Lowndes, in her day a remarkably successful practitioner of detective fiction and also a memoirist of repute, knew both Hunt and Ford. Susan Lowndes Marques here introduces a revealing and refreshingly unbuttoned account, written late in life and previously unpublished, in which

Belloc Lowndes recalls the period and the view taken of the couple in their social circle of that time. The prodigiously talented Rebecca West also knew both Ford and Violet Hunt, having met the couple when her unsigned review of *The New Humpty-Dumpty* identified Ford as its author. Six years later, West published *The Return of the Soldier*, and Seamus O'Malley looks at the relationship between that first novel and Ford's post-war masterpiece, *Parade's End*. Moving beyond the common themes of the shell-shocked officer and the insep-arability of war zone and home front, O'Malley reviews both writers' use of pastoral and asserts not only affinity but influence – from the younger to the older writer – arguing that Ford's novel can be seen as a more optimistic reworking of West's. Another wartime perspective emerges from the essay by Jörg Rademacher, who places Ford's influential poem 'In October 1914' (later re-titled *Antwerp*) in the cultural context of three contemporary German writers. Ford's poem was written before he had seen active service, and Rademacher sets it beside the work of two poets who died in the conflict and a novelist who survived it, finding unexpected affinities between them all.

Ford's post-war years in Sussex were followed by the move to France. At that time, he was in frequent contact with Herbert Read, whom he had met in 1917. Later to become one of the most celebrated and widely-read commentators on modern art, Read was then determined to make his mark as poet and novelist. Michael Paraskos recounts the story surrounding this crucial moment in Read's early career, a moment highly significant for Ford also, in the period im-mediately following his demobilization and his meeting with Stella Bowen. It was a relatively brief but certainly, for Read, a formative relationship, nicely illuminated here. Within a day of Ford and Stella arriving in Paris, Marcel Proust died. In a memorable section of *It Was the Nightingale* Ford cites that as a major impetus behind the writing of *Parade's End* and the two writers are often bracketed together with other modernists of their generation – but normally without much further comment. Here, starting with precisely that Fordian passage, John Coyle offers a corrective to this, with a suggestive analysis of mourning and rumour in the two writers' work, drawing out the differing aspects of memory characteristic of each of them. The early Paris years also included the early stages of two significant relation-ships with American writers for Ford. Susan Swartzlander writes about a famous collision: that between the brash new rising star Ernest Hemingway, who arrived in Paris in 1924, and the editor of *the transatlantic review,* just embarking upon the second major phase of his career. She tenaciously pursues the traces of Hemingway's responses to Ford's writing in his own texts, and his parodic opposition to Ford's influence. Christopher MacGowan surveys the relationship between Ford and William Carlos Williams, who finally met in Paris in early 1924. The story is illuminated here by MacGowan's perceptive and tactful analysis of Williams' national and familial history, and his exposition of the ways in which the two men's views of one another shifted over time, each finding or shaping a figure of both immediate value and representative significance.

From the mid-1920s, much of Ford's time was spent in America – and on journeys between the two continents. A 1927 shipboard meeting and possible romance, teasingly implied by the dedication in a copy he acquired of Ford's *A Mirror to France,* is the focus of Brian Ibbotson Groth's confrontation with this new biographical mystery, setting this suggestive detail beside Ford's poem, 'To Petronella at Sea' and exploring the possibility that 'Petronella' referred to Jean Rhys. Stephen Rogers's essay takes off from the brief mention in John Cowper Powys's *Autobiography* of his meeting with Ford in New York at the close of the 1920s. Considering the literary attitudes they shared (and those they didn't), it also discusses the changing cultural paradigms in the interwar period that moved these and other writers towards a greater didacticism and prophetic strain.

While the fortunes of the *transatlantic review* circle tend to bulk large in the postwar story, four other, smaller 'communities' come to mind. Two are closely related: Ford and Stella Bowen – and then their daughter Julie – in Sussex, from 1919 to 1922; and the later re-creation of many features of that milieu in *Last Post.* A central character of the novel, Mark's wife Marie-Léonie, was apparently based on Josette, the wife of the painter Juan Gris. They had been introduced to Ford and Bowen by Gertrude Stein in 1924 and during a holiday in Toulon in the winter of 1925-6, they all spent a good deal of time together. Their circle included Francis Carco, author of *Perversité* and Georges Duthuit, whose father-in-law, Henri Matisse, subsequently dined with Ford and Bowen early in 1926.[12] The following year, though, Gris died and the close relationship between Ford and Stella was by then drawing to its end. Ford was already spending much time in America, as he continued to do throughout the 1930s, when he supported and encouraged a remarkable number of young writers, a high proportion of them women who later achieved great distinction, including Eudora Welty, Jean Stafford and Elizabeth Madox Roberts. Listing such names highlights once more the inescapable fact that it has not been possible to deal with several of Ford's important literary relationships here. Two of the writers most closely associated with him, Jean Rhys and Violet Hunt, have been treated extensively in Joseph Wiesenfarth's recent book.[13] Another celebrated writer who can be mentioned in this connection is Caroline Gordon. She and her husband, the poet and critic Allen Tate, spent time with Ford in Provence, Paris and Tennessee, most famously in the summer of 1937, when Ford, Biala and Biala's sister-in-law were guests in the Tates' house, while the young Robert Lowell pitched a tent on the lawn and stayed for weeks.[14] The famous picnic at Cassis had taken root not only in Ford's *Provence* and Tate's poem, 'The Mediterranean', but had spread further, into the complex discussions about the cultural regeneration of the South which so exercised Tate, Andrew Lytle and others, and into Caroline Gordon's fiction. That summer of 1937 similarly grew and was transformed, spreading itself into letters, memoirs and legends – and also into Gordon's novel, *The Strange Children*.[15] This was, perhaps, the last of Ford's 'literary' communities, his death less than two years away, though he found kindred spirits at Olivet College in Michigan and among friends and neighbours in his beloved Provence. Years of shrinking cultural circles in one sense, then, yet he was concurrently engaged on the grand scale with the entire history of world literature. 'Writers walked through his mind and his life', Lowell wrote, recalling Ford's armfuls of Loeb classics and unpublished manuscripts:

> young ones to be discovered, instructed, and entertained; contemporaries to be assembled, telegraphed, and celebrated; the dead friend to be resurrected in anecdote; the long, long dead to be freshly assaulted or defended.[16]

(3) Successors

The final section of the volume looks at five figures who, though alive in Ford's lifetime (only just, in a couple of cases), were not 'confrères' in the same sense. Corwin Baden has fashioned, from a sparse array of sources – one letter, one brief meeting and a few critical references – the unfamiliar pairing of Ford and Richard Hughes, linking them not only by Ford's admiration for Hughes' early novels, *A High Wind in Jamaica* and *In Hazard*, but also the figure of Joseph Conrad, with whom Hughes was often compared. Graham Greene did meet Ford, but his writing career seems overwhelmingly post-Fordian, even in defiance of mere chronology. Bernard Bergonzi revisits that relationship and Greene's view of Ford as it emerges in his many writings about him, not least in his highly controversial edition of Ford's work for the Bodley Head, which severed *Last Post* from Ford's tetralogy. Angus Wrenn explores, provisionally yet not tentatively, the afterlife of Ford's work in the plays of Harold Pinter, taking as his point of departure a moment in Pinter's *Betrayal* – itself a wonderful exploration of the uncertain, the unreliable, the just possible – and looking particularly at Ford's 1910 novel *A Call* but also, more obliquely, at *The Good Soldier*. A. S. Byatt has written several times on Ford's work, showing herself to be one of his most intelligent and knowledgeable critics. Laura Colombino here trains her sharp gaze upon Byatt's fiction as well as her essays to compare the two writers' representations of the past, discovering links and affinities between them, focusing particularly on *Some Do Not . . .* and *The Virgin in the Garden*. One of Ford's staunchest admirers and most eloquent champions was the novelist and critic Anthony Burgess. William Mill examines the grounds of Burgess's admiration and looks at Ford's appearances in Burgess's novels and autobiographies, particularly at the comedic consequences of the recurrent play on names, changed and pseudonymous. Mill's essay concludes by revisiting Burgess's 1980 masterpiece, *Earthly Powers*, in which Ford appears as a character.

Of all the contacts reviewed here, in fact, it is Burgess who most brings Ford himself to mind: the tremendous energy and capacity for *work*, the huge appetite for literature and for life that both men shared. And 'Earthly' is, after all, *le mot juste*. Ford is not Utopian and his scale is a human one, though at its upper end, as we're reminded by the epithets he tended to prompt in his contemporaries – walrus, elephant, whale, pink and lemon giant, behemoth – and the envisaged place, that circle or community, if ideal, is still not unduly idealized. Ford may indeed have wondered, as John Dowell asks, why people can't have what they want when the things are 'all there to content everybody',[17] a question that has not lost its painful relevance. But he found his answers for himself: eco-warrior before his time, men, women and children around the dinner table – one made, perhaps, from the bottom boards of boats, set up on a beach where Aeneas might have landed, or Ulysses taken shelter, good food and wine and always, close at hand, or in memory's strong stream, the countless books and writers, those who danced and gave pleasure.

NOTES

1   Ford, *Memories and Impressions*, New York: Harper, 1911 – henceforth *MI*; p. 216.

2   Ford, 'Literary Portraits – I. Mr. Compton Mackenzie and "Sinister Street"', *Outlook*, 32 (13 September 1913), 354.

3   Ford, *Return to Yesterday*, London: Victor Gollancz, 1931, p. 20.

4   Ford, *Parade's End*, New York: Vintage, 1979, p. 144.

5   Sondra Stang, editor, *The Presence of Ford Madox Ford*, Philadelphia: University of Pennsylvania Press, 1981, p. 225.

6   Ford, 'The Poet's Eye – I', *New Freewoman*, I, 6 (1 September 1913), 108; 'Dedicatory Letter to Stella Ford', *The Good Soldier*, edited by Martin Stannard, New York and London: W. W. Norton, 1995, p. 3.

7   Ford, *Collected Poems*, London: Max Goschen, 1913 – henceforth *CP1*; p. 21.

8   See Richard Aldington, *Life for Life's Sake*, London: Cassell, 1968, p. 137.

9   Jessie Chambers, *D. H. Lawrence: A Personal Record*, Cambridge: Cambridge University Press, 1980, p. 110.

10 Ford, *The Critical Attitude*, London: Duckworth, 1911, pp. 56-7.

11 Ford, *New York Essays*, New York: William Edwin Rudge, 1927, p. 16.

12 See Max Saunders, *Ford Madox Ford: A Dual Life*, 2 volumes, Oxford: Oxford University Press, 1996, vol. 2, pp. 289-90.

13 Joseph Wiesenfarth, *Ford Madox Ford and the Regiment of Women: Violet Hunt, Jean Rhys, Stella Bowen, Janice Biala*, Madison and London: The University of Wisconsin Press, 2005.

14 The picnic, attended by Ford, Biala and the Tates, took place on 16th August 1932 (the day after the Feast of the Assumption of the Blessed Virgin Mary): see Ford's *Provence*, London: Allen & Unwin, 1938, p. 291. On the summer of 1937, see Ann Waldron, *Close Connections: Caroline Gordon and the Southern Renaissance*, New York: G. B. Putnam's Sons, 1987, pp. 15-25; Saunders, vol. 2, pp. 508-10; Allen Tate, 'Ford Madox Ford', in *The Presence of Ford Madox Ford*, p. 12; Robert Lowell, 'Visiting the Tates', in *Collected Prose*, New York: The Noonday Press, 1990, pp. 58-60.

15 In 'The Waterfall' (1950), a story incorporated, with changes, into *The Strange Children*, a writer whose most famous poem was written at Cassis recalls the picnic there which lasted three days: *The Collected Stories of Caroline Gordon*, Baton Rouge: Louisiana State University Press, 1991, p. 263. The fictional frame is fractured at one point in the story when the title of a painting is identified as 'Life at Benfolly' (the farm owned by Tate and Gordon) and the painter as 'Biala' (p. 268). There are other Fordian allusions in 'The Olive Garden' (pp. 306-16). The novel includes an explicit memory of 1937: 'That big Englishman and his wife and secretary and the young poet from Boston were all here then'. See Gordon, *The Strange Children*, London: Routledge & Kegan Paul, 1952, p. 105.

16 Lowell, 'Ford Madox Ford', in *Collected Prose*, p. 4.

17 Ford, *The Good Soldier*, p. 151.

'THAT SUBTLE AND DIFFICULT THING: A NATIONAL SPIRIT': FORD, ANGLO-SAXONDOM AND 'THE GORGEOUSLY ENGLISH' GEORGE BORROW

Helen Southworth

Ford's references to the now largely overlooked eccentric Victorian travel writer, amateur ethnographer and gypsiologist George Borrow (1803-1881), author most famously of *Lavengro* and *The Bible in Spain*, are numerous. Ford refers to Borrow in his critical work and in his non-fiction writing about place and he also uses a scene from Borrow's *Lavengro* as the source for two early poems. He employed Borrow creatively and nostalgically in *The Cinque Ports* (1900) and in the Pre-Raphaelite inspired *Poems for Pictures* (1900) early on in his writing career, and then returned to Borrow's work from a stylistic perspective in his later critical writings, such as *Thus to Revisit* (1921). And in what constitutes the most detailed discussion of his predecessor's work, in 1913 Ford wrote a quite lengthy review of Clement Shorter's biography of the man he provocatively labels 'the gorgeously English [...] George Borrow'.[1]

Ford read Borrow in the late nineteenth century; he tells us in his review of Shorter's *George Borrow and his Circle* that 'as a boy' he had '[Borrow's] the *Romany Rye* [*Lavengro*'s sequel] almost by heart' ('Mr. Clement Shorter' 678). Indeed Borrow was a popular figure among English writers, composers and artists at the turn of the century. At this time his books were taught in secondary schools and reprinted with regularity; thus Borrow frequently represents a childhood memory, revived in adulthood. The list of those, many modernists among them, who make reference to his life and work, sometimes cursory, sometimes detailed, includes Augustus John, Virginia Woolf, E. M. Forster, Wyndham Lewis, D. H. Lawrence, T. S. Eliot, Paul Nash, and Ralph Vaughan Williams. Ford shared an interest in Borrow with some of the *English Review* travel writer contributors, such as Borrovian biographer Edward Thomas whose *The Heart of England* was published in the same year as Ford's similarly titled *The Heart of the Country*, the second volume of *England and the English*.[2] It is possible that Ford's interest in Borrow was also spurred by his Pre-Raphaelite family ties. Ford's uncle by marriage, Dante Gabriel Rossetti, had Gypsies pose for his paintings. Ford's family lawyer, Theodore Watts-Dunton, was a friend of Borrow and the author of the immensely popular Gypsy novel *Aylwin* (1898). Ford at one point mocks Watts-Dunton for a contrived dedication to Gypsy lore with a reference to Isopel Berners, the love interest of Borrow's protagonist in *Lavengro*. Ford, forgetting that Isopel was a traveller but not a Gypsy, wrote that *Aylwin* 'was what his friends called bilge, and his innumeral poems seemed to be all devoted to proving that he had once been kissed by a Rommany lal ... a sort of watered-down Isopel Berners ...'.[3]

Borrow's idiosyncratic Englishness and his unorthodox approach to national identity appealed to Ford and his fellow modernists in the transitional years of pre-war England. Borrow's work sheds light on Ford's ideas about the relationships between town and country, and between nation and place. He associated Borrow with what he called 'Anglo-Saxondom': in *The March of Literature* Ford cites *The Bible in Spain*, Borrow's most popular book, as an example of the type of book in which 'Anglo-Saxondom particularly excels,' although it does not represent a peak at a period where 'great peaks,' he suggests, are few and far between.[4] The bohemian, impressionistic quality of Borrow's work spoke to Ford as he set out to record what he called 'that subtle and difficult thing', the 'spirit' of the English, in works such as *The Cinque Ports* and *England and the English*.[5] Borrow's 'foreignness', his Defoe-inspired, 'True-Born Englishman' emphasis on the mixedness of the English, represents a source for what Ian Baucom defines as Ford's place-based, rather than blood-linked, theories about national identity in his *England and the English*.[6] Borrow cites both Defoe's *Robinson Crusoe* and his *Moll Flanders* in *Lavengro* and indeed describes his book as an autobiography in the style of *Robinson Crusoe*.[7]

Borrow's oeuvre consists of mostly semi-fictional travel writing, focused first predominantly on Spain (*The Zincali* and *The Bible in Spain*) and, after approximately 1850, on his native Britain (*Lavengro*, its sequel *The Romany Rye*, and *Wild Wales*). Credited by biographers with knowledge of between thirty and forty foreign languages, Borrow engaged in translation, from Danish and Welsh, and in amateur philology, such as his study of the Romani language entitled *Romano Lavo-Lil*. He also collected and translated folk songs and poetry. As Ford himself notes, while Borrow frames his work as non-fictional ethnography and as autobiography, much of the content is factually dubious, which seems to have delighted Ford and, to a large extent, been the source of its value for him.[8] While best known for his Gypsies, most notably Jasper Petulengro, and for Isopel Berners, with whom Lavengro lives for a time in Mumpers' Dingle, both featured in *Lavengro* and *The Romany Rye*, Borrow's works are populated by a wide variety of eccentrics, many of them of mixed or uncertain national origin, and the relationship between races is a central theme in his work. Although Borrow's narrators spend time in cities, they are drawn to the countryside and to the wild and sequestered places found there. Borrow, in his semi-fictional manifestation as Lavengro, highlights his mixed Cornish and Norman heritage; he traveled extensively, first in the employ of the Bible Society for which he circulated the scriptures, as his *The Bible in Spain* subtitle makes clear: *Or, the Journeys, Adventures, and Imprisonments of an Englishman in An Attempt to Circulate the Scriptures in the Peninsula*. Having relocated in England he nevertheless maintained his peripatetic ways. Borrow's work is 'perambulatory', he is a 'man of the road' according to biographer Michael Collie, in the sense that there is a picaresque, an unanchored, topsy-turvy (to borrow Leslie Stephen's term for Borrow's universe)[9] quality to his work, one which, for Collie, translates into a patriotism free of 'the aspects of Empire that were a blight upon English life' (Collie 228). In this way, Borrow suggested an interesting precedent to writers and artists of Ford's generation as they negotiated questions of nationalism and cosmopolitanism, both in a general sense and in terms of writing.

The Cuckoo and the Gipsy, City and Country

Picking up on an oft cited passage, Ford prefaces his poem 'The Cuckoo and The Gipsy', originally published in the *Speaker* in 1898[10] and then as 'The Gipsy and the Cuckoo' in *Poems for Pictures and for Notes of Music* in 1900, with an epigraph from chapter IX of Borrow's *Lavengro* sequel, *The Romany Rye*.[11] This passage is a popular one because it captures the tenor of Borrow's book as a whole in its sympathy for the freedoms available to the itinerant and in its celebration of roguishness. Ford chose one series of lines for the original publication and then substituted it with a second more concise version of the same lines in *Poems for Pictures*: the speakers' names are erased in the second version. Both epigraphs are conversations between Gypsy Jasper Petulengro and the narrator, Lavengro, also called Romany Rye or Gypsy Gentleman. In the first of the two epigraphs, the Romany Rye questions Jasper about his life as a Gypsy. When Jasper says 'We are not miserable, brother', the Romany Rye asserts '[w]ell, then you ought to be, Jasper. Have you an inch of ground your own? Are you of the least use? Are you not spoken ill of by everybody? What is a gipsy?' Jasper then replies with a question about the identity of the bird 'yonder', to which the Romany Rye replies 'that's a cuckoo tolling, but what has the cuckoo to do with the matter?' The question is left open in anticipation of the poem. The second epigraph (which is a paraphrase) clarifies the connection further. The epigraph opens with Jasper's question about the bird, to which the Romany Rye replies simply 'that's a cuckoo'. Jasper then asks '[h]e's a roguish chaffing sort of bird, isn't he, brother?' When the Romany Rye agrees, Jasper continues with 'But you rather like him, brother? . . . Well, brother, and what's a gipsy?'[12]

The poem itself is a dialogue between two different but not inconsistent viewpoints, the Romany Rye's and the Gypsy's. Detailed further in the poem is the role of the Gypsy, and the cuckoo, in the maintenance of a traditional image of the countryside. Unlike the first epigraph, the speaker is not indicated in the poem. Jasper appears to be speaking, however, as the last line of the second stanza suggests: 'And the long white road more weary/ If we never came'. The third and last stanza changes form. Ford's poem closes on a series of questions challenging and rejecting an impulse, on the part of the non-Gypsy, to bring order to the natural disorder of the countryside: 'Would your May days seem more fair/ Were we chals deep-read in books,/ Were we cuckoos cawing rooks,/ All the brakes cathedral closes/ Where the very sunlight dozes,/ Were the sounds all organ tone and book and bell and prayer?' (*Selected Poems* 8).

When the poem first appeared it was accompanied by a 'dialogue pendant to [the poem]' entitled 'The Gipsy and the Townsman', suggesting the two should be read together. This connection is not made, however, in the first edition of *Poems for Pictures* or in the later *Collected Poems* (1936) where the two appear separately.[13] In the second of the two poems, Ford moves further from Borrow as he imagines a single but lengthier exchange between the Gipsy and the Townsman (the country and the city), notably *not* here the Romany Rye. The townsman comments that while it is '[p]leasant enough' (this repeated three times), to live outside presumably, in the summer time, in 'the seed-time', 'the hay-time', 'the grain-time', how, he asks, does the Gypsy fare during the winter, during the 'need-time-/ The grey-time-/ The rain-time-?' The Gypsy replies with a description of the countryside as bleak in the winter, but less so than the modern town: 'But there's smoke and wind and woe in the town/ Harder to bear/ There than here,/ On the saddest day of the weariest year' (*Selected Poems* 9).

Christina Rossetti's Pre-Raphaelite poetry likely influenced Ford's earlier poems, especially the love lyrics of *Poems for Pictures* alongside which these poems appeared.[14] Suggesting further Pre-Raphaelite ties, among the other poems included in the volume are one 'suggested by' George Meredith's poem 'Phoebus with Admetus' and a song drama entitled 'King Cophetua's Wooing', based on Alfred Tennyson's *The Beggar Maid* (written in 1833, published in 1842), and Edward Burne-Jones' painting *King Cophetua and the Beggar Maid* (1884). The first of the Borrow poems resembles Pre-Raphaelite poetry in the sense that it is nostalgic, suggested by another literary source, has a ballad-like dialogue form, and a romantic figure of sorts for a protagonist. The Gypsy focus and the shape (rhyme scheme, enjambment, internal rhyme, anaphora) and antiquated, pastoral tone of the poem is reminiscent of George Meredith's poems such as 'Juggling Jerry', focused on the Gypsy-like juggler (although the juggler asserts 'I, lass, have liv'd no gypsy, flaunting/ Finery while his poor helpmate grubs').[15]

'The Cuckoo and the Gipsy' is a nostalgic argument for pre-serving the countryside as it is and, in this way, it anticipates the nostalgia of *England and the English*, especially the second volume, *The Heart of the Country*. However, in his choice of Borrow, and of the Gypsy and cuckoo passage in particular, as a vehicle for a discussion of the relationship between the city and the countryside, Ford adds a twist to his nostalgia: the countryside is celebrated, but as a place that is unpredictable and untamed rather than as an entirely idyllic place.[16] The second of the poems, with its invocation of the smoky town and the only barely less hostile countryside makes this rejection of the pastoral even clearer. It stands apart from the more traditional first poem in terms of its contemporary tone and anticipates Ford's less romantic portrait of the hardships of the country alongside his celebration thereof in *The Heart of the Country*. Supporting such a reading of these poems, Ford repeats this rejection of a sentimental nostalgia for the countryside precisely in terms of Borrow in his later review of Shorter's biography, asserting that 'for, though the wind whispering in the sunlight through the yellow gorse is a pretty thing, it is very small baggage for life in the country, which is mainly compos-ed of mud, rain, rheumatism, and indigestion' ('Mr. Clement Shorter' 678). With these poems, especially the second, Ford engages with the Gypsy poem genre, moving away from the romanticized view of the Gypsy found in Matthew Arnold's well known 'The Scholar-Gipsy' (1853), in which the reader is urged to 'fly' from 'this strange disease of modern life', and writing more in the vein of John Clare, who, as Deborah Epstein Nord has argued, viewed the Gypsies from both a pastoral *and* a political perspective.[17]

This move away from pastoral nostalgia also reflects Ford's contradictory feelings about the work of the Pre-Raphaelites and what he perceived as its failure to engage with the contemporary world. His own aim, as stated in the preface to his *Collected Poems* in which he reprinted both 'The Cuckoo and the Gipsy' and 'The Gipsy and the Townsman', was 'to register my own times in terms of my own time' (*CP2*, 327). In 'Modern Poetry' Ford is disparaging about the capacity of the work of 'Lord Tennyson, of Browning, of Swinburne, of Rossetti, or of the late Mr Meredith' to 'stand the test of time', but then goes on, capturing his ambivalent stance, to celebrate the ballad: '[b]allads and folk-songs are never Great Poetry, but what exquisite pleasure they can give us, and what a light they can throw upon the human heart!'[18] This is consistent with what Paul Skinner describes as a 'lagg[ing] behind' of '[Ford's] poetic practice' in comparison to 'his [more forward-looking] critical pronouncements'. According to Skin-ner, despite his support of the modernist project in theory, in practice '[Ford's] own poems were 'longish things': he needed space, the rhythms of speech, the conversational sentence'.[19]

We might read the Borrow poems in terms of what Hugh Kenner describes, in his reading of the poems 'On Heaven' and 'The Starling',[20] as Ford's negotiation of a conventional framework with a contemporary idiom: 'words a person might say, not book-words, and sequences a person might speak',[21] in terms of '[Ford's] allegiance [at once] to tradition and to experimentation'.[22] Appropriately perhaps if we consider Meredith as source for the structure and tone of the Borrow poems, Ford considered Meredith as standing apart from the Pre-Raphaelites: he writes that Meredith, like Whistler, 'became early detached from the great swarm, to shine [a] solitary [planet] in the sky'.[23] Kenner highlights the prose writer in Ford, suggesting of the poem 'The Starling' that 'events are imagined like incidents in a novel. Juxtaposed, they do not state the poem's revelation; rather they are an occasion on which to meditate; meditating on them, the poet arrives at a revelation which he then explicitly states. It isn't a profound revelation, but the revelations at which one arrives by thinking seldom are' (Kenner 177). In the case of 'The Cuckoo and the Gypsy', the scene is literally one from a prose work. The exchange between Jasper and the Romany Rye provides, as Kenner contends of the events in 'The Starling', 'an occasion for meditation', specifically here on a question central to Ford's work and one he revisits in his writing about England, that is the relationship of the country to the city.

England's Melting Pot

In the same year that the Borrovian poems were published in *Poems for Pictures*, Borrow also appeared in Ford's *The Cinque Ports* (1900), subtitled an 'historical and descriptive' work, a study of the Kentish and Sussex ports. The first of two references, in a footnote in Ford's section on Winchelsea, is to Borrow's mention of a Swiss pilgrim who 'managed to earn a precarious living [in Catholic countries] by posing as coming from the shrine [of St James of Compostella]'.[24] A discussion of the flourishing of Winchelsea as a port via which pilgrims accessed Spain en route to the shrine provokes this mention. Ford appears to be referring to the Swiss soap boiler, former Walloon, Benedict Mol in Borrow's *The Bible in Spain*, encountered several times by the narrator over the course of the work. Mol in fact, somewhat inconsistently with Ford's rendition of events, is going to St James of Compostela to find buried treasure, the existence of which he has learnt from a dying man.[25]

The second mention of Borrow, a long quotation documenting the young Lavengro's reaction to bones in a Hythe crypt, falls in Ford's chapter on Hythe and Folkestone. Ford introduces the quotation, taken from Chapter Two of *Lavengro*, with an explanation of the contested origin of the bones as those of either victims of battles 'between Britons and Saxons, between Saxons and Danes, or between Hythe folk and the French' or, according to the 'more sceptical', of ordinary churchyard origin preserved in a Hythe crypt. He includes the extract in order to illustrate the power of the bones to stir the imagination (despite their uncertain origin). Thus, he cites Lavengro's conclusion that '[o]ne enormous skull must have belonged to a giant, one of those red-haired warriors of whose strength and stature such wondrous tales are told in the ancient chronicles of the north'. Ford explains in an accompanying footnote that Borrow believed the bones were of Danish origin, a fact which so caught his imagination as a boy that it led him to approach a study of Danish lore with particular application.[26]

Both of Ford's references to Borrow in *The Cinque Ports* are tied to the fantastical, magical quality of his predecessor's work and to his emphasis on eccentric figures. The origin of the Danish bones, and the idea of foreign invasion suggested thereby, which set the young Lavengro's imagination on fire while unverifiable, as Ford points out in *The Cinque Ports*, is nonetheless captivating enough to quote at length. The quixotic figure of Benedict Mol, only loosely tied to the point Ford makes, obviously also captures Ford's imagination to the point that he felt it merited inclusion.

In his preface, Ford describes his study, suggesting a tie to Borrow's picaresque, semi-fictional version of England, as 'neither archaeological nor topographical nor even archaeologico-topographical. It was to be *a piece of literature pure and simple*, an attempt, by means of suggestion, to interpret to the passing years the inward message of the Five Ports' (*CP* v-vi: my emphasis). Ford's aim, he says, is not accuracy, but suggestiveness – although a negative review of another work based on its inaccuracies determined him to verify all of his sources and to indicate those statements the truth of which he says seemed questionable.

The key to what Ford means by 'a piece of literature pure and simple' (and its relationship to Anglo-Saxondom) in *The Cinque Ports* might be found in yet another reference to Borrow in a chapter on 'Vers libre' in Ford's 'The Battle of the Poets' section of *Thus to Revisit: Some Reminiscences* (1921). Here Ford argues with diagrams that 'prose is a form as well adapted for the utterance of poetry as verse' and that if only the Anglo-Saxon could recognize this then 'Anglo-Saxondom would come into the comity of all nations' (*TR* 185). Ford asserts that:

> [...] the factual-propagandist, or the factual-biographic, work of prose, even as the propagandist or tendential piece of verse, may pass over into the division of literature – by virtue perhaps of its very inaccuracy. I do not know how high the reader may be inclined to rate George Borrow. I do not really know how high I rate him myself; but rate him high or low, you cannot get away from the

conviction that most of his facts are nonsense, whether in the *Bible in Spain* or in *Lavengro* – and that when they are not nonsense they are mendacities. Yet these very nonsenses and mendacities give to his work such literary qualities as it has – for, however they may libel the Man in Black, they make you intimate with the true George Borrow. (*TR* 190-1)

And he returns to Borrow a little later in the same piece, again in indirect praise of a creativity to which he himself seems to have aspired in, for example, his much loved but much attacked memoir of Joseph Conrad:

[T]he question of Immortality, of Literary Permanence, of Genius – in short, of poetry! – this question is simply one of personality. This statement should, of course, be accepted with some caution and in a reasonable spirit. I do not mean to say that every imaginative writer, as soon as he takes pen in hand, should give himself license to exaggerate, as Borrow did, his momentary impatience or to avenge his personal dislikes. But I do mean to say that the Public of to-day *has to go to imaginative writers for its knowledge of life – for its civilization.* For this, recorded facts are of no avail. (*TR* 192-3: my emphasis)

While Borrow is not mentioned in Ford's three volume *England and the English: An Interpretation* (1907), Ford repeats in his introduction to the first volume his Borrovian formula from *The Cinque Ports*. This work will not be 'encyclopaedic, topographical or archaeological', rather he will try to '"get the atmosphere" of Modern London'.[27] In this study of the English spirit, which Max Saunders describes as part fictional and part sociological, 'fall[ing] half-way between the novels of George Eliot and Thomas Hardy, on the one hand, showing rural life being transformed by the spread of the Industrial Revolution; and, on the other, the pre-war preoccupation with "The Condition of England"', suggesting a tie to works such as Borrow's *Lavengro*, Ford is at pains to assert the autobiographical, personal quality of his account.[28] In the second part of the trilogy, *The Heart of the Country*, for example, Ford offers, as he did in *The Cinque Ports*, 'his personal view of his personal countryside' (*EE,* 109). He has read others' work on the countryside, but this account will be based on his own first hand knowledge of England and the English.

As in Borrow's *Lavengro* and his *The Bible in Spain*, the anecdote is central to Ford's portrait of the English in *England and the English,* as is the encounter between the narrator and his subject and the frequently conversational tone of the work. Like Borrow, Ford's focus is the people. In *The Bible in Spain*, Borrow asserts that 'my favourite, I might say, my only study is man'.[29] In *The Heart of the Country* Ford, again suggesting ties to Borrow, turns to figures such as the tramp, in particular one named Carew, a figure Ford extols as 'the artist – the man who loves the road for his own sake: he has not any other ambitions than shade from the sun, long grass and eternal autumn weather', and to the peasant woman Meary who '[kept] all on gooing' in the face of life's harshest challenges.[30]

Echoing the earlier Borrow poems, we find a discussion of the relationship between the town and the country and the somewhat nostalgic assertion of the utopian quality of the country, especially in the first two volumes focused respectively on the town, on London specifically, and then on the country. Up against 'the Tom Tiddler's Ground of the Town' (a reference to one of Dickens's 'Christmas Stories'), Ford sets the 'Islands of the Blest that lie somewhere in the Heart of the Country' (*EE* 113). Ford's defence of the countryside, 'the cottage as the heart of the country', the labourer as 'the final pillar of the state', is in the Borrovian tradition (*EE* 198). Significantly citing W. H. Davies's work on tramps, Edward Thomas's writing 'on the life of the countryside' and Ralph Vaughan Williams' music, all of which have ties to Borrow, as working to the same end as Ford, Saunders describes *The Heart of the Country* as 'an attempt to put the culture back in contact with the land, and to allow a middle-class urban audience a vicarious contact with rural life' (Saunders 220).

The most intriguing tie between Ford and Borrow in terms of *England and the English* is Ford's decidedly Borrovian emphasis on the mixedness, the inherent foreignness, of 'the English People': 'that great, migratory people who in the course of centuries have taken root in some small islands and produced, in Town and Country alike, *that subtle and difficult thing: a national spirit*'.[31] The Borrovian influence is best seen in the third book, *The Spirit of the People*, where Ford substitutes a theory of race determined by place for one determined by blood. It is residence in England that makes one English, not one's blood, according to Ford. Ford describes himself as 'a quite ordinary man, with the common tastes and that mixture in about equal parts of English, Celtic and Teutonic bloods that goes to make up the usual Anglo-Saxon of these islands' (*EE* 232). Borrow's Lavengro likewise celebrates his own foreignness, his Cornish and Norman blood and his capacity to pass as a Gypsy, a Jew, an Englishman and an Irishman. 'There are no countries in the world', Borrow asserts in his preface to

Lavengro, 'less known by the British than these selfsame British Islands, or where more strange things are every day occurring, whether in road or street, house or dingle' (*Lavengro* xxiv). Thus, to Patrick Parrinder's list of writers of immigrant descent – he suggests Defoe and Benjamin Disraeli – as possible sources for Ford's 'non-fictional accounts of English history', including *England and the English*, we might add Borrow . . . (Parrinder 6).

A last possible tie between Ford and Borrow, and Borrow and Anglo-Saxondom, can be found in the work of the naturalist W. H. Hudson (1841-1922), another writer about place. Hudson, who was much admired and often mentioned by Ford, is frequently compared to Borrow. In *Portraits from Life*, Ford repeats what he characterizes as the popular view that Hudson's *Green Mansions* (1904) is 'Anglo-Saxondom's only rendering of hopeless, of aching passion [. . . .] He made you see everything of which he wrote, and made you be present in every scene that he evolved' (*PL* 45, 48). According to Ford, '[Hudson's] *Green Mansions* is the only English novel of passion; the *Purple Land* is the only English novel of Romance [...] *Nature in Downland, Hampshire Days, Birds in a Village,* and the *Shepherd's Life* are the only English books about England. And you must remember that Mr. Hudson is an American of New England stock' (*TR* 70). Ford characterizes Hudson as possessing a unique 'selflessness' which 'gives to [his] work the power to suggest vast, very tranquil space and a man absolutely at home in it' (*TR* 71). He suggests that it is perhaps precisely the fact that Hudson, who was born in Argentina of American parents, and had been for a long time 'racial[ly] absen[t] from these Islands [the British Isles]' that enabled him to '[escape] the infection of the amateurish way we handle the language when we write' (*TR* 74). Like others from Latin America (such as Cunninghame Graham whose work Ford also published in the *English Review*), Ford suggests, Hudson 'use[s] words as clean tools, exactly, with decency and modesty'; he 'escape[s] our conventionally insular way of looking at a hill, a flower, a bird, an ivy leaf [...] he is a native of Argentina, and La Plata, and Patagonia and Hampshire and the Sussex downlands – wherever the grass grows' (*TR* 75). Ford describes Hudson as at once an insider and an outsider in England in terms which could equally be applied to Borrow: 'a gipsyish man who had been in foreign parts, but knew the pedigree of every shepherd's dog on the Plain and the head of game that every coppice carried [...]'.[32]

'The gorgeously English' George Borrow

Ford's review of Clement Shorter's Borrow biography is appropriately
perhaps, in terms of his and Shorter's eccentric subject, ambiguous.
Shorter doesn't seem to like Borrow very much (he portrays him as
'rather a sneak, rather a liar and rather a hypocrite', according to Ford:
'Mr. Clement Shorter' 678) and Ford doesn't seem to like Shorter
very much either, his contact with the author's work up to this point
having consisted, he tells us early on, of 'little green slips from a
Press-cutting   agency,   [which]   have   contained   contemptuous
questionings as to who the devil I might be ...'.[33] Thus, Ford's review
of Shorter's book while superficially positive has a hint of sarcasm to
it, seen especially in his repeated parenthetical asides such as 'or so
Mr. Shorter tells us'. Ford is reluctant to comment on the quality of
Borrow's prose, which he says he read 'with immense enthusiasm' as
a boy. However he does seem (despite his approval of Borrow's
mendacities elsewhere) to side with Shorter on the point that if we
view, he says, 'art as a means of conveying vicarious experience',
Borrow might have added to the quality of his work had he stayed just
a little closer to the truth:

> [I]f only Borrow could have given us his real life – coloured as to facts if it
> must be, but yet credibly and consistently coloured; if he had given us some of
> the failures of Long Melford (and God knows poor Borrow must have known
> enough of failure); if he had made Isopel Berners a little less than eleven feet
> high; if he had let Mr. Petulengro once make a mistake – and so on, we should
> have had in *Lavengro* a book of immeasurable value and of very little less
> entertainment.

'[G]iven the proper environment', Ford concludes, 'Borrow might
have been a greater Defoe – a Defoe with a touch of poetry'.

The 'proper environment', which for Ford consists here of a
'cooperative' community of writers, preferably one that is 'cosmopolitan', provides the frame of the review and it is in this regard that we
get a clearer idea of Ford's own opinion of Borrow and of how
Borrow inspired him to think about Englishness and cosmopolitanism.
One also gains a sense of Ford's views on the importance of literary
contacts or what he calls 'group movements'. Opening the review
with the contentious statement (made by a reader in response to an
earlier piece) that '"cosmopolitanism is the slayer of art"', Ford muses
on the subject of what he considers 'the [positive] influence of foreign

work' 'even for very national writers', in which category he places 'the gorgeously English [...] George Borrow'. 'Even for very national writers', Ford insists, 'their art is an extraordinarily international affair. Where, for instance, would Borrow have been without his Spanish travel, his Welsh, Irish, Norse and gipsy studies (shallow as Mr. Shorter tells us they were) or his passion for the picturesque in the philology of fifty nations?' ('Mr. Clement Shorter' 678).

Despite this initial recognition of the important cosmopolitan quality of Borrow's work, over the course of the review Ford laments Borrow's comparative lack of cooperation and the reluctance of English writers in general, and he names Lamb, Fitzgerald and Stevenson, 'to meet, mix, and from day to day exchange views about their jobs'. In this way, he backhandedly undermines Shorter's focus on Borrow's so-called 'circle'. Offering a sense of his own prescription for the great 'English' 'novel' of the future, Ford, in closing, playfully imagines what might have happened to English literature had these writers opened their doors to the great French and Russian writers of their day:

> Consider what might have resulted had Lamb really had to match his wits against Théophile Gautier instead of having to potter round so much with gentlemen whose ideals were hot buttered toast and clear fires. Or imagine what might have happened to Borrow if he had come into weekly contact with the Goncourts, Flaubert, Maupassant, Gautier again, and even with Sainte-Beuve and Turguenieff. He could not have lied to them; they would have found him out. He could not have bounced before them; he would have felt a fool. He might have told marvelous anecdotes of others which would have appeared in the journals of the Goncourts or of ce cher Maxime. He would have met equals in intellect, in force of character, and in the love of words and dislike for accepted ideas. ('Mr. Clement Shorter' 678)

And one can only imagine what might have happened if Borrow and Ford, themselves in many ways 'equals in intellect, in force of character, and in the love of words and dislike for accepted ideas', had had the opportunity to share a jug of ale at an inn or a pot of tea in Mumpers' Dingle in the company of Isopel Berners!

NOTES

I would like to thank Ann Soutter, Mike Skillman, Ce Rosenow, Caleb Southworth and Paul Skinner for their suggestions on this chapter.

1   'Ford, Literary Portraits – X.: Mr. Clement Shorter and "Borrow and His Circle"', *Outlook* (London) 32 (November 1913), 677-8 – henceforth 'Mr. Clement Shorter'; 677.

2   Thomas published *George Borrow: The Man and his Books*, in 1912 and includes a chapter on Borrow in his *A Literary Pilgrim in England* in 1917.

3   Ford, *Portraits from Life*, Boston: Houghton Mifflin, 1937 – henceforth *PL*; p. 196.

4   Ford, *The March of Literature*, New York, The Dial Press, 1938, p. 698

5   Ford, *England and the English: An Interpretation*, New York: McClure, Phillips & Co., 1912 – henceforth '*EE* (US edition)'; p. xviii.

6   See Ian Baucom, *Out of Place: Englishness, Empire and the Locations of Modernity*, Princeton: Princeton UP, 1999, pp. 17-20; see also Paul Peppis, *Literature, Politics and the English Avant Garde: Nation and Empire, 1901-1918*, Cambridge: Cambridge UP, 2000; and Patrick Parrinder, '"All that is Solid Melts into Air": Ford and the Spirit of Edwardian England' in *History and Representation in Ford Madox Ford's Writing*, ed. Joseph Wiesenfarth, Amsterdam and London: Rodopi, 2004 – henceforth 'Parrinder'; pp. 7-8.

7   Michael Collie, *George Borrow: Eccentric*, Cambridge: Cambridge University Press, 1982 – henceforth 'Collie'; p. 17.

8   Ford, *Thus to Revisit: Some Reminiscences*, New York: Octagon Books Inc., 1966 – henceforth *TR*; pp. 190-93.

9   Leslie Stephen, 'Country Books', *Hours in a Library, Vol. III*, London: John Murray, 1919, p. 191.

10 Ford, 'The Cuckoo and the Gipsy', *Speaker*, 18 (August 20, 1898), 232.

11 George Borrow, *The Romany Rye*, Oxford: Oxford UP, 1984, pp. 55-6. This same passage is included by E. V. Lucas in his anthology *The Open Road* and by renowned Romany scholar John Sampson in his gypsy anthology *Wind on the Heath*, and it is referred to by Sampson student Dora Yates.

12 Ford, *Selected Poems*, edited by Max Saunders, Manchester: Carcanet, 1997 – henceforth *Selected Poems*; p. 8.

13 Ford, *Collected Poems*, New York: Oxford UP, 1936 – henceforth *CP2*. Ford, *Poems for Pictures and for Notes of Music*, London: John MacQueen, 1900.

14 Pamela Bickley, 'Ford and Pre-Raphaelitism' in *Ford Madox Ford: A Reappraisal*, ed. Robert Hampson and Tony Davenport, Amsterdam and New York: Rodopi, 2002, p. 64.

15 George Meredith, 'Juggling Jerry', *Poems*, New York: Scribner, 1923, p. 171. In a 1909 obituary for Meredith, Ford identifies 'Love in the Valley' as a poem he particularly admired: *English Review*, 2 (June 1909), 409-10.

16 In 'Ford Among the Aliens', Andrzej Gasiorek argues that in *The Soul of London*, the first volume of *England and the English*, 'the very terms that Arnold construed as diametric opposites, seeing in "culture" a solution to "anarchy", are here superimposed, giving rise to a way of thinking and writing that sees a potential in the diversity that the great nineteenth century writer could only

disparage as chaos'. A similar argument might be made about the second volume of the trilogy in terms of Ford's portrayal of the countryside. *Ford Madox Ford and Englishness*, eds. Dennis Brown and Jenny Plastow, Amsterdam and New York: Rodopi, 2006, p. 76.

17 Deborah Epstein Nord, *Gypsies and the British Imagination 1807-1930*, New York: Columbia UP, 2006, p. 48.

18 Ford Madox Ford, *The Critical Attitude*, London, Duckworth, 1911, p. 183.

19 Paul Skinner, 'Poor Dan Robin: Ford Madox Ford's Poetry' in *Ford Madox Ford: A Reappraisal*, pp. 91, 84-5. For Skinner, 'the poems of the nineteen-tens are the most, and most fascinatingly, transitional, as Ford presents what were often, at that time, unfamiliar materials for poetry in an extensive variety of metrical forms' (p. 99).

20 Ford, 'On Heaven' (*On Heaven and Poems written on Active Service* 1918) and 'The Starling' (*High Germany* 1912).

21 Hugh Kenner, 'The Poetics of Speech' in Richard Cassell, editor, *Ford Madox Ford: Modern Judgements*, London and Basingstoke: Macmillan, 1972 – henceforth 'Kenner'; p. 176.

22 Sondra J. Stang and Carl Smith, '"Music for a While": Ford's Compositions for Voice and Piano', *Contemporary Literature*, 30: 2 (Summer 1989), 216.

23 Ford, *Ancient Lights*, London: Chapman and Hall, 1911, p. 25.

24 Ford, *Cinque Ports*, Edinburgh: William Blackwood and Sons, 1900 – henceforth *CP*; p. 72. This is Borrow's and Ford's spelling of Compostela.

25 Borrow, *The Bible in Spain*, London: J. M. Dent & Co., 1842 – henceforth *Bible in Spain*; p. 129.

26 *CP* 219-20. In George Borrow, *Lavengro: The Scholar, The Gypsy, The Priest*, New York: Grosset and Dunlap, 1927 [1851] – henceforth *Lavengro*; p. 12.

27 Ford, *England and the English*, edited by Sara Haslam, Manchester: Carcanet, 2003 – henceforth *EE*; p. 3.

28 Max Saunders, *Ford Madox Ford: A Dual Life*, Vol. 1, Oxford: Oxford University Press, 1996 – henceforth 'Saunders'; p. 220.

29 *Bible in Spain*, 48. Thanks to Ann Soutter for noting that this is from Pope's *An Essay on Man*: 'the proper study of mankind is man'.

30 *EE*, 132, 174. Perhaps a reference to the 'King of the Beggars', Bamfylde Moore Carew.

31 My emphasis. *EE* (US edition), p. xviii.

32 *PL* 53. Ford makes a similar argument about Conrad's advantage as an outsider in 'Mr. Joseph Conrad and Anglo-Saxondom' (*TR* 91-2).

33 'Mr. Clement Shorter' 677. Ford refers to Shorter's criticism of his work in a letter of 1910 to Edgar Jepson: *Letters of Ford Madox Ford*, edited by Richard M. Ludwig, Princeton: Princeton University Press, 1965, p. 45.

TROLLOPE RE-READ

Monica C. Lewis

The works of Anthony Trollope experienced an extraordinary revival in England in the first half of the twentieth century, a revival that only intensified with the onset of World War II. Richard Altick outlines how, when the new 'entertainments' provided by the new century were restricted by the onset of the Second World War, people turned to reading – and turned to Trollope in particular as their author of choice:

> During the Second World War . . . the English people, deprived of many of their favorite recreations and seeking respite from often intolerable emotional and physical strain, turned to the printed word as they had never done before. Hampered by a severe shortage of paper and other essential materials as well as of labor, publishers could not possibly keep up with the demand for books and periodicals of every description [. . . .] The printed word, whether in comic papers or precious dog-eared volumes of Trollope, was an indispensable part of everyone's life.[1]

Beginning in the late 1920s and lasting through the Second World War, sales and studies of Trollope boomed. As libraries and bookstores struggled to keep Trollope's novels on the shelves, critical assessments of Trollope's works appeared more and more frequently in literary publications of the day. One of Trollope's earliest and most emphatic twentieth-century reviewers was none other than Ford Madox Ford.

At first glance, Ford's evaluations of Trollope as an Englishman and as an author are ambivalent at best. In Ford's critical view, Trollope is the premier historian of Victorian England. At the same time, Ford, despite his own aspirations to the role of socio-literary historian, sees himself as an author ultimately aligned against Trollope and the England that Trollope supposedly stood for, an England of 'comfortable classes' and 'cathedral closes'.[2] Nevertheless, Ford demonstrates in his criticism a continual regard for Trollope's approach to narrative, and indeed Trollope's narrative style influenced the development of Ford Madox Ford's literary voice in perhaps unexpected ways. No less a novel than *The Good Soldier* (1915) echoes two of the narrative concerns most pressing for both Trollope and Ford: the function of the storyteller and the construction of character, the character of the English gentleman in particular.

Perhaps the most unequivocal evidence of Ford's admiration for Trollope is found in the far-reaching *March of Literature* (1938), where Ford ranks Trollope, alongside Jane Austen, as the best of the English novelists, declaring Trollope to be 'inimitable' and rejoicing in his dominance over moralists like Charles Dickens on the shelves of American bookstores.[3] In his acutely sentimental holiday essay 'And on Earth Peace' (1926), ostensibly a review of Trollope's *Chronicles of Barsetshire*, Ford exhibits a more tempered enthusiasm for Trollope, one predicated on Trollope's supposedly 'pacific' tendencies:

> It was, Trollope's England, a land of deep peace; of the century of the Pax Britannica that extended from Waterloo to Mons, and though few people can have been less pacifist none can have been more pacific than the author of 'Framley Parsonage'. (*NYE* 15)

The distinction is telling. Amid the century of 'Pax Britannica' Trollope was pacific, Ford suggests, but was no pacifist. Indeed, Ford imagines that Trollope might actually have hated Ford and the English literary tradition he feels he has come to represent:

> I have spent pretty nearly [a] half-century in combating the tendencies expressed in Trollopism and the Pax Britannica. I have always been against the comfortable classes, the cathedral closes, the author's comments. If Trollope could have he would have hated me and my friends and the authors I love and all our Gallicisms. (*NYE* 16)

Ford doubts whether or not he would be 'English' enough for Anthony Trollope; Ford's rejection of cathedral closes, comfortable classes, and, notably, of authorial intrusions, makes him more Gallic than English, separating Ford and his peers from the Pax Britannica of Victorian literature. But ironically, Trollope is ultimately, for Ford, the Victorian author who best illustrates how to interrogate the idea of 'Englishness' in literature.

Still earlier evidence of Ford's appreciation of Trollope, an appreciation less tempered by Christmas Yule, exists in the form of published reviews, beginning with 'Phineas Re-Read', a review of *Phineas Finn, the Irish Member* and *Phineas Redux* in November of

1911. In this critique of what he calls Trollope's 'Irish novels', Ford's admiration for Trollope intersects with their complementary literary concerns.

> Trollope is – he might be – as valuable to England as Green's 'Short History of the English People', on the one hand, or as Clarendon's 'History of the Rebellion' might be on the other. For he is the historian of England of the 60s and 70s.
>
> Yet in his own day he was not taken seriously, and for him, as a writer, that was a very great boon. Instead of being Mr. Thackeray the moralist, whom it was possible to take seriously because he was a moralist [. . .] Trollope was just nobody in particular.[4]

Trollope is at once a Ford-certified historian and a 'nobody in particular'. And ironically, it is this very narrative anonymity, as Ford reads it, which makes the Victorian author so appealing to a modern historian and storyteller. Trollope is not 'nobody in particular' as a result of pacific tendencies or personal shortcomings; rather, Ford can take a certain pleasure in characterizing Trollope's narrative presence as 'nobody in particular' because Trollope avoids the most grave of narrative sins – the inclusion of moralizing narrative intrusions. Consider Ford on moralization, characterization, and the responsibilities of the English novelist as set forth in a 1913 review:

> The statement of morals, the formulation of ethical codes, appears to me to be no business of the novelist. His business is to draw pictures of possible – of as far as he can normal – conditions; the reader's business being to draw the morals. To delude the novelist with the idea that he is stout fellow enough to be a moralist is to perform a wicked action [. . . .] The drawing of character – at any rate as practiced in the English novel – is, if not a wicked proceeding, at any rate a very dangerous one . . . .[5]

For Ford, statements of morals and formulations of ethical codes fall outside the realm of the novelist; it is the reader who must come to any moral judgements for him- or herself. The business of morals is dangerous territory for the novelist, and it is a danger closely linked to the business of character. Trollope recognized this; Ford, in turn, recognized it in Trollope. Both Trollope and Ford fashion author-narrators who engage in a self-conscious dialogue with the reader regarding the creation, construction, and depiction of character; the representation of morality in character was a concern for Trollope in the nineteenth century just as it was for Ford in the twentieth. The complexity of character that both authors acknowledge – an

acknowledgement that subsequently involves and engages the reader
in a consideration of character – lies at the heart of Trollope's
importance to Ford. It is also inextricably linked to the question, for
Trollope and for Ford, of what constitutes an English 'gentleman', as
seen, for example, in their portrayals of the Reverend Francis Arabin
and Edward Ashburnham, respectively.

Volume II of Trollope's *Barchester Towers* (1857), titled 'Mr.
Arabin', begins as follows:

> The Rev Francis Arabin, fellow of Lazarus, late professor of poetry at
> Oxford, and present vicar of St Ewold, in the diocese of Barchester, must now
> be introduced personally to the reader. He is worthy of a new volume, and as
> he will fill a conspicuous place in it, it is desirable that he should be made to
> stand before the reader's eye by the aid of such portraiture as the author is
> able to produce.

The storyteller continues:

> It is to be regretted that no mental method of daguerreotype or photo-
> graphy has yet been discovered by which the characters of men can be
> reduced to writing and put into grammatical language with an unerring
> precision of truthful description. How often does the novelist feel, ay, and the
> historian and also the biographer, that he has conceived within his mind and
> accurately depicted on the tablet of his brain the full character and personage
> of a man, and that nevertheless, when he flies to pen and ink to perpetuate the
> portrait, his words forsake, elude, disappoint, and play the deuce with him, till
> at the end of a dozen pages the man described has no more resemblance to the
> man conceived than the signboard at the corner of the street has to the Duke
> of Cambridge?[6]

The concern here is at the level of language, the difficulty of finding
the correct words to correspond to a man's character – a man,
presumably, that the narrator 'knows', rendering the attempt at an
accurate description all the more frustrating. Trollope's writing is full
of such questioning, and the recognition of the narrator's ultimate
fallibility at the level of the written word is telling. The recognition of
the impossibility of 'reducing' character to words and the difficulties
of 'putting into grammatical language' with 'an unerring precision of
truthful description' the human condition – or the condition of just one
human – are difficulties that Trollope makes evident to the reader for
a very particular purpose. By recognizing his own fallibility the
author-narrator requires the reader to make his or her own moral
judgements. Words, for Trollope and for his readers, 'forsake, elude,

disappoint, and play the deuce', rendering the pinning down of an ultimate truth, on the level of narrative or the level of morality, impossible. In his consideration of 'The Morality of Irony and Unreliable Narrative in Trollope's *The Warden* and *Barchester Towers*', Paul Lyons argues that 'the unreliably omniscient narrator [of *Barchester Towers*] destabilizes any notion of reliability, restating in the conflict between fiction and reality the classical problem of words not being things but arbitrary symbols for things to which the reader must bring meaning'.[7] Neither the narrator nor the reader can rely solely on the words printed on the page for an accurate assessment of character; the reader must bring his or her own meaning, must make his or her own judgements in regard to characters and morals. In his efforts to paint a portrait of a man in words, Trollope's author-narrator in *Barchester Towers* faces the same dilemma as *The Good Soldier*'s narrator John Dowell – how does one depict the measure of a man?

Dowell's initial portrait of Captain Edward Ashburnham paints him as 'an Englishman and a gentleman' – as a man of superficiality and sentimentality.[8] Dowell recalls first seeing Ashburnham one night in a hotel in Germany:

> [. . .] his yellow moustache was as stiff as a toothbrush and I verily believe that he had his black smoking jacket thickened a little over the shoulder-blades so as to give himself the air of the slightest possible stoop. It would be like him to do that; that was the sort of thing he thought about. Martingales, Chiffney bits, boots; where you got the best soap, the best brandy, the name of the chap who rode a plater down the Khyber cliffs; the spreading power of a number-three shot before a charge of number-four powder . . . by heavens, I hardly ever heard him talk of anything else. Not in all the years that I knew him did I hear him talk of anything but these subjects. (*GS* 31-32)

Here Dowell portrays Ashburnham as an obsessively superficial gentleman – as someone whose depths, perhaps, cannot be sounded by an outsider and an American. And indeed, Ashburnham's is a character that others can understand but which Dowell fails to comprehend, that of the 'good soldier'.

> Good God, what did they all see in him; for I swear that was all there was of him, inside and out; though they said he was a good soldier [. . . .] For all good soldiers are sentimentalists – all good soldiers of that type. Their profession, for one thing, is full of the big words, courage, loyalty, honour, constancy. (*GS* 33)

The disconnect between 'big words' like 'courage', 'loyalty', 'honour', and 'constancy' and what Dowell suspects must be the true character of the man he claims to 'know' reflects Dowell's (and Ford's) cognizance of the difficulty of putting an English gentleman on paper, and the dangers inherent in attempting to assign a moral character to any man – difficulties and dangers foregrounded by the claims of Trollope's own author-narrator.

Indeed, Part Three, Section IV of *The Good Soldier* begins with a discursive disclaimer much like the one Trollope's author-narrator uses to introduce the Reverend Arabin:

> It is very difficult to give an all-round impression of any man. I wonder how far I have succeeded with Edward Ashburnham. I dare say I haven't succeeded at all. It is even very difficult to see how such things matter. (*GS* 177)

Dowell continues soon after:

> For who in this world can give anyone a character? Who in this world knows anything of any other heart – or of his own? I don't mean to say that one cannot form an average estimate of the way a person will behave. But one cannot be certain of the way any man will behave in any case – and until one can do that a 'character' is of no use to anyone. (*GS* 182)

The construction of character matters very much to Trollope – else he would hardly take the time to elaborate upon the difficulty of constructing one – and this same sort of reflection upon the construction of character is what alerts readers of *The Good Soldier* to the fact that despite Dowell's claims to the contrary, 'such things' *do* matter. And indeed, the difficulties inherent in the construction of character *are* of use to the storyteller and to the reader alike, as they allow Trollope's author-narrator and Ford's character-narrator both to reflect upon the elusive nature of character and to place the burden of passing moral judgement upon the reader. Dowell's assertion that 'one cannot be certain of the way any man will behave in any case' does not only reflect the difficulties that the chronicler of a modern character faces. Dowell is also unsure of Ashburnham because Ashburnham's character is inextricably linked to the words that constitute his story. Ashburnham's character is a work in process – it is revealed to the reader and to Dowell himself *as* Dowell recounts the saddest story he has ever heard. For Dowell as storyteller, words 'forsake, elude, disappoint, and play the deuce', just as Trollope warned that they would. The ontological, linguistic difficulties that Trollope identified as inherent in the portrayal of a character, the character of a nineteenth-century English 'gentleman' in particular, find an echo in the work of Ford Madox Ford as the literature of the twentieth century continues to question the modern-day constitution of an officer and a gentleman.

NOTES

1   Richard Altick, *The English Common Reader: A Social History of the Mass Reading Public, 1800-1900*, Columbus, Ohio: Ohio State University Press, 1998, p. 366.
2   Ford Madox Ford, 'And On Earth Peace', *New York Essays*, New York: William Edwin Rudge, 1927 – henceforth *NYE*; pp. 12-20 (p. 16). 'And On Earth Peace' was first published in *New York Herald Tribune Books* on December 26, 1926.
3   Ford Madox Ford, *The March of Literature: From Confucius' Day to Our Own*, New York: Dial Press, 1938, p. 787.
4   Ford, 'Phineas Re-Read: A Review of Phineas Finn, the Irish Member and Phineas Redux by Anthony Trollope', *Daily News* (1 November 1911), 4. Henceforth 'Phineas Re-Read'.
5   Ford, 'Literary Portraits VIII: Professor Saintsbury and the English "Nuvvle"', *Outlook* (London), 32 (1 November 1913), 606.
6   Anthony Trollope, *Barchester Towers*, Harmondsworth: Penguin, 1994, p. 167.
7   Paul Lyons, 'The Morality of Irony and Unreliable Narrative in Trollope's *The Warden* and *Barchester Towers*', *South Atlantic Review* 54:1 (January 1989), 47.
8   Ford, *The Good Soldier*, New York: Oxford University Press, 1990 – henceforth *GS*; p. 30.

THE PROPHET AND THE SCEPTIC:
GEORGE ELIOT AND FORD MADOX FORD[1]

Sara Haslam

Despite Ford Madox Ford's relative silence on the subject of George
Eliot (there is scant reference in the eight-hundred page *March of
Literature* to the best-known woman novelist of her day[2]), this essay
explores both a range of her influences on Ford's development as a
writer, and some possible reasons for the limited nature of his
comment. Ford does himself acknowledge some of her influences
upon him; others are left for the critic or reader to discern or to
experiment with. The most significant of those in the latter category is
mediated by Henry James, I will suggest, on the occasion when he and
Ford first met.

Although Ford says almost nothing about Eliot in *The March of
Literature* – Victorian women novelists do not in general feature
strongly in what Alan Judd terms an 'idiosyncratic survey'[3] – he
seems to have read a fair proportion of her books. His mother,
Catherine, probably started him off when young with at least two of
Eliot's titles (she 'enjoined on' him the reading of *Silas Marner* and
The Mill on the Floss).[4] Altogether Ford talks about reading, over a
period of twenty years, *Silas Marner*, *The Mill on the Floss*, *Scenes of
Clerical Life*, *Romola*, and *Adam Bede* (though this was, perhaps,
abandoned in favour of a Trollope novel).[5] Of these he makes further,
and positive, reference to 'Janet's Repentance', the third of the tales
published in *Blackwood's Magazine* in 1857, collected as *Scenes of
Clerical Life*. In addition, Ford expresses awareness of Eliot's
translation of Strauss's *Life of Jesus*, but otherwise her philosophical
interests remain uncommented on. There is also no mention of her
most successful novel, *Middlemarch*,[6] though as I have argued
elsewhere I think he read this too.[7] In the remainder of this essay I will
detail Ford's treatments of Eliot, both discussing them in their own
right, and additionally attempting to construct a narrative of his critical
relationship with her. Ford's opinion of her, and thus her influence on
him, develops and alters in what is, I will argue, a notable fashion,

through the years in which he wrote about her: 1911, 1919, 1929, and 1931.

Whatever technical or imagistic impression Eliot's depiction of Bulstrode's demise may have made on Ford (see note 7), it is safe to say that the idea of the character's immoral and repressed embodied past returning to confront him would not have appealed to this now twentieth-century author. Ford was still, in the first years of the new century, grappling with the serious question of what kind of novelist he wanted to be, and a few years before he published his essay 'On Impressionism', he wrote a most damning critique of Eliot.[8] Originally appearing as one of his editorials in the *English Review*, this critique was re-published in the chapter 'English Literature of Today: I' in the book *The Critical Attitude* in 1911.[9] His treatment of Eliot has pride of place in the chapter: her name is the first a reader encounters. It is her tendency to (in a wonderful image) 'dilat[e] upon sin', and simultaneously to adopt the status of 'writer as prophet' he most abhors (*CA* 56).[10] In a close second place come her departure from the simple authorial processes of observation and recording ('like Frankenstein', he says, she evolves 'obedient monsters who had no particular relation to the life of her day'), and her formlessness. Notably in this section, as is often the case in Ford's literary criticism, he makes his case in part by pairing her with a companion novelist, Anthony Trollope.[11] Trollope, in Ford's opinion, both records and observes, and in addition has no ambition to be a 'great figure'. Despite the harshness of Ford's judgement of Eliot, the comparison with Trollope is neither simple, nor does it quite have the effect one might expect. After all, Ford writes that Eliot *was* a 'great figure', while Trollope could produce a 'good "household article"'.[12] More significantly still, in terms of the wider narrative, Ford's appreciation of Trollope is lukewarm at best, and is a very long way from its height in *The English Novel* – where he stands 'absolutely alone' (though with Austen, Shakespeare and Richardson, *EN* 112-3) – and *The March of Literature*.

Neither Eliot nor Trollope comes off especially well in this instance, then: Trollope, as well as writing that 'household article', is 'never remarkably engrossing' (*CA* 56). It seems clear that at this point in Ford's aesthetic development, he is most concerned to make a principled stand against the Victorians, whoever they may be. But he wants particularly to consign Eliot to the past, and to emphasise how the writing world has progressed since she held sway:

> She was taken more seriously than any writer of to-day ever has been [. . . .]
> Yet, to the great bulk of educated criticism of to-day, George Eliot has
> become a writer unreadable in herself and negligible as a critical illustration.
> (*CA* 55)

Ford is, in some ways, constructing literary history. His desire, and
need (he has not had a 'hit' since *The Soul of London* in 1905), to be
in the forefront of a different and new generation of writers is shown
in part in his representation of the passage of literary/historical time
later in the same essay. He talks of Ibsen writing *A Lady from the Sea*
'a great many years ago' (*CA* 75); this play appeared in 1888. Also in
this essay, and its companion, 'English Literature of Today: II', it is
those novelists most often acknowledged as Ford's own major influences, Joseph Conrad and Henry James, who are treated positively
(*CA* 89). John Galsworthy – just – manages to hold on to a place at the
table (*CA* 88). George Eliot's influence, however, is most active in
Ford at this stage when he is classifying the kind of writer that he felt
was both outdated, and furthest from what he wanted as a model: a
moraliser, an inventor, a preacher, a thinker. (As such she was also
largely representative of the kind of Victorian he was trying
desperately to evade in his personal life in 1911.) But while Ford may
have been displaying his perspicacity, his desire to 'make it new', and
his independence in this critical view, he did not in fact get there on
his own. He was still three crucial years from producing *The Good
Soldier*, and his critical opinion of Eliot was one that was more
common than any other at this time.

Ford admits as much when, at the start of his essay, he cites the
'great bulk of educated criticism of today' (*CA* 55). Certainly things
had changed a great deal in the years prior to 1911 in this respect. One
critical highpoint in Eliot's reception was the essay by Leslie Stephen,
published in the *Cornhill Magazine* in February 1881, just after her
death.[13] 'In losing George Eliot', he wrote, 'we have probably lost the
greatest woman who ever won literary fame'.[14] Like Henry James
after him, Stephen also wrote of some things coming to an end with
Eliot's death. He believed that her works 'may hereafter appear as
marking the termination of the great period of English fiction which
began with Scott' (Haight 136). By the time Ford was coming to
authorial consciousness, however (*The Brown Owl* was published in
1891), the critics had largely adopted a very different tone.[15] Writers
such as W. E. Henley, Arnold Bennett, and George Saintsbury attacked her moralism, her coyness about sex, her 'feminine style', and her

brain, as I go on to discuss.[16] It was not until 1919 that any serious critic sought to reappraise Eliot's work. That critic was Virginia Woolf, and in an uncanny coincidence, this was the same year that (as far as I am aware) Ford next wrote about Eliot, in an essay about Woolf herself.[17]

Though it is not strictly within the scope of this essay, I would like to discuss briefly not the reason for the change in critical temperature around Eliot at the turn of the century – though it is tempting to make links between this and the social climate[18] as well as the progress of a new generation of writers – but the manner in which it was expressed. My argument about Ford will be relevant here too, however, because of the gender politics of the affair. Such politics mean it is a shame that, while one aspect of Ford's developing creative self had to break with the past, another – that aspect that was in tune with the rights, abilities and expectations of women and was expressed in 1913 with a publication for the Women's Freedom League – should have missed an opportunity.[19] Ford wrote in *The March of Literature* that the 'academic' critic despises Jane Austen because her 'subjects are merely domestic' (*ML* 717). Though he is not necessarily saying that he admires her for this reason,[20] he is displaying ignorance of the fact that women novelists were often despised by critics because they did not stick to the 'domestic'. Eliot thought, and thought in the abstract, even as she attempted to create detailed portrayals of everyday things. The size, and nature, of her brain, plays a surprisingly large role in Eliot criticism – famously, when she was 31 the country's leading phrenologist, George Combe, studied her head and surmised, 'she has a very large brain, the anterior lobe is remarkable for length, breadth, and height' (Ashton 3).[21] No doubt as a result, 'the poor woman was not content simply to write amusing stories', as Stephen puts it. Thus 'she is convicted upon conclusive evidence of having indulged in ideas' (Haight 137).

'Convicted' is *le mot juste*. W. E. Henley, characterizing himself in an essay adopting a Bunyanesque style as the Eliot 'Sceptic', wrote that when she 'put away her puppets and talked of them learnedly and with understanding ... [he] recalled how Wisdom crieth out in the street and no man regardeth her, and perceived that in this case the fault was Wisdom's own' (Haight 161). To George Saintsbury, *Adam Bede* was 'of course [...] extremely clever'. It did well (evidently despite its cleverness) only because Charlotte Brontë was 'dead or dying, – I forget which', and Dickens' 'best work was done' (Haight 167). Trollope admits her greatness in his autobiography in 1883, then produces a killer 'but' relating to her 'intellect', which is different from most 'tellers of stories': to him she was an analyst rather than a creator.[22] (Years before, congratulating her on *Romola*, he warned her not to 'fire too much over the heads' of her readers[23]). It is Eliot's ability and desire to abstract (or her 'wide intelligence' in Stephen's phrase, Haight 141) that 'may explain', Gillian Beer suggests, 'why many who hear a woman's voice in Jane Austen's writing, do not do so in George Eliot's'.[24] Including Ford? Would this have troubled him? I don't think so. There may be a muted sexism in the way he criticises her narrative persona in 1911 (her 'inflation' and assumption of a God-complex are, perhaps, particularly unbearable because she is female) but that is all. And of course the kind of writer Ford believed in and turned out to be was a world apart from Eliot's high certainties and intrusive narration. What I am suggesting is that Ford may well have found it hard to judge Eliot on her merits in the contemporary critical climate. And perhaps this is why, though he would always ultimately have rejected her method-ology, he seems to make no allowance for the relationship between the need for secrecy as to her sex and the construction of that narrative voice;[25] for the bravery and unconventionality of her private life;[26] and for the sheer force of will and dedication to their shared craft that it must have taken for her to publish what she did, when she did.[27] He didn't have another chance to do so, for he never wrote about her in such detail again. By 1919, critical opinion about Eliot was on the move once more, and Ford's too, as I have suggested, had altered.[28]

He wrote a series of articles in the *Piccadilly Review* in that year. The series had the title 'Thus to Revisit'.[29] There were five articles in all, and two of them mention George Eliot. The first, called 'The Novel', takes as its subject Gilbert Cannan's *Time and Eternity*[30] and Woolf's *Night and Day*.[31] The first thing that strikes the reader coming fresh to this piece from the *Critical Attitude* is the change in Ford's frame of reference. It has increased enormously. Though his subject in 1911 was strictly English Literature, this would not have prevented Ford from mentioning writers from elsewhere. And in the first paragraph of the essay in 1919 ten authors feature, of whom only four are British. Ford's strongly held views about the importance of construction and form seem also to have been moderated. 'But I should like to add', he informs the reader in 1919, 'that I do not wish to be taken as thinking [...] that all formless narrative is to be regarded with contempt' (*CE* 187). To discuss Cannan and Woolf (and thereby to address the question of 'where we really stand'), Ford's structure is the interplay between what he terms Novels – possessing 'unity of form, culminations and shapes' – and Romances – 'containing digressions, moralizations, and lectures'.[32] Mr Cannan, who pre-war was one of 'les jeunes', and Woolf, of whom Ford claims 'to know nothing' have written respectively, Ford thinks, a Novel, and a Romance.[33]

George Eliot is invoked first of all as soon as Ford begins to write in any detail about Woolf. His mind returns her to him as the supreme model of intellectual womanhood. Confronted, and perhaps made to feel inferior, by Woolf's novel, and her example of what he somewhat startlingly terms a 'super-educated' woman, Ford hears the voice of his childhood, which for now is the same as the 'voice of George Eliot', speaking to him instead. Woolf's contemporary voice is, then, inflected by his memory of childhood and simultaneously of Eliot. Happily for Ford, though, this new Eliot 'has lost the divine rage to be didactic' (*CE* 188). As a result, Woolf's book is 'modern' to him, but is also both 'interesting and suggestive', and helps to turn his initial suppositions about Novels as opposed to Romances on their heads. Where Woolf is a 'mistress of inclusion', Cannan is a 'master of excision'; but she is 'moral-less', while he is a 'virulent […] and an incoherent moralist'. Woolf as 'spiritual descendant' of George Eliot (and other nineteenth-century writers) serves in this context both to reveal the fashion in which some steam has gone out of Ford's ire regarding Eliot, and to re-direct our sense of her influence primarily from the writerly to the psychological (*CE* 189).

The second of his mentions of Eliot in the *Piccadilly Review* series (in 'II. The Realistic Novel') should not dispel this sense, but does briefly re-introduce the writerly influence. Here, Ford is genuine in his admiration for Eliot's achievements in what he terms the 'domestic school' of realism, and he seems able unproblematically to place her in a tradition from which he might now feel a safe distance. The relevant section comes immediately after that titled 'Dostoevsky as a Model', published in the *Critical Essays* (pp. 190-2) and reads as follows:

> Of the more unassuming, gentle, and probably more valuable school which you might call the English domestic school of realism – the school, or rather the tendency, which once gave us the works of Trollope, 'Janet's Repentance', by George Eliot, and *Mary Barton* by Mrs. Gaskell, it is

difficult nowadays to discover much trace. Yet it is a national vein which
might well be worked more assiduously.

Ford's choice of adjectives is notable, as is his focus on the last of
Eliot's three tales. Early critics debated which was the best of them,
but largely agreed about the deftness of the realism throughout –
although they termed it something different. 'Now and then we get a
novel', writes one anonymous reviewer, 'like these *Scenes of Clerical
Life*, in which the fictitious element is securely based upon a broad
groundwork of actual truth'. S/he continues, 'in the *Scenes of Clerical
Life* we have a happy example of such copying [from Nature faithfully
and heartily]'.[34] Another reviewer describes Eliot as a novelist who
'can paint homely every-day life and ordinary characters with great
humour and pathos, and is content to rely on the truth of his pictures
for effect'.[35] By contrast, in his edition of *Scenes of Clerical Life*,
David Lodge regards 'Amos Barton' as the most successful, and this
is because of his assessment that in the two later tales, as Eliot 'grew
in eloquence, wisdom, social vision and psychological penetration',
she also tended 'to idealize her main characters and to moralize her
narratives into patterns of reward and retribution'.[36] Which sounds
exactly like the Eliot to whom Ford also would object, and not at all a
'gentle' or 'unassuming' proponent of realism. Nonetheless, Ford is
attempting to resurrect a 'national vein' that he believes is both
valuable, and at risk of becoming unworked by writers, and is seeking
to draw it to the attention of those who should mind. A key example
for him (whether 'super-educated' or not) is George Eliot, and she is
now clearly in a very different place of influence for him from where
she was in 1911.[37]

Ford next wrote about Eliot ten years later. During the
intervening years he wrote the texts that best project a comprehensive,
panoramic vision in his work: the four novels that make up *Parade's
End*. Some of the references to Eliot in 1929 have already been
commented on in this essay. They appear in *The English Novel*, and
relate to his mother's encouragement to read Eliot, and also place her
in lists of novel writers one must read (*EN* 103, 111). There's a
notable echo of Woolf's opinion that *Middlemarch* was written for
'grown-up people' as an adjunct to one such list (the novels he has
mentioned are *Evelina*; *Castle Rackrent*; *Sense and Sensibility*; *Mary
Barton*; *Scenes of Clerical Life*; *Villette*; the *Barchester Towers* novels
and the works of Rutherford and Gissing). He calls these 'attempts at

rendering English life that are above the attention of adults with the mentality of French boys of sixteen' (*EN* 103) [and gives no clue why he singles out French boys in this way...]. Perhaps Woolf's opinion in 1919 is shown to resonate in Ford's developing appreciation of Eliot after all.

The final reference to Eliot of Ford's critical life is in *Return to Yesterday*, the volume of memoirs covering the years 1894 to 1914. This was published in 1931, and Max Saunders describes it both as a 'magnificent' volume, and as 'one of [Ford's] most morbid books, giving a harrowing account of his 1904 breakdown, [and] elegizing his dead friends James, Crane, Conrad, Meary Walker, and Marwood [...].[38] George Eliot features in his elegy for Henry James. As I first began compiling Ford's references to Eliot, I felt that this one was the least significant. Though it comes at the end of the first chapter, a chapter dedicated to James (and, to a lesser degree, Conrad), its embedded nature encouraged only a cursory glance. It is convoluted in structure, referring, as it does, to a story James was telling that he had, himself, only been told. Yet the memory resonates, despite, or perhaps because of, its structure. It communicates something highly significant about Ford's relationship to James and to Eliot in a specific, familial, context.

'[James] had once heard', begins Ford, 'that Secretary to the Inland Revenue recount how he had seen George Eliot proposed to by Herbert Spencer on the leads of the terrace at Somerset House'.

> 'You would think', Mr James exclaimed with indignation, his dark eyes really flashing, 'that a man would make something out of a story like *that*: but the way he told it was like this': and heightening and thinning his tones into a kind of querulous official organ Mr James quoted: '"I have as a matter of fact frequently meditated on the motives which induced the Lady's refusal of one so distinguished; and after mature consideration I have arrived at the conclusion that although Mr Spencer with correctness went down upon one knee and grasped the Lady's hand he completely omitted the ceremony of removing his high hat, a proceeding which her sense of the occasion may have demanded..." Is that', Mr James concluded, 'the way to tell *that* story?'[39]

James' displeasure may have been real, but in contrast to his view several people managed to 'make something' out of this story, not least its original teller. (It is highly unlikely that Herbert Spencer ever proposed to Eliot – more likely, in fact, that it was the other way around.[40] Also the idea that a woman who, roughly three years later would leave the country to live with a married man, would object to a proposal because a man was wearing a 'high hat' is ridiculous.) James himself makes something of this story of his 'mentor' as he passes it on to a youthful and admiring visitor.[41] Ford remembers his 'eyes really flashing', communicating the drama of which 'a man' should be capable – and thus, of course, begging the question, 'what of a man who is not?' Ford, too, makes something of it. The anxiety of influence of which he was certainly in the grip as he heard this story – it was his first meeting of James – became more pronounced as he conjured with the occasion in *Return to Yesterday* years later: 'I do not imagine that Mr James had the least idea what I was, and I do not think that, to the end of his days, he regarded me as a serious writer [...] he was the most masterful man I have ever met' (p. 16). Ford's 'awe' is not dispelled, and the anxiety might well have been compounded, by James's 'vivid display of dislike' for members of Ford's family and associates that day, which climaxed in the story of George Eliot. James had heard the story from, and is mocking as he retells it, Ford's own uncle, William Rossetti. Ford certainly had his own feelings about the suffocating 'greats' of his youth, but Eliot will have been in part tainted by this general assault on the Victorians in which James indulged, doubtlessly projecting a complex version of his own fraught and potent relationship with her as he did so.[42]

I was, I think, wrong about the significance of this final mention of Eliot. Though by date of publication it came last, in true Ford fashion the scene it described happened first. The meeting with James took place on 14 September 1896, when Ford had published little, and long before he wrote anything about Eliot. Partly as a result of this meeting, it will have been difficult for Ford ever to be objective about her. James' story is a highly productive one, about sex, repression, rejection, observation, and about who can and who cannot tell a story – according to the Master's rules. As he tells it, James implicates teller and listener as well as protagonist. Ford in part used his elegy for James to re-establish and re-imagine his sense of inferiority to him, and thus by extension to George Eliot – the Master's Mistress? – too.[43]

NOTES

1   Thanks to Max Saunders, Joseph Wiesenfarth and Angus Wrenn for their comments during the preparation of this essay.
2   Her name appears in two lists of writers on page 753: *The March of Literature*, London: George Allen & Unwin, 1939, 1947 – henceforth *ML*. On Eliot's fame: 'After the success of *Adam Bede* (1859)', writes David Carroll, 'George Eliot received unflagging attention from [the] critics until the end of her career': *George Eliot: The Critical Heritage*, London: Routledge & Kegan Paul, 1971 – henceforth 'Carroll'; p. 1. He has already noted in his introduction that he was 'taken aback at first simply by the number' of contemporary reviews of her novels. Brian Spittles puts Eliot in both the list of the three most eminent Victorian women, and the three most important novelists of the period: *George Eliot: Godless Woman*, London: Macmillan, 1993, p. 1.
3   Alan Judd, *Ford Madox Ford*, London: HarperCollins, 1990, p. 17. In *ML* there is one mention of Charlotte Brontë, a couple of Gaskell (though she's not in the index), and that's about it for women novelists – although Christina Rossetti does better. Jane Austen, among the greatest of writers for Ford, receives much longer treatment.
4   The verb does not necessarily suggest an unpleasant experience. These are the first titles in a list that also includes *Wuthering Heights*, *Sidonia the Sorceress*, *Lorna Doone* (a great favourite), *The Woman in White*, *The Moonstone*, *Diana of the Crossways*, and *Far from the Madding Crowd*. In *The English Novel: From the earliest days to the death of Joseph Conrad* (1929), Manchester: Carcanet, 1983 – henceforth *EN*; p. 108.
5   'We can take up with interest *Barchester Towers* in a hand from which nervelessly *Adam Bede* drops', he wrote in 1911: *The Critical Attitude*, London: Duckworth and Co. – henceforth *CA*; p. 56.
6   See Carroll 27; Rosemary Ashton, *George Eliot: A Life*, London: Penguin, 1997 – henceforth 'Ashton'; p. 329; Gordon S. Haight, ed. *A Century of George Eliot Criticism*, London: Methuen & Co., 1966 – henceforth 'Haight'; p. xi.
7   See my book *Fragmenting Modernism: Ford Madox Ford, the Novel and the Great War*, Manchester: Manchester University Press, 2002, pp. 209-15. Here I note the similarity in the images Eliot uses to display Bulstrode's crisis (light and dark, windows, glass and double reflection) to those Ford finds to describe his impressionism in 'On Impressionism' in 1914.
8   Ford may have been thirty-eight (a year older than Eliot when she first published fiction), and the author of 29 books, but 1911 – the year I go on in the essay to discuss – was a very difficult year. His relationship with Violet Hunt was fraught; the title for the first relevant chapter in Max Saunders' biography is a contemporary quotation from Ford, 'art is very bitter'. Yet he showed in this year, according to Saunders, the ability to 'rise from the ashes of his past life' in two of the four books that he published: *The Simple Life Limited* and *Ancient Lights and Certain New Reflections*. Max Saunders, *Ford Madox Ford: A Dual Life*, vol. 1, Oxford: Oxford University Press, 1996, p. 320.
9   'The Critical Attitude and English Literature of To-Day', *English Review* 3 (October 1909), 481-94, became chapter 3 of *The Critical Attitude* with minor changes, according to David Harvey, *Ford Madox Ford: 1873-1939: A Bibliography of Works and Criticism*, Princeton: Princeton University Press, 1962; *CA* 55-78. The Eliot critique is the subject of the first few pages.

10 Earlier in the same text he sets out his diametrically opposed view of the job of writer: 'his actual and first desire must be always the expression of himself […] the expression of his view of life as it is, not as he would like it to be': *CA* 32-3.

11 An earlier example of such pairing is Shaw and Barrie, *CA* 34-9. In *ML* 715-20 he does something similar with Austen and Trollope.

12 In this way, it is, perhaps, like other examples of Ford's criticism, when he is reacting, and judging, on several levels at once.

13 Lord Acton's description of her as 'the most illustrious figure that had arisen in literature since Goethe' was another (quoted by Oliver Elton, in *A Survey of English Literature, 1830-1880*, in Haight 190).

14 In Haight 136-49 (136).

15 The crucial period was between 1885 (when Lord Acton's review of Cross's *George Eliot's Life* was published in the *Nineteenth Century*), and 1890.

16 See Haight 161-2; 169-70; 166-68. See also Carroll 41-3. Carroll writes that Henley 'seeks to ridicule' Eliot (42).

17 Woolf's essay was written for the Eliot centenary, and was published in the *Times Literary Supplement* in November 1919. It addresses the way in which the late Victorian version of a deluded woman had held sway, and asks 'at what moment, and by what means' her spell was broken. Her answer has quite a lot to do with Eliot's sex (Haight 183).

18 Though the Women's Social and Political Union wasn't founded until 1903, Emmeline and Christabel Pankhurst founded the Women's Franchise League in 1889, and the Married Women's Property Acts were passed in 1870 and 1882. Eric Hobsbawm suggests that, while the movement for (middle class) women's emancipation 'accelerated during the 1880s', in addition a 'growing number of bourgeois males were no longer required to do productive work, and many of them indulged in cultural activities' instead. Lucky George. See Eric Hobsbawm, *The Age of Empire 1875-1914*, London: Weidenfeld & Nicolson, 1995, p. 202. His larger discussion about the 'New Woman', in Chapter 8, is, of course, also relevant.

19 *This Monstrous Regiment of Women*, which took its title from John Knox's 'infamous diatribe against female rule' in 1558. And in February 1911 Ford had written to the editor of the *New Age* defending his support of the right of women to vote. 'I am accustomed to say and to believe', he wrote, 'that there is no real difference between man as man and woman as woman'. See Joseph Wiesenfarth, *Ford Madox Ford and the Regiment of Women*, Madison, WI: The University of Wisconsin Press, 2005, pp. 25, 27.

20 He admires her character drawing, her humour, her gossip.

21 Ashton continues to detail the admiration of her mental faculties expressed by John Chapman, Herbert Spencer, Charles Dickens, and George Henry Lewes. In 1851, some months before her meeting with Combe, she was lodging at 142 Strand, the office of the radical London publisher John Chapman, and working as the unofficial editor of his publication, the *Westminster Review*. The unusualness of this position for a young woman at this time, states Ashton, 'can hardly be overestimated' (p. 4).

22 This is an extract from his autobiography, published in 1883, quoted by Haight 150. Even Henry James, of whom more later, found her guilty of 'an excess of reflection'. The quotation comes from his review of Cross's *Life of George Eliot* in the *Atlantic Monthly*, 1885. In Fred Kaplan, *Henry James: the imagination of genius*, London: Hodder & Stoughton, 1992, p. 350.

23 In a letter dated 28 June 1862, quoted by Carroll 195.

24 Gillian Beer, *George Eliot*, Brighton: The Harvester Press, 1986, p. 17.

25 This issue is evidently of interest to Jenny Uglow, who writes well about it in her biography:

> She was delighted at the success of her impersonation, a fictional trick in itself and one which questions her realism in an intriguing way. She drew many portraits from life [...] but the authorial comment [...] comes not from the 'real' memory of Marian Evans but from a man, granted the status, education and social confidence she had been denied. The mask also sets her free, in one swoop, to rewrite her own history. She now had power over that complex, demanding Midland society which had so constrained her – she could control actions, pin down motives, re-design fates. *George Eliot*, London: Virago, 1987, pp. 83-4.

26 Woolf says in her essay in 1919 that her decision to go alone to Weimar with G. H. Lewes in 1854 was 'of profound moment to her and still matters to us' (Haight 184).

27 Even the most unimaginative and unsympathetic opponent of Eliot's didacticism might struggle to remain unmoved by the letters Lewes wrote to her publisher, John Blackwood, as she was publishing her first stories. Her fear in the face of publication (Ashton calls this a 'terrible diffidence', p. 164), and necessary cultivation of masculine disguise, meant that Herbert Spencer was highly unpopular for helping to 'out' her as the author of *Adam Bede*.

28 David Carroll describes the 'unexpected ups and downs' in her reputation (p. 1). Ford changes his mind about other writers too of course. Think of the difference in his assessment of Dostoevsky in 1914, and in 1938, in the final section of *ML*. His 1914 essay on *The Idiot* is reprinted in Saunders and Stang eds, *Critical Essays*, Manchester: Carcanet, 2002 – henceforth *CE*; pp. 126-9.

29 Two other series of the same name, originally in the *Dial* and the *English Review*, were republished in *Thus to Revisit: Some Reminiscences*, in 1921. This series was not, but has been republished in *CE* 186-202.

30 *Time and Eternity: a tale of three exiles* was published in 1919 by Chapman and Hall (London). It has three long chapters, the subject of each is one of the exiles of the title, who share lodgings: Mr Perekatov, a Russian Jew; Valerie du Toit, a young, rich, Dutch South African; and Stephen Lawrie, a young Scots socialist.

31 Ford could not have read Woolf's essay on Eliot before writing this piece. Her essay was, as has been indicated, published in the *TLS* on 20 November; his appeared in the *Piccadilly Review* on 23 October. His positive view of Eliot here, then, especially in the second piece I go on to discuss, is more striking than his opinion in 1911.

32 *CE* 186-7. In *The English Novel*, Ford opposes 'novels' to 'nuvvels'. The latter are beset by 'continually brought in passages of moralizations' by their authors – Fielding, say, or Thackeray (*EN* 77).

33 Ford may well have known nothing of Virginia Woolf. Although she and Leonard had instituted the Hogarth Press in 1917, *Night and Day* was only Woolf's second novel.

34 This unsigned review appeared in the *Atlantic Monthly* in May 1858 (Carroll 66).

35 'George Eliot' now appeared on the title page, but was still assumed to be male. 'The suspicion is pretty general', as it was put in the *Saturday Review* (later in the same review from which this quotation is taken), 'that George Eliot is an assumed name, screening that of some studious clergyman, a Cantab, who lives, or has lived the greater part of his life in the country, who is the father of a family, of High Church

tendencies, and exceedingly fond of children, Greek dramatists, and dogs' (Carroll 67).

36 George Eliot, *Scenes of Clerical Life*, ed. David Lodge, Harmondsworth, Middlesex: Penguin, 1973, p. 18. A little later in his introduction he does concede that 'Janet's Repentance' contains 'some of the best writing in *Scenes of Clerical Life*' (p. 28). The debate about Eliot and her realism is vociferous and complex, and it is one to which many critics contribute, in detail, throughout the twentieth century, Lodge included. Many of the relevant texts can be found in K. M. Newton, ed., *George Eliot*, London: Longman, 1991. Newton says in his introduction that while 'her reputation as a novelist of the first rank has never perhaps been entirely secure', the critical debate about her works has 'been productive at several important stages in the history of modern criticism', p. 1.

37 In the years 1911-1919 Ford had published *The Good Soldier* of course, but also (in addition to many other titles) *Henry James*.

38 Saunders, *A Dual Life*, vol. 2, pp. 373, 380.

39 Ford Madox Ford, *Return to Yesterday* (1931), ed. Bill Hutchings, Manchester: Carcanet, 1999, p. 18.

40 142 Strand (see note 21) backed almost on to the Thames, and Ashton writes that Chapman had acquired a key to the gate at the back of Somerset House, 'where he and his boarders could walk up and down'. However, though Spencer may well have walked there with Eliot, he was not in love with her, but she with him. She wrote him love letters that Ashton calls 'extraordinary' in their frankness and unconventionality. Eliot herself supposed 'no woman ever before wrote such a letter as this' (Ashton 79, 98-100).

41 Richard Freadman, *Eliot, James and the Fictional Self*, London: Macmillan, 1986, p. 31. Freadman discusses the range and intensity of Eliot's influence on James, and quotes James on her: 'George Eliot belongs to that class of pre-eminent writers in relation to whom the imagination comes to self-consciousness only to find itself in subjection' (p. 32).

42 Cornelia Pulsifer Kelly writes that publication of *Felix Holt* brought James back to his writing life on an 'epoch-making day' in 1866 (*The Early Development of Henry James*, University of Illinois Studies in Language and Literature, vol. XV, Feb-May, 1930, p. 60). But James envied, as well as admired, her, and himself suffered an anxiety of influence, as both Freadman and Kelly point out. Freadman talks of a 'desperate and defensive struggle for artistic and psychic individuation' in James' relationship with Eliot (p. 32). As a post-script to the comments about Eliot's brain, it is tempting to quote a letter from James in Rome to Grace Norton in March, 1873, in which he writes that '[A] marvellous mind throbs on every page of *Middlemarch*. It raises the standard of what is to be expected of women [...] We know all about the female heart; but apparently there is a female brain, too'. *Henry James Letters*, vol. 1, 1873-1875, ed. Leon Edel, London and Basingstoke: Macmillan, 1974, p. 351. (In context, this is at least in part a tongue-in-cheek remark.)

43 Earlier in this essay I quoted Ford in *The Critical Attitude* on the subject of 'the great bulk of educated criticism of to-day'. I omitted, at that point, a crucial phrase from the quotation. In full (with my emphasis), he wrote that George Eliot 'was taken more seriously than any writer of to-day ever has been, *or ever will be* taken'.

FORD AND TURGENEV

Max Saunders

Ford's 'Literary Contacts' take various forms: his contacts with other writers, or with their work; other writers' contacts with him, or his work; but also contacts of other kinds – whether with people, places, things, or ideas – which are mediated by literature. Ford's own friendships were intensely literary contacts, mostly either with other writers, or with others deeply committed to literature. His contacts with places, countries, histories, were also intensely literary ones. For Ford, to be in London, Paris, New York, Provence, the Romney Marsh, was to be in contact with its cultural history. Conversely, his sense of place was shaped by his contact with literature.

A manuscript fragment in Cornell University's Ford collection brings together these ideas in suggestive ways. It is headed 'Books for Exchange: II', and is closely related to a recently rediscovered 'Literary Causerie' Ford published in 1905 on Flaubert.[1] The latter begins: 'I had some men of letters in my study the other evening and one of them began talking of exchanging books – of exchanging, that is, the names of our really intimate consolers'. The fragment is mostly about Turgenev's *Sportsman's Sketches*, which is the first book Ford mentions in the Flaubert essay. Though the title of 'Books for Exchange: II'. suggests a continuation of the published essay, its opening appears to follow on from this opening paragraph – 'They are the books that always ring true to our particular notes, that we may rely upon always to distract us' – rather than to follow on from the end of the Flaubert essay. In its incomplete state it's impossible to be sure whether it is a draft of another essay, or an abandoned passage from the published one. Its connexion with the Flaubert causerie means that it too was written soon after Ford's 1904 breakdown; and it is possible that he felt it too revealing of his fragile mental state to publish. It is precisely for that honesty about how mental distress affects his relation to literature that it is so illuminating, and it is published here for the first time:

Books for Exchange
II.

I think that the indispensable characteristic of the books that one offers one's friend in exchange for his is just that one – that it [*sic*] should grasp one, that it should hold one, at just those times when the mind most needs to be held: at just those times when, through distractions, illnesses, weaknesses or troubles, the mind seems to slip off from the pages of a book as you may see a newly fledged sparrow slide awkwardly down the slope of a roof. – It is just then that the mind most needs the solace of books – & it is just then, as a rule, that books most find us. Then indeed one's book for exchange is most precious – & it is then that I turn to the *Sportsman's Sketches* of Tourguénieff.[2]

I have read it so often at such moments – when I have been below the line of physical & mental health – that I seem almost to have reserved it for such moments, &, tenderly as I have always loved it, I was astonished when I took it up this morning, being moderately sane, [clothed?] and cheerful. Its colours seemed to be brighter than I had imagined: I seem to have seen it in a newer and brighter light. What is more, I have begun with the sketch of *Hor and Kalinitch* & have read right through to the end of *Lebedyan* – the last in the first volume of M[rs] Garnett's version: I have lost so much time, gained so much pleasure, & have a little muddled my ideas of what I had meant to say – so that, now, when I rather want to look up a quotation in the second volume I am afraid & refrain. . . . . . .

Tourguenieff, like Flaubert, is astonishingly little known in England: since he has no *Madame Bovary* for this country's locked book closets, he is hardly even known at all. Yet there is little doubt that he is actually – by acclamation – the greatest writer that the XIXth century produced – for if, excluding Russia (which would place him first) & Great Britain (which ignores all foreign writers) we canvassed the nations of Europe & the United States of America for the name of the second writer of that period, we should find that, unanimously they would accord that place to Tourguenieff, reserving, naturally, the first place to some countryman of their own, each in its turn. This is a pretty fair test. – And, indeed, I have heard it triumphantly borne out, even in this country. – For, the most-looked[-]up-to British critic of letters of the present day, being asked his opinion of XIXth century foreign writers in general replied: "Oh, they're a dirty minded, physically dirty set of fellows. – Except of course Dumas!" – But, being asked about Tourgenieff, he replied: "Oh well: yes. He was a sportsman & a gentleman."

This, of course, is a point of view, like another: but it is curious to how little extent the impression that I, personally, get from the *Sportsman's Sketches*, is that of a sportsman. It is true that the touring over Russia in search of birds to shoot was the actual occasion of the journeys during wh. Turguénieff saw the scenes that [he] has recorded in the book. Yet, practically the only description of actual shooting that one comes across is the passage in *"Lgov"* – where three "guns" come into the middle of a pond full of very [*illegible*] wild ducks & "We could not, of course, get at all the duck that were shot; those who were slightly wounded swam away; some which had been quite killed fell into such thick reeds that even Yermolaï's little lynx eyes could not discover them, yet our boat nevertheless was filled to the brim with game for supper."[3]

And this passage is too much like the description of an Imperial or Royal battue to be characterised as inspired with the spirit of a sportsman. – Shooting, in fact, was with Tourguenieff, precisely not a sport: it was a recreation that gave him a matchless opportunity for observing things between shot & shot, or between walk & walk.

This is one of Ford's earliest testimonials to a writer who was to remain a talismanic figure throughout his career; and the earliest to the book that Ford was often to cite as one of those that mattered most to him.[4] Constance Garnett's translation of *A Sportsman's Sketches* appeared in 1895, so Ford, who was a close friend of the Garnetts, is likely to have known it for a decade already. His maps of literary history may shift and evolve: Stendhal, Jane Austen, and W. H. Hudson are often but not always mentioned. Chekhov appears occasionally. More modern writers tend to figure in Ford's later pantheon (Joyce, Pound, Hemingway). But Turgenev remains a crucial figure for Ford, representing an unparalleled observer; a poetic writer; an enigmatically natural stylist; the embodiment of a human sympathy and compassion who appears to function in Ford's imagination as an antithesis to the more aloof and ironical stance, sometimes verging on cruelty, of writers like Flaubert, James, or George Moore.

In this manuscript Ford's contact with fellow-writers takes the form of discussing contacts with others' books. But the books Ford most admired and discussed tend to be by those he had known person-ally. This isn't to say he didn't admire earlier writing. The first 800 or so pages of *The March of Literature* testify to his passion for a vast range of earlier styles and forms. He hadn't known Flaubert (d. 1880) or Maupassant (d. 1893), the writers who contributed most to his ideals of style, form, and technique. But the writers to whom, along with these two, his criticism returns most often, are those he knew and admired in person as well as on the page: especially James, Crane, Conrad, W. H. Hudson, Pound, and Joyce. Turgenev figures in this category, since Ford had met him when he was brought to visit Madox Brown's studio. The young Ford, probably then not quite eight, offered Turgenev a chair, in what he described later as 'the earliest incident of my chequered and adventurous career'. It is the personality which impressed Ford in the man that he re-encounters in the books:

> I was conscious simply of a singular, compassionate smile that still seems to
> me to look up out of the pages of his books when – as I constantly do, and
> always with a sense of amazement – I re-read them.

This was written more than thirty years after 'Books for Exchange',
but echoes its astonishment on re-reading Turgenev. 'When one is
suddenly introduced to such immensenesses', said Ford, one 'believes
that one is being visited by some supernatural manifestation'. But
Turgenev's compassion for 'anything that was very young, small, and
helpless' spared him from the mortal terror 'that visits one when one
sees Gods'.[5]

Turgenev always retained this sense of godlike supremacy in
Ford's memory. 'For me Turgenev is the greatest of all writers', he
wrote.[6] He told Bowen that he thought Turgenev's *Letters of a
Sportsman* 'the finest things that were ever written', adding: 'I would
rather have written "Bielshin Prairie" than have done anything else in
the realm of human achievements [. . .]'.[7] Given the strength of these
judgements, it appears that Ford's literary contact with Turgenev has
been underestimated in comparison to his engagement with Flaubert,
James, Conrad, or Pound. The rest of this essay will chart his critical
discussions of Turgenev, and then consider the influence of Turgenev
on Ford's writing.

Ford's critical comments on Turgenev also reflect his own
aesthetic development. His earliest remarks, written when Ford was at
his most prolific as a poet, tend to emphasize Turgenev's poetic
qualities:

> Tolstoy the novelist gave us exact and very wonderful observations of life:
> Dostoievsky gave us the most wonderful registrations of mental abysms, of
> darkness, of profound and irremediable gloom. But Tourguenieff gave the
> world a tender, exact, and poetic rendering of human life. There is nothing
> in the world more poetic than some of the sketches in "A Sportsman's
> Letters", there is nothing in the world that more pitifully sums up the
> enigmas of human lives than "Fathers and Children," nothing that puts more
> piteously the case of humanity bound down by and bowing down to the
> conventions of humanity itself than the story of Lisa in the "House of
> Gentlefolk."[8]

This view of Turgenev as poet is carried on into Ford's later accounts.
In his memoir of Conrad he recalls their discussions of him. Indeed,
an important component of Ford's admiration for the Russian is that it

was shared by the novelist-friends he most admired – Conrad and James:

> We talked of Turgenev – the greatest of all poets; *Byelshin Prairie* from the *Letters of a Sportsman*, the greatest of all pieces of writing: Turgenev wrapped in a cloak lying in the prairie at night, at a little distance from a great fire beside which the boy horse-tenders talked desultorily about the Roosalki of the forests with the green hair and water nymphs that drag you down to drown in the river.[9]

A decade later he was still granting the same story in the same book the same pre-eminence. And, true to his dictum that poetry should be as well-written as prose, he still celebrates it as a poem; though the terms of appreciation have perhaps sharpened into those of the Modernist poetics Ford was instrumental in advancing:

> Or if I want to remember a magic verbal projection of the concrete there is the picture of the boy Alyusha and the rushes and the horses in the firelight of Turgenev's Byelshin Prairie which, in its entirety seems and has always seemed to me to be the most marvellous poem in the world.[10]

This emphasis on the poetic perhaps arises because *A Sportsman's Sketches* is not a novel, but a series of anecdotal essays, dealing with natural description and encounters with people, written in autobiographical form. But it was the writing and criticising of novels that especially exercised Ford, and another main emphasis of his discussions of Turgenev is his pre-eminence as a *novelist* too. An essay of 1919, for example, does what Ford's criticism often does: contrasts the ideal of the novel with something else, sometimes what he dismissively calls the 'nuvvle', sometimes the second-rate novel, or as here, the 'romance':

> Let us say that amorphous, discursive tales containing digressions, moralisations and lectures are Romances, and that Novels have unity of form, culminations and shapes. In the Romance it matters little of what the tale teller discourses, so long as he can retain the interest of the reader; in the Novel every word – every word – must be one that carries the story forward to its appointed end. The Romances then would be the *Satyricon*; *Don Quixote*; *Tom Jones; Vanity Fair*; or the *Brothers Karamzeff*, of Dostoievsky; the Novels – well, there are very few Novels. There are the *Neveu de Ramau*, of Diderot; *Le Rouge et le Noir*, by Stendhal, *Madame Bovary*, and *Education Sentimentale*, of Flaubert; practically all the imaginative writings of Turgenev, and of the late Mr. James.[11]

In an ironic review of E. M. Forster's *Aspects of the Novel*, Ford argues that 'it is perfectly true to say that Anglo-Saxondom has no first-rate novelist in the sense that Turgeniev, Chekhov, Stendhal, and Flaubert were first rate', though he adds: 'One may make a reservation in favour of Conrad and Henry James to whom we are too near to judge with any certainty'.[12] Thus Turgenev is one of those who sets a standard of aesthetic excellence. In one of his wartime books of propaganda, Ford includes him in a list of artists who:

> by means of a certain impeccability and austerity in the handling of words, of paint, or of musical resolutions, stand perfectly unchallenged by nation and nation [. . . .] They provide at once the thoughts which we think, the language with which we express our thoughts, and the standards with which we measure our achievements and the achievements of our fellows[.][13]

One component for Ford of this eminence is a quality at the heart of his concept of Impressionism: aloofness, detachment, objectivity, the eschewing of any desire to moralize.[14] That is what, for Ford, sets such writers apart from Victorian novelists like Dickens or Eliot. Henry James prized Turgenev for the way 'He felt and understood the opposite sides of life'.[15] It is his feeling for others which prevents his taking sides against them. Ford would have admired Turgenev's tendency (which was also his own) to be attacked from all sides – as when *Fathers and Sons* angered both the radicals and conservatives for its treatment of the Nihilist Bazarov. Ford echoes James's sentence in his praise of Conrad, where the 'opposite sides of life' have become internalised, into the inner conflicts of individuals. Conrad, he said, could 'see vividly the opposing sides of human characters' (*MS* 93). And later in the same book, he praises Turgenev as having 'had the seeing eye to such an extent that he could see that two opposing truths were equally true' (*MS* 208). 'Flaubert, then, evolved the maxim that the creative artist as Creator must be indifferently impartial between all his characters', wrote Ford. 'That Turgenev was by nature . . . because of his own very selflessness'. Left at that, this might sound a counsel of sentimentality. But Ford takes up the liberal virtue of openness to opposing views into the domain of aesthetics. Not only do true novelists present characters with opposing views and opposing sides, but they also take opposing views of them. 'To noble natures like those of Flaubert and Turgenev', says Ford, 'the mankind that surround them is insupportable . . . if only for its want of intelligence' (*MS* 209). This might seem surprising of the gentle Russian – whereas

Flaubert's scorn for bourgeois cliché is legendary. But Ford develops the idea to suggest that the requisite multiple perspective is not only psychological, but also spatial and temporal:

> That is why the great poet is invariably an expatriate, if not invariably in climate, then at least in the regions of the mind. If he cannot get away from his fellows he must shut himself up from them. But if he is to be great he must also be continually making his visits to his own particular Spasskoye [Turgenev's estate]. He must live always both in and out of his time, his ancestral home, and the hearts of his countrymen. (*MS* 209)

There is much self-analysis here too, of course, especially in the way Ford takes Turgenev as a model for his own habit of expatriation: his need to write about places and times from the outside as well as the inside.

From one point of view, then, Turgenev stands as an exemplar of conscious art: 'at once the most gifted and the most technically perfect of all writers' (*AL* 185-6). Yet – paradoxically – Ford, usually so committed to the technical analysis of writing, also repeatedly remarks on the impossibility of analysing Turgenev's achievement.

> It is useless to say that he is greater than Shakespeare, but he has, in common with Shakespeare, the quality of being unapproachable, and he lacks some of Shakespeare's faults. He is so unapproachable, because, as a writer, you can learn nothing of him. His methods are undiscoverable; you might imitate him, but you would never get any further. And, inasmuch as the figures that he draws are more actual, less typical, than those that Shakespeare drew, and inasmuch as the human vicissitudes that he narrates are less legendary, he is a writer more humane. Lisa is a more womanly figure than are Cordelia, or Portia, or Anne Page, just because the mental struggles through which she went are the struggles through which we all have to go at one time or another and in one form or another.
>
> And if we go to a novelist to learn what life is, to whom can we go with a surer faith than Tourguenieff? That makes him, of course, have less significance for Russia, since Russia desires first to hear what to do as a nation. But we whose national problems are solved pretty well and in a rule-of-thumb way have leisure to set before us the problem of how to live tolerantly, and, in a high sense, gently, with our individual fellow-men. (*CE* 40)

Even in the fullest, best, and last sustained account Ford wrote of Turgenev, in his penultimate book *Mightier Than the Sword*, though he says much both about Turgenev's personality, and about the impossibility of separating it from those of this creations, he notes that 'contrary to the habit of writers of my complexion I have here said

nothing about the "technique" of my subject', and adds: 'It can't be
done. No one can say anything valid about the technique of Turgenev'
(*MS* 212). In this respect Ford couples Turgenev with W. H. Hudson,
much of whose naturalist prose is formally close to that of *A Sportsman's Sketches*. He was fond of quoting Conrad saying to him about
Hudson: 'You can't tell how this fellow gets his effects!'; 'He writes
as the grass grows. The Good God makes it be there. And that is all
there is to it!'[16] Ford transfers the comment to Turgenev, saying: 'As
with Hudson, the stylist, the dear God made Turgenev's words to
come, as He made the grass grow. It is there and there is no more to
say about it' (*MS* 213). From one point of view, such inscrutability is
the perfection of Impressionist aesthetics: 'And the main canon of the
doctrine of Impressionism had been this: The artist must aim at the
absolute suppression of himself in his rendering of his Subject' (*TR*
138). Writers like Hudson and Turgenev seem to Ford to achieve this
'absolute suppression' of the self in their writing thanks to their ability
so utterly to lose themselves in observation:

> I suppose that the chief characteristic of great writers – of writers who are
> great by temperament as well as by industry or contrivance – is self-
> abandonment. You imagine Mr. Hudson watching a tiny being and his whole
> mind goes into the watching: then his whole mind goes into the rendering [. . .
> .] Turgenev is such another as Mr. Hudson and I can recall no third. (*TR* 70)

In one example, though he still doesn't analyse it, Ford does attribute
Turgenev with a 'self-consciousness' as far as his *art* is concerned, but
which seems – by another paradox – founded on his 'selflessness' as
an observer:

> Turgenev, I mean, watched humanity with much such another engross-
> ment as Mr. Hudson devotes to kingfishers, sheep, or the grass of fields and
> rendered his results with the same tranquillity. Probably, however, Turgenev
> had a greater self-consciousness in the act of writing: for of Mr. Hudson you
> might as well say that he never had read a book. The Good God makes his
> words be there. . . . Still, in the *Sportsman's Sketches*, in the *Singers*, the *Rattle
> of Wheels*, and in *Bielshin Prairie* above all – you get that note: – of the
> enamoured, of the rapt, watcher; so enamoured and so rapt that the watcher
> disappears, becoming merely part of the surrounding atmosphere amidst
> which, with no self-consciousness, the men, the forests or the birds act and
> interact. I know, however, of no other writers that possess this complete
> selflessness. (*TR* 70-71)

That idea embodies another Impressionist paradox, according to which it is the most selfless art that best expresses the writer's personality. Ford connects Turgenev's technical inscrutability with his biographical opacity: 'No, of Turgenev's technique one can say with assurance no more than one can say with certainty of his personality or of his relations with Madame Viardot' (*MS* 213). Doubtless Ford wished that his own private life had been less susceptible of public analysis. But what is at stake here is a way of thinking about the relation between artists and their work. He argues that Turgenev eludes biographers because he identified with the people and passions he observed to such an extent that his identity combines with theirs:

> Turgenev was by turns and all at once, Slavophil and Westerner, Tsarist and Nihilist, Germanophile and Francophobe, Francophile and Hun-hater, insupportably homesick for Spasskoye and the Nevsky Prospekt and wracked with nostalgia for the Seine bank at Bougival and the rue de Rivoli. All proper men are that to some degree – certainly all proper novelists. But Turgenev carried his vicarious passions further than did anyone of whom one has ever heard. He would meet during a railway journey some sort of strong-passioned veterinary surgeon or some sort of decayed country gentleman. . . . And for the space of the journey he would be them. . . . (*MS* 208-9)

Substitute English or American terms for the Russian ones and there is oblique autobiography here too. But the force of that autobiography is to say that novelists' lives are best expressed by their fiction:

> One knows nothing about him. One knows less about him even than about Shakespeare. He moves surrounded by the cloud of his characters as a monarch by his courtiers [. . . .] (*MS* 205)

This process by which a writer's identity is expanded by observation is matched, for Ford, by a corresponding process in reading. Our last paradox of Impressionism is that a writer like Turgenev can render an impression so that it expands the consciousness of the reader. If the impression is compelling and vivid enough, it can insinuate itself into your own repertoire of impressions and memories of impressions. Ford sometimes makes the claim – at first sight an astounding one – that experiences he has read about have become his own experiences. For example, he writes of Hudson:

> He shared with Turgenev the quality that makes you unable to find out how he got his effects [. . . .] When you read you forget the lines and the print. It is as if a remotely smiling face looked up at you out of the page and told you things.

> And those things become part of your own experience. It is years since I first
> read *Nature in Downland*. Yet [. . .] the first words that I there read have
> become a part of my own life. They describe how, lying on the turf of the high
> sunlit downs above Lewes in Sussex, Hudson looked up into the perfect,
> limpid blue of the sky and saw, going to infinite distances one behind the other
> [. . .] little shining globes, like soap bubbles. They were thistledown floating in
> an almost windless heaven.
>   Now that is part of my life. I have never had the patience – the
> contemplative tranquillity – to lie looking up into the heavens. I have never in
> my life done it. Yet that is I, not Hudson, looking up into the heavens [. . .]
> (*MS* 70-71)

This might appear a naïve claim that art is vicarious experience. But
the Fordian reader is not in the position of the man who leaps up from
the audience to interrupt the intolerable violence of *King Lear*. Ford
isn't confusing art and life, and distinguishes clearly between Hudson,
who did have the patience to make this observation, and himself, who
didn't. Rather, it is that Hudson's self-abandonment opens up a space
which enables the reader to inhabit the subjectivity of the narrative.
Reading is an experience; reading masterly impressionism expands
your repertoire of memorable experience.

     Such a claim begins to look more interesting than the naïve
theory of vicarious experience if we ask why it is that the writers who
seem to Ford most to dissolve the boundaries between reading and
experiencing are also those whose techniques are least susceptible of
analysis. One way of approaching an answer is to consider a case
where a writer's technique is advertised – as, say, in the kind of
Thackerayan authorial intrusion that Ford frequently denounces. In
such a case, technically-conscious readers like Ford have their
attentions drawn to the techniques. That is, when you can find out how
writers get their effects, you are conscious of their *writing*. What Ford
values in the prose of Hudson and Turgenev is that the unobtrusive-
ness of its technique short-circuits his critical attention, making him
disattend to the fact that he is reading; which in turn makes him more
susceptible to the impressions. It is only the supreme examples of
impressionism that are able to bypass Ford's formidable technical self-
consciousness, and thus take him out of his own consciousness. The
point is not that he becomes unable to distinguish between his own
experience, and Turgenev's or Hudson's; but that during the act of
reading, or while contemplating the impressions in memory, the force
of the presentation suspends that distinction; distracts attention from
thinking about whose subjectivity we are experiencing. What Ford

most admires in literature, then, is the ability of selfless writing to make happen selfless reading; reading in which the self loses self-consciousness that it is reading, which in turn facilitates the suspension of consciousness of the self:

> Mrs Constance Garnett, whose translation of Turgeniev's works has given me, I think, more pleasure than anything else in the world except, perhaps, the writings of Mr. W. Hudson. Whenever I am low, whenever I am feeble or very tired or pursued by regrets, I have only to take up one or the other of these writers. It does not much matter which. For immediately I am brought into contact with a wise, a fine, and infinitely soothing personality. I assimilate pleasure with no effort at all, and so weariness leaves me, regrets go away to a distance, and I am no more conscious of a very dull self [. . . .] Word after word sinks into the mind, pervading it as water slowly soaks into sands. You are, in fact, unconscious that you are reading. You are just conscious of pleasure as you might be in the sunshine. (*AL* 188-9)

Which returns us to the 'Books for Exchange' manuscript, and its gratitude to Turgenev for what we might now call a therapeutic effect, of taking the depressed mind out of itself. Of course Ford's own renderings of these writers must needs be renderings of his readings, which brings to bear a different kind of consciousness; more mediated, or more aware of writing's mediation, than they might sound. But that would be another essay.

To conclude this one, let us consider the influence of Turgenev on Ford's writing. It is Ford's discursive impressionism, rather than his fiction, that owes the greatest debt to *A Sportsman's Sketches*. Their more recent translator, Richard Freeborn, describes how their 'pictorial aspect' is complemented by what he calls a 'sociological aspect':

> which involves a Turgenev who cannot help being a member of the nobility, of the landowning class, and who to that extent is both a stranger to the world of the peasants and a frankly curious observer anxious to describe this world to his readers.[17]

Put thus, Turgenev's influence on Ford's writing about English peasant life, in *The Heart of the Country, Women & Men,* and *Return to Yesterday*, as well as in his early poetry, becomes clear. Indeed, the whole project of the trilogy *England and the English* can be seen as applying the method of *A Sportsman's Sketches* to English life, whether rural or urban. Whether he's describing a London match-seller, the view from a train window, or the lives of peasants like

Meary Walker, Meary Spratt, or Ragged Arse Wilson, Turgenev's
narrator is the model for his class-awareness, sympathetic curiosity,
and pictorial impressionism. Indeed, the term 'impression' is the one
Turgenev uses for the experiences he is rendering (see, for example,
Sketches 164, 250).

There are also traces of Turgenev through Ford's fiction; and
readers with 'the seeing eye' will have noted already how that phrase
of Dowell's recurs in Ford's writing about Turgenev.[18] It is possible
Ford had the 'Hamlet of the Shchigrovsky District' in mind when
conceiving *The Good Soldier*: a tragicomic love story, told by a
narrator perpetually on the brink of absurdity, to a mostly silent
listener.

Writing of 'Bezhin Lea' (or 'Bielshin Prairie') Freeborn says:
'A special magic haunts the picture that Turgenev offers us and
suggests that such beautiful July days are a part of innocence, of
boyhood, clothed in the magic of recollection' (*Sketches* 13). 'The fact
that he was drawing on memory may account for the brilliant lustre',
Freeborn writes of the stories, 'so evocative and even nostalgic, which
surrounds the best of them' (*Sketches* 10). Turgenev was a master of
nostalgia; in the remembered passion of *Spring Torrents*; or in seeing
the opposing sides of generation conflict in *Fathers and Children* by
thinking himself back into forward-looking youthfulness. The magical
lustre of nostalgia is also the subject of Ford's and Conrad's *Romance*:
'And, looking back, we see Romance – that subtle thing that is mirage
– that is life'.[19] *A Sportsman's Sketches* is sometimes translated as
Memoirs of a Sportsman.[20] Otherwise Turgenev wasn't as prolific an
autobiographer as Ford.[21] But since Turgenev looms so large in Ford's
first volume of memoirs, *Ancient Lights*, and behind his writing about
England, it is not fanciful to see him as a guiding presence in Ford's
other reminiscences; which helps account for his return in *Mightier
Than the Sword*. Another way of putting this is to see Turgenev as
anticipating Ford's interest in the relation between autobiography and
impressionism. A marvellous passage in 'Forest and Steppe' remembers how sensations in the natural world reanimate someone's autobiographical imagination. (Note how the attention to the dog, racing
forward after scents and movements, and to the birds and animals it
disturbs, permeates the texture of introspection here):

> Your breathing is calm, though a strange anxiety invades your soul. You walk
> along the edge of the forest, keeping your eyes on the dog, but in the

meantime there come to mind beloved images, beloved faces, the living and the dead, and long-since dormant impressions unexpectedly awaken; the imagination soars and dwells on the air like a bird, and everything springs into movement with such clarity and stands before the eyes. Your heart either suddenly quivers and starts beating fast, passionately racing forward, or drowns irretrievably in recollections. The whole of life unrolls easily and swiftly like a scroll; a man has possession of his whole past, all his feelings, all his powers, his entire soul. (*Sketches* 250)

Ford, writing one of his characteristic (and characteristically Turgenevean) books about places and memories, recognised: 'Try how he will, an Impressionist's book about an actual place or an actual man is bound to assume a rather reminiscential air'.[22]

It is this combination of pictorial impression and psychological effect that gives Turgenev's descriptions of place their 'magical' quality. They are never just visual, but also 'spiritual' – that is, in his terms, experiences that involve the soul. Transformative encounters with landscape tend only to appear in Ford's historical fiction before the war, when the characters have more reason to be out of doors; and also in his poetry. His early novels of modern life are more urban and social in their emphases. But the enforced exposure of the Western Front changed that. It is to the haunting remembered wartime landscapes of *No Enemy* and to *Parade's End* that we need to turn to find an equivalent. (It is true the landscapes of *The Heart of the Country* are intensely psychological, but written very much under the shadow of Ford's 1904 breakdown, and tend to give an impression of the landscape as oppressive.) Perhaps the best example is the dog-cart ride Christopher Tietjens and Valentine Wannop take on the Romney Marsh, submerged in a transcendental silver mist, which both provides the magical backdrop against which they fall in love, but also obscures General Campion's car, which smashes into them, anticipating the danger and destruction to come. In 'Clatter of Wheels' Turgenev describes a very different, and more comical (though potentially disastrous) ride, at one point of which the narrator is woken by a strange splashing noise:

What on earth had happened? I was lying in the carriage as before, but all around it, and barely more than a foot below its edge, a flat area of water, illuminated by the moon, was fragmented and criss-crossed by tiny, distinct ripples. I looked toward the front and there was Filofey sitting on the box, his head fallen forward, his back bent, solemn as an idol, and further ahead still, above gurgling water, I could see the bent line of the shaft and the horses' heads and backs. And everything was so still, so soundless, as if it were in an

> enchanted kingdom, a dream, a fairy-tale sleep. Fantastic! Then I looked
> towards the back from under the hood of the carriage. We were indeed in the
> very middle of a river [. . . .] (*Sketches* 232-3)

Just as a memory of this episode seems to me to underlie the dog-cart
ride at the end of Part One of *Some Do Not . . .*, so another of the
Sportsman's Sketches seems to inform *Last Post*. In 'Living Relic',
the peasant girl Lukeria was engaged to be married. In her excitement
she is unable to sleep, and, hearing a beautiful nightingale song, is
drawn outside to listen to it. She thinks she hears her fiancé calling
softly to her in the dark, and accidentally slips off the porch and has a
bad fall, receiving internal injuries that result in almost complete
paralysis. She now appears to conflate time: she is still young, but
appears ancient and wizened, her face yellowed like an icon (hence
the title). She lies in a wattle hut in the summer, receiving visits from
friends, and impressions of the natural scene. Though her story is
entirely different, her situation is exactly that of Mark Tietjens as he
approaches death in the final novel of *Parade's End*. Like Mark, she
has developed an acute awareness of animal life: 'If there's a mole
digging underground, I can hear it. And I can smell every scent, it
doesn't matter how faint it is!' (*Sketches* 216). She is unable to sleep
for pain. Rather than thinking (of the pain, of the past) she just
perceives (*Sketches* 216): an exemplar of what Ford was to call 'will-
less impressionism' (*MF* 18). Lukeria is thus a figure within
Turgenev's text of the kind of unegotistical observation the author
aims at, and that Turgenev particularly represents for Ford. 'Who can
enter into another's soul?' she asks. Filofey, the feckless cart driver
says much the same when quizzed whether another cart of rowdy
travellers might contain robbers: 'How's that to be known? D'you
think it's possible to get inside another's soul, eh? Another's soul is a
mystery' (*Sketches* 219, 242). It's proverbial wisdom for the peasants,
but a technical question for Impressionist writers. Ford too, as some of
the comments quoted here show, often wondered about the possibility
of abandoning his own consciousness and imagining his way into
another. And it was the few writers whose work made him feel that
had happened, without his being able to say exactly why, who meant
most to him, and whose books he wanted to exchange with his other
contacts – his friends, and his readers.

NOTES

1 'Books for Exchange: II', autograph manuscript, 3 leaves, Carl A Kroch Library, Cornell University; transcribed by Max Saunders (with editorial conjectures in square brackets), and published here with kind permission of Michael Schmidt and the Division of Rare and Manuscript Collections, Cornell University Library. 'A Literary Causerie: The Less-Known Flaubert', Academy, 69 (11 November 1905), 1175-76. See Saunders, 'Ford Madox Ford: Further Bibliographies', English Literature in Transition, 43:2 (2000), 131-205.

2 There are slight variations in Ford's spelling of the Russian novelist's name, both within this manuscript, and throughout his writings on him. Some of the titles of Turgenev's works are also referred to variably in the discussions quoted here by Ford and by others. I have let these variants stand without editorial comment, except where the differences might cause confusion.

3 *A Sportsman's Sketches*, translated by Constance Garnett, volumes 8 and 9 of *The Novels of Ivan Turgenev* (London: William Heinemann, 1895), 8, p.127. Garnett has 'dinner' instead of 'supper'.

4 There is an earlier discussion in a letter to Galsworthy dated conjecturally as from October 1900: *Letters of Ford Madox Ford*, ed. Richard Ludwig, Princeton: Princeton University Press, 1965, p. 12.

5 Ford, *Mightier Than the Sword*, London: Allen & Unwin, 1938 – henceforth *MS*; pp. 191-93, 241. Ford, *Ancient Lights*, London: Chapman and Hall, 1911 – henceforth *AL*; pp. 186-88. Cf. *AL* 186: 'I remember Turgeniev personally only as a smile'.

6 Ford, *Return to Yesterday*, London: Gollancz, 1931, p. 129.

7 Ford to Bowen, 28 Aug. 1918: *The Correspondence of Ford Madox Ford and Stella Bowen*, ed. Sondra Stang and Karen Cochran, Bloomington and Indianapolis: Indiana University Press, 1994, p. 9. Garnett's translation gives the name of the Prairie as 'Byezhin'.

8 'Literary Portraits: [X, but says VIII]. Maxim Gorky', *Tribune* (28 September 1907), 2. Reprinted in Ford, *Critical Essays*, ed. Max Saunders and Richard Stang, Manchester: Carcanet, 2002 – henceforth *CE*; p. 40.

9 Ford, *Joseph Conrad: A Personal Remembrance*, London: Duckworth, 1924, p. 35.

10 Ford, 'Hands Off The Arts', *American Mercury*, 34 (April 1935), 402-08 (p. 407).

11 Ford, 'Thus to Revisit . . . . I. – The Novel' *Piccadilly Review* (23 October 1919), 6: *CE* 186-7.

12 Ford, 'Cambridge on the Caboodle', *Saturday Review of Literature*, 4 (17 December 1927), 449-50. *CE* 279.

13 Ford, *When Blood is Their Argument*, London: Hodder & Stoughton, 1915, pp. 80-81.

14 See Saunders, 'Impressionism, Fiction, and the Location of the Ethical', in Astrid Erll, Herbert Grabes and Ansgar Nünning, eds., *Ethics in Culture: The Dissemination of Values through Literature and other Media*, Berlin/New York: de Gruyter, 2007.

15 Henry James, *Partial Portraits*, London: Macmillan and Co., Limited, 1888, p. 296.

16 Ford, *Thus to Revisit*, London: Chapman & Hall, 1921 – henceforth *TR*; pp. 69-70.

17 Richard Freeborn, 'Introduction', *Sketches from a Hunter's Album*, Harmondsworth: Penguin, 1985 – henceforth *Sketches*; pp. 10-11. All references to the text are to this edition.

18 Ford, *The Good Soldier*, London: John Lane, 1915, p. 19.

19 Ford and Conrad, *Romance*, London: Smith, Elder, 1903, p. 462.

20 See for example, Henri Troyat, *Turgenev*, London: W. H. Allen, 1989, pp. 41, 43.

21 A single volume of *Turgenev's Literary Reminiscences and Autobiographical Fragments* was assembled by David Magarshack, London: Faber, 1959.

22 Ford, *A Mirror to France*, London: Duckworth, 1926 – henceforth *MF*; p. 19.

OPPOSING ORBITS: FORD, EDWARD GARNETT AND THE BATTLE FOR CONRAD

Helen Smith

'Fancy the Bodley Head coming to an end. It makes one shiver to see time effacing one's landmarks'[1] remarked the sixty-three year old Ford Madox Ford in a letter to the publisher Stanley Unwin written in 1937. The Bodley Head was not the only loss to the publishing world early that year as Ford noted in a hastily scrawled postscript: 'Garnett too! He was a pretty vindictive foe of one – or rather of what I stood for, but I had a certain affection for him'. Ford's reaction to the news of the death of Edward Garnett, the publisher's reader, editor and critic, is intriguing. Was there, as he initially suggests, a personal antipathy between Ford and the man he had known since his youth and whom he once described as 'London's literary – [...] if Nonconformist – Pope'?[2] What was it that Ford 'stood for' that Garnett so opposed, and why, if Garnett really was a 'vindictive foe', did Ford retain a residual affection for him? Clearly this was a relationship with a considerable history.

That history goes back to Ford's and Garnett's childhood. Ford met Edward and his siblings on visits to his grandfather Ford Madox Brown and his uncle William Rossetti, both of whom were friendly with Edward's father, Dr Richard Garnett, who ended his lifelong career at the British Museum as Keeper of Printed Books. The members of the younger generation saw a great deal of each other but as Edward's son David recalls, there were considerable temperamental differences between the two families:

> [...] the young Garnetts [...] were sceptical, unworldly and over-critical, and the Hueffer boys [. . . .] were credulous, worldly (without being worldly-wise) and over-confident. The young Garnetts were inclined to regard the Hueffer boys as half egregious asses and half charlatans. The Hueffers, who originally respected the Garnetts, became more and more exasperated by their sceptical attitude and their strait-laced almost puritanical contempt for success and notoriety, which constituted the breath of romance for Ford and Oliver.[3]

Edward Garnett was five years older than Ford and in those days tended to consider him rather as a sixth former might a twelve year old. Garnett's sister Olive described one such evening in 1894 when Edward 'treat[ed] Ford like a well meaning baby. "Are you awake?" stroking his hair, patting him on the back etc'.[4] Although Ford was frequently the butt of Garnett's teasing, he also benefited from Edward's editorial advice early in his career. As 'reader' for T Fisher Unwin, Garnett used his influence to help Ford – he was particularly impressed by *The Shifting of the Fire* which his employer published in 1892 – although this did not prevent him from ruthlessly censuring the younger man's work. 'Edward criticised Ford's MSS [of his biography of Ford Madox Brown] severely' notes Olive in September 1895:

> German – cumbrous – slovenly – vague – will generalise about things of which he knows nothing etc etc – He took trouble trying to make it better, underlining bad English, crossing out useless things & so on. But I can't help feeling for Ford [. . . .] Of course it is kind of Edward & good for Ford.[5]

Despite such strictures, Ford recognised the considerable work Garnett put in on the biography: 'Thanks for all you've done – I don't know why you do it'[6] he wrote in grateful acknowledgement – sentiments that were to be echoed by numerous writers who received the benefit of the Garnett blue pencil during the course of his career.

Arthur Mizener argues that although Ford respected Garnett, they never got on,[7] whilst Ford's disciple, Douglas Goldring, claims he had been told that Garnett had 'a sort of *physical* antipathy'[8] to Ford and goes on to suggest that Edward, whom Goldring unjustly maintains was remarkably ugly, was jealous of Ford's popularity with women. As Garnett was never short of female company and had intimate relationships with several women this theory is suspect to say the least. If Garnett was envious of Ford it is more likely that he coveted the remarkable fluency and ease with which he wrote: Garnett himself found writing a tortuous business, especially at the beginning of his career. Both Mizener's and Goldring's comments may be coloured by their knowledge of the subsequent souring of the relationship. It would be wrong to attribute a single cause to the eventual rift, which seems to have come about gradually. Both men moved in the same circles and were keen prospectors of new writing talent: a competitive edge may well have developed and the advancing years may have lessened the tolerance of those temperamental differences noted by David Garnett. As for the protagonists themselves, Ford informed Garnett in 1928 that just before Joseph Conrad died, 'he told me [...] that you had "got your knife terribly into me" about something I had said or done to you',[9] while four years earlier Garnett confided to Olive how 'I used to come down on [Ford's] gorgeous embroideries in the early days – with the result that he shunned me, and as he never could stand criticism our relations practically ceased before the war'.[10]

Nevertheless, it seems that when in 1905 Garnett told John Galsworthy 'Hueffer has at last been boomed, boomed furiously! and has come into his own. I am so very, very glad'[11] his pleasure was genuine. Early correspondence suggests that a true friendship did then exist and in 1900 Ford had dedicated *Poems for Pictures* to Garnett. Olive Garnett's diary details many pleasurable joint excursions and it is clear that Garnett and Ford met frequently in those days. Later Ford was a frequent guest at the weekly literary lunches Garnett hosted at the Mont Blanc restaurant in Soho where he met men like Galsworthy and W. H. Hudson. Even Douglas Goldring concedes that Garnett '"launched" [Ford] into the circle in which he subsequently moved'.[12]

In 1898 the two men became neighbours when Ford and his wife Elsie rented a cottage from Garnett's sister-in-law close to The Cearne, the home of Edward and his wife Constance near Edenbridge, Kent. It was probably in September of that year that Garnett strolled over to Ford's cottage bringing with him Joseph Conrad, whose literary career he had been supervising for the past five years. That introduction turned out to be a landmark in the lives of both Ford and Conrad and it is through the Polish ex-mariner that we can glean much about the subsequent relationship between Edward Garnett and Ford Madox Ford.

Shortly after this meeting Ford and Conrad decided to write a novel together: exactly who suggested this collaboration remains unclear. In *Joseph Conrad: A Personal Remembrance* Ford suggests that Conrad consulted those who had 'taken part in his launching as a writer'[13] and names W. E. Henley, Marriott Watson and Garnett as likely candidates. A letter Conrad wrote to Garnett however, suggests that the latter was sceptical about the arrangement from the outset: 'I reckon Ford told you. I reckon you disapprove. "I rebel! I said I would rebel." (d'you know the quotation). I send you here Henley's letter over the matter'.[14] Conrad could be certain Garnett would recognise the quotation from Turgenev's *Father and Sons* as he had himself used it in his preface to his wife's translation of the novel. Although the words are spoken by Bazarov's grief-stricken father after his son's death, Conrad's allusion may be aimed more at the novel's title, figuring himself as the rebellious 'son' acting against the advice of his literary 'father'. Garnett features in the first fruit of the collaboration, *The Inheritors*, thinly disguised as Lea, the publisher's reader. The portrait is positive; the narrator recalls how

> Lea had helped me a good deal in the old days – he had helped everybody, for that matter. You would probably find traces of Lea's influence in the beginnings of every writer of about my decade, of everybody who ever did anything decent […] For many years I had been writing quite as much to satisfy him as to satisfy myself [. . . .][15]

Despite this eulogy, Garnett came to view the collaboration with a distinctly jaundiced eye. In a 1936 review of Edward Crankshaw's study of Conrad, Garnett argues that 'Conrad was attracted by Ford's remarkable talent for romancing, by his great faculty of improvisation and […] since these qualities were foreign to his own genius Conrad hoped by collaboration to turn out a popular novel'.[16] Garnett berates Crankshaw for 'swallow[ing] all the glaring misstatements and exaggerations' of Ford's *Joseph Conrad*, and rejects Crankshaw's assertion (based on Ford's account of his relationship with Conrad) that it was 'necessity for craftsmanship' which led Conrad to Ford's door. According to Garnett it was the need for quick money ('a popular novel'), not craftsmanship, which was the determining factor in Conrad's decision. Garnett's dismissal of any artistic motive was surely calculated to undermine the various claims Ford makes in *Joseph Conrad* regarding his deliberations with Conrad about technique. Garnett sums up his reservations about the project by declaring:

> Ford was in spirit a German romantic, and Conrad a Slav realist in his psychological insight. And the two elements could not mix, though this is by no means to say that the literary intercourse of the two men was unfruitful.[17]

The reference to Conrad the 'Slav realist' is significant as it strikes at the core of the aesthetic disagreement between Garnett and Ford.

Edward Garnett and Ford Madox Ford did agree on one thing: that the English novel at the turn of the twentieth century was damagingly insular, in dire need of rejuvenation and that salvation was to be found abroad. Ford was convinced that writers in England should look across the Channel in order to find inspiration: Garnett was equally adamant that the Russians were the only true exemplars. Not only did Garnett send his protégés away to read the Russian masters, he tirelessly promoted their work in his critical columns and wrote several introductions to his wife Constance's translations. More controversially, he consistently characterised Joseph Conrad as a 'Slavic' writer in his influential reviews of his work. Even as early as 1898, when he wrote the first general appraisal of Conrad in the *Academy*, Garnett was drawing comparisons with the Russians. For the Polish Conrad, to whom all things Russian were anathema, this insistence on the 'Slavic' qualities of his art became increasingly exasperating. His mounting fury eventually boiled over in 1911, when Garnett wrote him a private letter accusing him of pouring his hatred of all things Russian into *Under Western Eyes*. 'There's just about as much or as little hatred in this book as in the *Outcast of the Islands*' came the testy reply; 'I don't expect you will believe me. You are so russianised, my dear, that you don't know the truth when you see it – unless it smells of cabbage-soup when it at once secures your profoundest respect. I suppose one must make allowances for your position of Russian Embassador [sic] to the Republic of Letters'.[18]

Conrad was not the first to make caustic capital out of Garnett's Russophilia. A few months before the spat over *Under Western Eyes*, Ford published *The Simple Life Limited*, the first novel he wrote under the pseudonym Daniel Chaucer. Two years previously Ford's sexual and financial entanglements had resulted in a breach with both Garnett and Conrad, the details of which are too long and complicated to be rehearsed here.[19] *The Simple Life Limited* contains satirical sketches of both his former old friends: Mr Parmont, the cynical critic, is clearly modelled on Garnett, whilst Conrad features as the novelist Simeon Brandetski, who anglicises his name to Simon Brandon. The narrator reports on Parmont's view that 'It was only Russians who could write because they hadn't any conventions, they went straight to life, they went straight to nature'[20] and later it is claimed that 'Russia had played during all Mr Parmont's life since he had left school the part of a tremendous ground bass, rising occasionally to an uproar that drowned the noise of all the other advanced movements in Europe' (*SLL* 206). There is more than a germ of truth in Ford's satire. Furthermore, the final clause of that sentence hints at his irritation with Garnett's insistence that Russian writers were the true guides to literary greatness, rather than Ford's beloved Flaubert and Maupassant.

The writing of *The Simple Life Limited* may have purged some of Ford's bitterness towards Conrad, for in December 1911 he published a warm appreciation of his former collaborator in *The English Review*. This is the first but by no means the last time that he describes Conrad as 'Elizabethan'. Was this the beginning of a long campaign by Ford specifically to counter the 'Slavic' image of Conrad Garnett had been cultivating so assiduously?[21] The 'Elizabethan' Conrad reappears in Ford's memoir of his collaborator, published very shortly after the latter's death in 1924 in which Conrad's England is an 'immense power standing for liberty and hospitality for refugees; vigilant over a pax Britannica that embraced the world [...] ready to face Russia with fleet or purse when or wherever they should meet' (*JC* 58). Was Ford picking up on complaints Conrad had made in Ford's earshot during his lifetime about Garnett's 'Slavic' obsession? Conrad certainly was not above playing Garnett and Ford off against each other, as Ford was to discover when Garnett published his *Letters from Conrad* in 1928. It is also noticeable that Ford frequently mentions how important French writers were to Conrad in his various reminiscences: 'That which really brought us together' Ford declares in *Joseph Conrad*, 'was a devotion to Flaubert and Maupassant' (*JC* 36), while in *Thus to Revisit* Ford paints a picturesque scene of the pair 'Buried deep in rural greenness' reading 'nothing but French: you might say it was Flaubert, Flaubert, Flaubert all the way'.[22] The French theme re-emerged in 1928, when Ford wrote an introduction to 'The Sisters', a novel Conrad had started in 1895 but subsequently abandoned on Garnett's advice. Ford's introduction proffered some interesting (if unreliable) theories about the conflicting directions in which Conrad was then being pulled by his friends, and Garnett in particular.

According to Ford, 'The Sisters' and the short story 'The Return', which was later published in *Tales of Unrest*, 'are indications of the gradually weakening desire that Conrad had to be what I would call a "straight" writer, as opposed to the relatively exotic novelist of the sea and the lagoons which fate, the public and some of his friends forced him to become'.[23] Later in the introduction Ford names W. E. Henley and Garnett as those friends who pushed an apparently unwilling Conrad 'in a marine direction'. In a letter informing Garnett of the abandonment of 'The Sisters', Conrad tells him 'You have killed my cherished aspiration'[24] which if we are to believe Ford, consisted in a desire 'to be a Dostoievsky who should also be a conscious artist writing in English or preferably in French'.[25] This is a highly contentious statement which more than anything reflects *Ford's* own agenda and vision of the writer he would have liked Conrad to become. In 1918 Conrad wrote to Hugh Walpole acknowledging receipt of Walpole's study of his work. 'The only thing that grieves me and makes me dance with rage' writes Conrad 'is the cropping up of the absurd legend [...] about my hesitation between English and French as a writing language. For it is absurd [...] there was never any alternative offered or even dreamed of'.[26] Ford may regret the loss of the 'gorgeous vision' that he claims would have opened up had Conrad followed his alleged Franco-Dostoevskian desires, but a swift perusal of either 'The Sisters' or 'The Return' reveals that in both instances Conrad was attempting to do something to which his talents were ill-suited. After Garnett had adversely criticised 'The Return' Conrad conceded 'Never more! It is evident that my fate is to be descriptive and descriptive only. There are things I *must* leave alone'.[27] Garnett had finally persuaded him to cease trying to render introspective states in a pseudo-French style in order that Conrad might fulfil *Garnett's* idea of his true destiny: to be the great 'Slavic' novelist of English fiction.[28]

At this point it is worth returning to the remarks Garnett made about the collaboration between Conrad and Ford and why he considered it to be ill-starred: 'Ford was in spirit a German romantic, and Conrad a Slav realist in his psychological insight'. Just what Garnett meant by these comments with regard to Ford can be gauged from a review he wrote in 1925. That he quotes a Russian is nicely ironic:

> It was Turgenev who declared that he had an unbounded admiration for the German imagination and for the German Romantic faculty of day-dreaming, because it could transform anything into everything at its will or pleasure. Mr Ford has certainly inherited the ancestral faculty.[29]

The event which provoked this sardonic reference was the publication of *Joseph Conrad: A Personal Remembrance,* Ford's controversial memoir of his collaborator, which was to add another sour chapter to the story of the relationship between Garnett and Ford.

Garnett's irritation with the factual inaccuracies of Ford's book is all too apparent in his first review of it which appeared in the *Nation and Athenaeum* on 6 December 1924. Although he concedes that Ford has captured many of Conrad's mannerisms and 'conveys excellently' the atmosphere of Conrad's home, The Pent, Garnett takes Ford severely to task for 'embellishing his "portrait" with fantastic inventions'[30] – some of which Garnett goes on to enumerate. Ford's preface, in which he emphasises the novelistic qualities of the memoir, is given short shrift by Garnett:

> To accept a fiction-biography would be to invite the three-card trick from every ingenious manipulator. In the magic name of 'impressionism' a man can magnify, distort, or suppress facts and aspects to his own glorification, he can dye everything with his own hues and belittle others, and then, on being brought to book, he can turn round reprovingly and protest 'But this is a work of art!'

No biography is ever entirely 'factual'. The selection of which 'facts' to include and the biographer's subsequent interpretation of them effectively distorts every written account of a life. The biographical subject will always be the biographer's creation and in that sense a 'fictional' figure. Edward Garnett was too shrewd a reader not to be very well aware of this. Garnett's major objection is that Ford made free with the factual integrity that supposedly separates the novel from biography and that he did so not in the interests of Conrad (which might have been more excusable), but for his own greater glory. In enumerating the credentials that qualify him to sit in judgement on Ford, Garnett adopts a tone that is positively patrician, not only pointing out that he knew Conrad before, during and after the time Ford describes but also that he had introduced the two men and 'had known Mr Ford as a lad of eighteen, [and] sponsored his early works'. The review closes with Garnett rather darkly promising that the publication of Conrad's letters will 'no doubt throw interesting light on various statements in "A Personal Remembrance," and separate the wheat from the chaff'.

Three days after the publication of the review Garnett appears to have set about the task of winnowing himself. In a letter to his sister Olive he asks her to 'send me a list of what you think are Ford's misstatements in the book'.[31] From this it might be assumed that Garnett's second review of *Joseph Conrad*, which appeared in *The Weekly Westminster* in February 1925, would be more scathing than his initial attack in *The Nation*, but actually it is the mellower of the two.

In this second review, Garnett again acknowledges that 'there is a good deal of true insight [...] clever description and [...] genuine atmospheric observation'[32] in Ford's memoir. However it is Ford's descriptions of the conversations he had with Conrad regarding the technique of novel writing (in which the French feature prominently) that Garnett singles out for particular criticism. Whilst conceding that Conrad may well have participated in these literary arguments, Garnett proposes that 'the disquisition itself is Mr Ford's creation'. He goes on to recall a conversation he himself had with Conrad in which the latter claimed he had 'never understood' the technicalities of writing and concludes that whilst Conrad did indeed experiment with the novel form 'he followed his instinct and had no sacrosanct plan when he commenced a novel'. David Garnett's comments about his father are instructive:

> [Edward] had little use for theory and could seldom bolster up his opinions by inventing one. He arrived at his opinions, especially his aesthetic ones, by instinct, and by sympathy. He was intensely sceptical and never more so than when confronted by theories of aesthetics. He did not believe there were any rules and preferred that there should be none.[33]

It is impossible to state precisely where the truth lies – Ford and Garnett base their conflicting claims on unverifiable accounts of discussions. However what becomes clear is that both attempt to cast the recently dead Conrad in their own image: this rivalry is not confined to petty, personal jealousy as to who enjoyed the greater friendship with Conrad, although undoubtedly an element of that does exist. 'It is natural for the planets that circle round the sun each to believe that his orbit is of particular importance' writes Garnett. 'It is important for the planet, but not for the sun'.[34] Quite. What is at stake here is not so much Conrad's posthumous reputation, but Garnett's and Ford's own battle as to who exerted the greater literary influence, not just in the case of Conrad, but also perhaps in the wider world of letters in the early twentieth century.

It is evident from Olive Garnett's diary that Edward was making plans to publish his correspondence with Conrad at the same time as he was writing his first review of Ford's memoir.[35] What is not clear is whether he decided to include a letter Conrad specifically instructed him to burn in an attempt to undermine Ford's account of the collaboration, although the promise that the publication of Conrad's letters would 'separate the wheat from the chaff' strongly suggests that he did. Conrad wrote the letter in question, in which he describes

the collaboration on *The Inheritors*, in March 1900. No wonder Ford
was upset when he read it:

> I set myself to look upon the thing as a sort of skit upon the political (?!)
> novel, fools of the Morley Roberts sort do write [. . . .] And poor *H*[ueffer]
> was dead in earnest! Oh Lord. How he worked! There is not a chapter I
> haven't made him write twice – most of them three times over.
> [...] H has been as patient as no angel had ever been. I've been fiendish.
> I've been rude to him; if I've not called him names I've *implied* in my remarks
> and in the course of our discussions the most opprobrious epithets. He
> wouldn't recognize them. 'Pon my word it was touching...
> You'll have to burn this letter – but I shall say no more. Some day we shall
> meet and then —!³⁶

The impression Conrad gives here is that it is he who is the
master craftsman, standing over Ford, the rather inept literary
apprentice. In his introduction to *Letters from Conrad* Garnett notes
the 'variety of appealing tones Conrad had at his command both when
addressing old friends and new acquaintances'³⁷ and Conrad was
doubtless well aware that Garnett would appreciate his scathingly
humorous description. Conrad's eagerness to dismiss *The Inheritors*
and his own contribution to its composition (which was indeed small)
may also reflect a desire to dissociate himself from a novel written for
the marketplace for which he knew Garnett had such scorn – although
the latter was always acutely conscious of the emptiness of Conrad's
purse and as Garnett was by then reader for Heinemann, who
published *The Inheritors*, he was probably instrumental in ensuring its
acceptance.

It was the young American collector of Conradiana, George T.
Keating, who sent Ford a copy of the US edition of *Letters to Conrad*
with the offending letter especially marked. To add insult to injury,
Garnett had decided to sell his collection of letters from Conrad and
W. H. Hudson in New York. Lot 187 comprised 'An interesting letter
about Hueffer's collaboration with Conrad in the writing of "The
Inheritors"', with the most scathing sentences quoted in the catalogue
for all to see.³⁸

This combination of circumstances prompted Ford to contact his
old sparring partner once more. Pointedly marked 'Private and not for
publication in <u>perpetuity</u>' Ford opens the letter by claiming that what
distresses him about Garnett disobeying Conrad's instructions to burn
the letter is not on account of 'the sarcasms against myself' to which
he is 'fairly indifferent' but because publication 'discredits the

memory of that unfortunate man'.[39] However what follows suggests that Ford was not as untouched by Conrad's 'sarcasms' as he professes:

> At that time he [Conrad] was living in my house and I was letting my own family go short in order to keep him and I was giving my whole time to giving him moral support and to putting his affairs in order – and to writing his books. All that is nothing. [...] That Conrad then should have written such a letter about myself at just that time is nothing but discreditable – and if I resent, as I do with a good deal of sadness, your printing this letter it is entirely for the sake of Conrad and not in the least for my own sake.[40]

There is a shrillness about that list of good deeds and although Ford is absolutely right in saying that Conrad does not emerge with a great deal of credit, Ford's wounded, almost melodramatic tone betrays him: he doth protest his indifference too much. Both Garnett and Ford would assert that they were acting as assiduous 'keepers of the flame' – in publishing the letter Garnett could argue that he was letting Conrad speak for himself about the collaboration and that the letter explodes Ford's inaccurate claims, whilst Ford wishes to suppress it because it displays Conrad in a negative light. Once again, although Conrad is the ostensible subject of the dispute, the whole affair is as much about the personal rivalry between Garnett and Ford and their respective claims to influence.

There are a couple of points in Ford's letter where this becomes apparent. After denying that he ever broke with Conrad or vice-versa Ford concedes:

> I felt and expressed a slight coldness to him ever repudiating his [*sic*] French influence in his work but in the course of a clandestine [...] interview that I had with him he acknowledged that he lived amongst so pronounced a group of pro-German or Anti-French that he had been driven to thinking that an Anti-French pronouncement would at that date be politic.

Ford still propagates his own vision of Conrad as a champion of the French, although his assertion that his former collaborator publicly renounced that influence as a result of outside pressure says little for the steadfastness of Conrad's principles. Towards the end of the letter Ford tells Garnett that 'as we never did agree about anything in literature I see no possibility of our now doing so' – a remark which suggests that Ford is as much preoccupied with the old literary antagonisms with Garnett as he is with Conrad's epistolary perfidies.

So what are we to make of Ford's final summation of his relationship with Garnett in the letter to Stanley Unwin? Although Garnett and Ford came to regard each other less than cordially, Ford may well have recalled the days of their earlier friendship with nostalgia and affection. That he was unable to decide whether Garnett's supposed animosity was directed against him personally, or rather against what he 'stood for' is unsurprising: from its earliest days theirs was a relationship in which the personal and the professional were inextricably linked. On the face of it, the Franco-Russian battle between Ford and Garnett would appear to be a strictly aesthetic discord. However as their dealings with Conrad suggest, it was also intimately bound up with issues of personal jealousy, competitiveness and betrayal. What is beyond dispute is both men's passionate commitment to their literary ideals and their contribution to, and influence in, the Republic of Letters in the early twentieth century. Edward Garnett and Ford Madox Ford brought many young and inexperienced authors into their own particular and distinctive orbits; their conflict over whose representation of Conrad should prevail thus has significant implications in the wider universe of literary modernism itself.

NOTES

1   Ford Madox Ford to Stanley Unwin, 24 January 1937, Allen & Unwin Archive, University of Reading. Ford has misdated this letter as Garnett died on 19 February 1937. Quoted with the kind permission of Michael Schmidt, the executor of the Ford estate. The Bodley Head suffered financial difficulties in the 1930s, but the landmark managed to survive, producing (among other things) uniform editions such as *The Bodley Head Ford Madox Ford*, discussed in Bernard Bergonzi's essay in this volume.
2   Ford Madox Ford, *Mightier than the Sword*, London: George Allen & Unwin, 1938, p. 59.
3   David Garnett, *The Golden Echo*, London: Chatto & Windus, 1953, pp. 35-6.
4   Olive Garnett, diary entry, 'November 17th Saturday' 1894. Reprinted in *Olive & Stepniak: The Bloomsbury Diary of Olive Garnett 1893-1895*, ed. Barry Johnson, Birmingham: Bartletts Press, 1993, p. 133. Thomas Moser draws attention to this episode, pointing out that Ford later frequently appears as a baby in his own writings and in the comments of his friends. Thomas Moser, *The Life in the Fiction of Ford Madox Ford*, New Jersey: Princeton University Press, 1980, p. 21.
5   Olive Garnett, diary entry 'Saturday 28th' [September] 1895, *ibid.*, p. 205.

6   Ford to Garnett, undated letter, Harry Ransom Center, University of Texas at Austin. Quoted with the kind permission of Michael Schmidt, the executor of the Ford estate.

7   Arthur Mizener, *The Saddest Story: A Biography of Ford Madox Ford*, London: The Bodley Head, 1972, p. 38.

8   Douglas Goldring, *The Last Pre-Raphaelite*, London: Macdonald, 1948, p. 64.

9   Ford to Garnett, 5th May 1928, unpublished letter, Northwestern University Library, Chicago. Quoted with the kind permission of Michael Schmidt.

10 Edward Garnett to Olive Garnett, 9 December 1924, unpublished letter, Harry Ransom Center, University of Texas at Austin.

11 Garnett to John Galsworthy, 8 May 1905, in Garnett, ed., *Letters from John Galsworthy 1900-1932*, London: Cape, 1934, p. 59.

12 Goldring, *The Last Pre-Raphaelite*, p. 65.

13 Ford Madox Ford, *Joseph Conrad: A Personal Remembrance*, London: Duckworth, 1924 – henceforth *JC*; p. 49.

14 Conrad to Garnett, 7 November 1898, *The Collected Letters of Joseph Conrad* (vol. 2), ed. Frederick R Karl and Laurence Davies, Cambridge: Cambridge University Press, 1986, p. 115.

15 Joseph Conrad and Ford Madox Ford, *The Inheritors* (1901), foreword by George Hay, intro. David Seed, Liverpool: Liverpool University Press, 1999, p. 35 and p. 37.

16 Edward Garnett, 'A New Study of Conrad'. (Review of *Joseph Conrad: Some Aspects of the Art of the Novel* by Edward Crankshaw), *London Mercury*, 34 (1936), 67-69.

17 *Ibid.*

18 Conrad to Garnett, 20 October 1911, *Collected Letters of Joseph Conrad* (vol. 4), ed. Frederick R. Karl and Laurence Davies, Cambridge: Cambridge University Press, 1990, p. 488.

19 Max Saunders gives a full account of Ford's break with Conrad in Chapter 17 of *Ford Madox Ford: A Dual Life*, vol. 1, Oxford: Oxford University Press, 1996.

20 'Daniel Chaucer' (Ford Madox Ford), *The Simple Life Limited*, London: John Lane, 1911 – henceforth *SLL*; p. 204.

21 Joseph Wiesenfarth discusses Ford's description of Conrad as 'Elizabethan' and the issue of Conrad's 'Slavonism' in 'Approaching Ford Madox Ford's *Joseph Conrad: A Personal Remembrance*' in *Inter-Relations: Conrad, James, Ford and Others*, ed. Keith Carabine and Max Saunders, Lublin: Maria Curie-Sklodowska University and New York: Columbia University Press, 2003, pp. 133-47. Wiesenfarth points out that Ford presents Conrad as 'an Elizabethan poet writing modern novels and argues that 'Conrad as poet stands Slavonism and romance on end' (p. 139). It is interesting to note that in his first appreciation of Conrad Garnett specifically links Conrad's poetic qualities with Russian (for which read 'Slavic' – the terms were interchangeable as far as Garnett was concerned) writing. In his *Academy* article of 15 October 1898 Garnett writes: 'This faculty of seeing man's life in relation to the seen and unseen forces of Nature it is that gives Mr Conrad's art its extreme delicacy and its great breadth of vision. It is pre-eminently the poet's gift, and is very rarely conjoined with insight into human nature and a power of conceiving character. When the two gifts come together we

have the poetic realism of the great Russian novels. Mr Conrad's art is truly realism of that high order'. 'Mr Joseph Conrad', *Academy* (15 October 1898), 82-3. Garnett was not one of those who saw Conrad as a 'romantic realist': in his review of *Nostromo* he again refers to Conrad's 'method of poetic realism' which Garnett maintains is 'intimately akin to that of the great Russian novelists'. Garnett, 'Mr Conrad's Art', *Speaker* (12 November 1904), 138-9. Garnett's notion of 'poetic realism', which is given further definition in some of his reviews of the Russian novelists, resembles Walter Silz's description in his study of the German Poetic Realists. According to Silz, such a writer 'selects and poeticizes, like the memory'. This technique accords closely with that of Conrad, who as Mara Kalnins argues 'was acutely aware of how both [literal and fictional] truth are altered by memory and by the creative imagination'. Walter Silz, *Realism and Reality: Studies in the German Novelle of Poetic Realism*, Chapel Hill: University of North Carolina Press, 1954, p.12. Mara Kalnins, introduction to *A Personal Record* and *The Mirror of the Sea* by Joseph Conrad, London: Penguin, 1998, p. xxv. Garnett's view of Conrad may thus in some respects be closer to that of Ford than Wiesenfarth suggests.

22 Ford, *Thus to Revisit*, (1921) New York: Octagon Books, 1966, p. 39.
23 Ford, introduction to 'The Sisters' by Joseph Conrad, ed. Urgo Mursia, Milan: Urgo Mursia & Co., 1968, p. 12.
24 Conrad to Garnett, 23/24 March 1896, *Collected Letters of Joseph Conrad* (vol. 1), p. 268.
25 Ford, intro., 'The Sisters', p. 13.
26 Conrad to Hugh Walpole, 7 June 1918, *Collected Letters of Joseph Conrad* (vol. 6), ed. Laurence Davies, Frederick R Karl and Owen Knowles, Cambridge: Cambridge University Press, 2002, pp. 227-8.
27 Conrad to Garnett, 29 September 1897, *Collected Letters of Joseph Conrad* (vol. 1), p. 387.
28 The question of whether Ford or Garnett exerted the greater influence on Conrad divides scholars. Zdzis aw Najder for example, refutes Jocelyn Baines' claims for Ford's superiority, arguing that 'Conrad's friendship with Garnett had a greater impact on what and how he wrote'. Najder, *Joseph Conrad: A Chronicle*, trans. Halina Carroll-Najder, Cambridge: Cambridge University Press, 1983, p. 237.
29 Edward Garnett, 'Instructive and Amusing' (review of *Joseph Conrad: A Personal Remembrance* by Ford Madox Ford), *Weekly Westminster* (14 February 1925), 473.
30 Edward Garnett, 'Romantic Biography' (review of *Joseph Conrad: A Personal Remembrance* by Ford Madox Ford), *The Nation and the Athenaeum,* 36 (6 December 1924), 366-8.
31 Edward Garnett to Olive Garnett, 9 December 1924.
32 Garnett, 'Instructive and Amusing'.
33 David Garnett, *The Flowers of the Forest*, London: Chatto & Windus, 1955, p. 155.
34 Garnett, 'Instructive and Amusing'.
35 In a diary entry for 3 December 1924 Olive notes 'Copied Conrad's letter [to Olive] for inclusion in Edward's volume'. Olive's diary for the years 1890-1895 has been published in two volumes edited by Barry Johnson, the first volume, *Tea*

and Anarchy! covers the years 1890-1893, (London: Bartletts Press 1989, see note 4 for details of the second volume). The complete diary is in the possession of Olive's great niece, Mrs Caroline White, who has kindly granted me permission to quote from it.

36 Conrad to Garnett, 26 March 1900, *Collected Letters of Joseph Conrad* (vol. 2), p. 257.

37 Edward Garnett, introduction, *Letters from Conrad 1895-1924*, (ed. & intro. Garnett), London: Nonesuch Press, 1928, p. xxv.

38 *The Historic Edward Garnett Conrad-Hudson Collection.* Catalogue of the American Art Association Inc, New York City: 1928, p. 36.

39 Ford Madox Ford to Edward Garnett, 5 May 1928, unpublished letter, Northwestern University Library. Quoted with the kind permission of Michael Schmidt.

40 *Ibid.*

MARIE BELLOC LOWNDES ON FORD
AND VIOLET HUNT

Susan Lowndes Marques

Marie Belloc Lowndes (1868-1947) was a prolific author of 'why-dunnits', penning Hitchcock's first film, *The Lodger* and less famously creating the character Hercules Perot, a French detective supporting a strong accent, with a penchant for solving murders in the English upper middle classes.[1] She was also the sister of the controversial Catholic poet, Hilaire Belloc. However, Marie Belloc Lowndes is, and should be, best remembered as a unique and singularly well positioned memoirist of her age.[2]

Four volumes[3] of her memoirs were published in the early forties, and a selection of letters and diaries in 1971. An enormous number of her letters have also been published in selections of many correspondents – Henry James, Phillip Sassoon, Osbert Sitwell, Katherine Mansfield, Edward Grey, H. H. Asquith – to name but a few. In spite of this, the bulk of her letters are as yet unpublished. Together with these letters and diaries are a vast amount of articles written on specific topics. These vary from cultural and travel pieces to short stories, but the large majority of the material consists of biographical sketches. One such example is this piece about Ford Madox Ford.

Marie Belloc Lowndes was tirelessly social and enjoyed meeting and mixing with people from all walks of life. She was, of course, particularly interested in writers, and would seek introductions to the youngest, least prominent as well as the firmly established. These writings also crossed borders, especially in the early part of her journalistic career, when her frequent visits to Paris yielded interviews with the great masters of nineteenth-century French literature. What characterized her work, both fiction and non-fiction, was a deep concern with people's private lives, especially affairs of the heart. She was unquestionably a gossip, but gossip often leads one to details that might never otherwise be discovered.[4] It may also be true that gossip is of dubious truth-value, as seems to be the case with some of the claims she makes in her piece on Ford. What is interesting, in my view, is even if all the information is not accurate, it perhaps provides an insight into what people thought of the person in question at the time. A gossip does not necessarily invent information, but may merely reproduce what she or he has heard, without confirming its provenance or veracity.

Marie Belloc Lowndes met Ford through Violent Hunt. Her earliest reference to Ford is in a diary entry on December 2nd, 1911, when the couple made their first appearance as 'bride and bridegroom' at a dinner party she attended; though, as her reminiscences of them show, she had met him at least two years earlier.[5] She must have met with both of them regularly at various social occasions, although I get the impression she was never particularly close to either Ford or Hunt. Indeed she profoundly disagreed with Hunt's version of Lizzie Siddall's death in *The Wife of Rossetti* (1931). The following type-script, published here for the first time, was written after the Second World War; and she died in 1947, so it must date from 1945-47.

> Ford Madox Hueffer was not only a remarkable writer, he was a fine historical novelist, and it is to me surprising when I read accounts of the novelists of his day, to find no mention of *The Fifth Queen* and *The Fifth Queen Crowned*. For years I never went up Whitehall, without remembering certain passages of these two books. They give a more vivid picture of the London of Henry the Eighth than any novel I have ever read.
>
> On the declaration of war in 1914 Ford Madox Hueffer immediately joined the Army, to the anguished distress of Violet Hunt. Though his good knowledge of German would have been of great value to the British Staff, no one seems to have thought of utilizing it.[6] Also it must be admitted he would have found it difficult to have found respectable sponsors. In those days that fact counted for much. To me there was something repugnant in Ford Madox Hueffer's personality. He was fat, and stuffy looking, but he must have had a considerable attraction for women. This was proved by the fact that after he had parted from Violet Hunt, and settled in Paris, a charming woman became attached to him.[7] After a while he went to America, and settled in New York, there also he found a woman of means who called herself his wife.[8] Years after his death I received a letter in which the writer informed me that she was Ford Madox Hueffer's widow, and asked if she could come and see me – when we met she had evidently been devoted to him, and believed the ceremony of marriage they had gone through, I think, in Paris, had made her his wife.[9] At that time it was within my knowledge that though he had never been divorced he had gone through the ceremony of marriage with two other women.[10]
>
> Ford Madox Hueffer was brilliantly clever, and had he possessed character he might have become very famous.
>
> There must have been a strong prejudice against Ford Madox Hueffer in the London literary world, for it is a singular fact that I never met him except

in Violet Hunt's house. Even at a time when it was believed that she was his wife, many of her old friends gave up seeing her for the reason that they intensely disliked him.

In 190[9] I stayed in [Suffolk] at Aldeburgh with Edward Clodd. The day after our arrival Violet came into my room and begged me earnestly to ask Mr. Clodd to invite Ford Madox Hueffer to join the party. When I objected that I did not know him, which at that time was true, she told me she had already spoken to Mr. Clodd and had said that I knew and liked Ford Madox Hueffer and greatly wished him to join the party. This made me indignant and my indignation was still further aroused when I discovered, as I soon did, that Mr. Clodd did not like what he knew of Hueffer. I told him that Violet had made a mistake and that I had no wish for Mr. Hueffer to be invited. It was then revealed that Violet had already written and asked him to come, but as our host pointed out that there was no room in the house for another guest, she went off and took lodgings for him in what was then a small fishing town. She then got me to coax – that was her word – Mr. Clodd to allow Hueffer to come every evening to supper. This he unwillingly did. Years later I read in one of the great American papers a fantastic account of that week.[11] Almost every well known British writer was mentioned as being there, and I especially remember that my brother was included among Mr. Clodd's supposed guests. To the best of my belief the two men had never met, and did not meet later on.[12] What gave me great pleasure was the presence of Thomas Hardy. He was at the time a widower – and a far from happy man.

Violet Hunt was never in any way in what was ordinarily called 'Society'. But at one time she was a bright star in the London Bohemian literary world. Her affair with Oswald Crawfurd[13] was widely known, but never spoken of by her, or indeed if I remember rightly by anyone else. I never once saw him at South Lodge. They had a flat, of which they shared the rent, somewhere near St. James Street. The affair must have begun when she was very young, and went on for many years. In those days she was really enchantingly pretty, recalling girls painted by Leighton and Burne-Jones. She was exceedingly graceful, with good features and lovely, naturally curling hair. She had a beautiful figure and, generally speaking, a very pretty way with her. I don't believe for a moment that anyone nicknamed her 'the modest Violet'. To my mind *Sooner or Later* is a very remarkable book. It is the story of the Oswald Crawfurd liaison. She really loved Crawfurd, and when he married a very wealthy widow it broke her heart. To the best of my belief she had no other lover till she met Hueffer.[14] Quite a number of men wished to marry her, especially one really distinguished diplomat who went on caring for her for years.

I never believed her stories as to her intimacy with Holman Hunt and his circle.[15] I was in that circle, and used to go to the Holman Hunts frequently as a young married woman. I never met her there, and never heard any of them mention her. Holman Hunt, though he did marry his deceased wife's sister, was austere and humourless.

What strange to say was true, poor Violet had some very devoted friends. There was something about her attaching and touching. To compare her to Colette is grotesque.[16] As if one compared a pretty fluffy kitten to a tigress. Colette, in my view, was a great writer, but Violet Hunt at her best was extremely good, especially when dealing with the macabre. It is absurd as well as unkind, to say that she was in great need for social reasons of a husband. She could have married again and again, certainly four or five times. To say that to be married was a dream of Violet's life is a complete misunderstanding of her character. She was a born Bohemian.

I think her affair with Hueffer grieved her friends owing to his being a man of indifferent reputation, but I never heard an unkind remark said about the business, excepting after the astonishing, utterly uncalled for series of lies which they both told, but especially Violet told, concerning the supposed German divorce and marriage.[17] It was at first completely accepted as having happened. I have a letter from Arnold Bennett in which he described her coming to Paris on her way back from, I suppose, Westphalia.[18] He quite believed the tale – that the Grand Duke had made him one of his subjects because he, Ford, was so distinguished, that then the Grand Duke had divorced Ford from his English wife (all German sovereigns had this power of divorce, the German Emperor constantly exercised it).

On her return Violet wrote round to her friends telling them the story and everyone believed her. Then her name was 'Mrs. Hueffer' in the Telephone Directory.

NOTES

Marie Belloc Lowndes' misspelling of Ford's name ('Maddox') has been corrected throughout.

1   Belloc Lowndes tried to appeal to the Society of Authors after Agatha Christie published *The Mysterious Affair at Styles* in 1920, Poirot's first appearance, but received the response that you could not copyright characters, only plots.
2   S. Hynes, 'View from the Tea Table' in *Times Literary Supplement* (17 September 1971), 1108: 'She was in many ways the ideal memoirist of that world; she was well-connected and knew everybody, she was tirelessly social (she seems to have dined out nearly as often as Henry James did, often at the same table, and she was a shrewd observer. [....] It gives a valuable tea-table view of the First World War, the rumours, the anxieties, the indiscretions of politicians in society, [...] a close-up of the abdication crisis, [....] the 1945 election. [....] raw material of careful literary history'.
3   Marie Belloc Lowndes, *'I, Too, Have Lived in Arcadia'*, London: Macmillan & Co., 1941; Marie Belloc Lowndes, *Where Love and Friendship Dwelt*, London: Macmillan & Co., 1943; Marie Belloc Lowndes, *The Merry Wives of Westminster*, London: Macmillan & Co., 1946; Marie Belloc Lowndes, *A Passing World*, London: Macmillan & Co., 1948; Susan Lowndes ed., *Diaries and Letters of Marie Belloc Lowndes 1911-1947*, London: Chatto & Windus, 1971.
4   'Contrary to what people may say about gossip, there is in fact widespread agreement [...] that those at the heart of the most powerful institutions, including the university, the corporate world, and the political arena, frequently rely upon

gossip as a source of crucial information inaccessible by other means'. Maryann Ayim, 'Knowledge through the grapevine: Gossip as inquiry', in *Good Gossip*, edited by R. F. Goodman and A. Ben-Ze'ev, Kansas: University Press of Kansas, 1994, p. 86.

5   'I went to a most extraordinary Party at Elizabeth Aria's. The guest of honour was H. G. Wells. The Ford Madox Hueffers also made their first appearance as bride and bridegroom'. Susan Lowndes ed., *Diaries and Letters of Marie Belloc Lowndes 1911-1947*, p. 27.

6   In fact Ford enlisted in July 1915. For the first year of the war he wrote propaganda, sponsored by his friend the cabinet minister C. F. G. Masterman. He tried to get a Staff job, but MI6 blocked the application on the grounds that his German ancestry made him unsuitable for intelligence work. See Ford, *War Prose*, ed. Max Saunders, Manchester: Carcanet, 1999, p. 4

7   The Australian painter Stella Bowen.

8   Ford had a relationship with Rene Wright from 1926-8, but as he was still unable to obtain a divorce from his wife Elsie Hueffer, they never married, nor is it recorded elsewhere that they claimed to be married.

9   This could be either Stella Bowen (1893-1947), or the American painter Janice Biala (1903-2000), with whom Ford lived during the 1930s. It is perhaps more likely to be Bowen (who had moved back to England during the 1930s). Both Bowen and Biala were referred to as 'Mrs Ford', though neither they nor Ford claimed to have married. However, it is possible that after his death either woman felt it necessary to make the claim so as to be able to benefit from any posthumous income from his work.

10 Besides Ford's first and only legal wife, Elsie, this presumably refers to Violet Hunt. The doubts Belloc Lowndes casts below on Ford's and Violet's stories about his German divorce and their marriage might suggest otherwise; but perhaps she means that she doubted the divorce but believed they had gone through a marriage ceremony, however illegal.

11 Ford wrote about this house party many times: in 'Literary Portraits – IX: Mr. Thomas Hardy and " A Changed Man"', *Outlook*, 32 (8 November 1013), 641-2; and later in *Return to Yesterday*, London: Victor Gollancz, 1931, p. 304, and *Portraits from Life*, Boston: Houghton Mifflin, 1937, pp. 103-4. The magazine version Belloc Lowndes refers to is 'Thomas Hardy, O.M.: Obiit: 11 January, 1928', *New York Herald Tribune Books* (22 January 1928), 1-3.

12 Ford certainly knew Hilaire Belloc, whom he discusses in *Return to Yesterday*, particularly pp. 381-4.

13 Oswald Crawfurd (whose name Belloc Lowndes writes as 'Crawford') was British Consul in Oporto, and the editor of the *New Quarterly Magazine* and the illustrated journal *Black and White*. See Barbara Belford, *Violet: The Story of the Irrepressible Violet Hunt and Her Circle of Lovers and Friends – Ford Madox Ford, H. G. Wells, Somerset Maugham, and Henry James*, New York: Simon and Schuster, 1990, pp. 71, 80.

13 Barbara Belford, who had access to Hunt's copious diaries, shows that she did indeed have other lovers, including Wells and Maugham.

15 Belford, p. 29, says that Hunt's father, the painter Alfred William Hunt, was a friend of Holman Hunt's.

16 Douglas Goldring had recently written that Hunt 'was regarded as an English Colette': *South Lodge*, p. 42. London: Constable, 1943.
17 Max Saunders, *Ford Madox Ford: A Dual Life*, Oxford: Oxford University Press, 1996, vol. 1, pp. 346-52, discusses these stories of a marriage.
18 She had been visiting Ford who was living in Giessen, in Hesse.

THE COMPLEXITY OF TRUTH:
FORD AND THE RUSSIANS

Anat Vernitski

In his dedication to his memoir *Ancient Lights*, published in 1911, Ford bequeaths to his daughters Christina and Katharine a rejection of the uncompromising truths that characterized the Great Victorians. Having explained that his childhood was marred by a consciousness of being sinful and stupid, being made to feel so mainly by his father (music critic of *The Times*) and grandfather (pre-Raphaelite artist), Ford wishes his children to avoid the same destiny.[1] Refusing to follow the greatness of his elders, Ford wants them to inherit his own emphasis on impressions instead of hard facts. He stresses that his book is a 'book of impressions' (*AL*, xiv). In *Ancient Lights*, he states that he is not interested in the accuracy of facts, but, at the same time, he insists on the sincerity of his impressionable writing. He professes to have 'for facts a most profound contempt' and wants to express 'the spirit of an age, of a town, of a movement' (*AL* xv).

As to facts, Ford suggests to the reader that:

> when you have a little time to waste, I should suggest that you go through this book carefully, noting the errors. To the one of you who succeed in finding the largest number I will cheerfully present a copy of the ninth edition of the Encyclopaedia Britannica, so that you may still further perfect yourself in the hunting out of errors. (*AL* xv)

Interestingly, the image of a reader painstakingly looking for errors in the *Britannica* appears later in the first book of Ford's tetralogy *Parade's End*, in *Some Do Not . . .*, published in 1924. In the chapter introducing Tietjens, he is described as occupying himself in the months following his wife's leaving him for another man 'in tabulating from memory the errors in the *Encyclopaedia Britannica*, of which a new edition had lately appeared'.[2] It is a measure of the extent to which Tietjens suffers from shell-shock that he is later reduced to reading the *Britannica* to recover his memory of facts (*PE* 170). Facts are a great loss to Tietjens, and his turning to what he regards as an inferior source to aid the reconstruction of his memory is surely a useful device, enabling Ford to distance himself from his protagonist.

Taking into account Ford's views, it is interesting to trace his ambiguous attitude towards political convictions, as he is both attracted to and repelled from the one-sided view of truth inherent in all political thought. An interesting case of political activists with whom Ford had a long-standing association is that of Russian revolutionary exiles.

Since his youth, Ford was acquainted with Russian revolutionary exiles who were established in London in the 1880s. This acquaintance came about through his relatives the Rossettis and his friends the Garnetts. Edward Garnett, the publishers' reader who was instrumental in the career of Joseph Conrad, was acquainted with a number of Russian émigrés in Britain. His wife, Constance Garnett, became eventually one of the most prolific translators of Russian literature into English. Both she and Olive Garnett, Edward's sister, were especially attached to Sergei Stepniak (Kravchinskii), with whom Ford was also acquainted, and Stepniak's influence is paramount in the choice of works Constance translated. Olive eventually visited Russia and published a book of stories entitled *Petersburg Tales* (1900) and a novel *In Russia's Night* (1918). Helen and Olive Rossetti, Ford's cousins, even edited (as teenagers!) the anarchist magazine *The Torch*, to which a number of British and foreign anarchists contributed.[3]

The Russian revolutionaries that Ford was associated with would not have shared his mistrust of facts and emphasis on personal impressions. They were people who, in Russia and later in the West, became vaguely known as 'Nihilists'. The Nihilists were the young Russian revolutionaries of the 1870s, and this name was popularized by Turgenev in his novel *Fathers and Sons*. The revolutionary protagonist of that novel, the student Bazarov, is interested exclusively in scientific and objective truth. In a central scene in the novel, Bazarov's friend Arkady tells him of Arkady's uncle's complicated love life. Bazarov listens to the long story with disdain, and comments that it would be a better use of their time to study an insect.

The Russian revolutionaries Ford knew were spiritual sons of the fictional Bazarov. Establishing scientific truth was for them a reaction to autocracy and superstition.[4] When Ford was growing up he got to know a number of Russian revolutionary exiles who were acquainted with the Garnett and Rossetti families. The main figures were Petr Kropotkin, Sergei Stepniak (Kravchinskii) and Felix Volkhovskii. These Russian exiles were by persuasion either Anarchists or 'Populists' (narodniki), members of secret organisations, some of them even guilty of assassination (notably, Stepniak had murdered the Head of the St Petersburg Secret Police). They continued, even in exile, to advocate the idea of terrorism as a means to influence the Russian authorities in relaxing autocracy and improving human rights in Russia.

However, when these revolutionaries arrived in Britain, they decided to abandon terrorist activities in favour of propaganda in order to influence the British public. By raising awareness abroad to human rights abuse in Russia, they wanted to make the Russian authorities change their policies. They decided that the close ties between the British and Russian royal families and the important role of Britain in European politics could help initiate changes in Russia via British public opinion.

The Russian exiles, together with a number of British socialist thinkers and writers (including George Bernard Shaw), founded the Friends of Russian Freedom. Moreover, strong personal ties were formed between the Russians and English intellectuals in London. For example, both Constance Garnett and her sister-in-law Olive Garnett were in love with Stepniak, and close friends of Volkhovskii.[5]

In his memoirs, Ford describes his meetings with the Russians. He portrays Stepniak as 'huge, flat-featured, with small, fiery black eyes and an enormous black beard' and Volkhovskii as 'small, lean, grey and always humorous'.[6] Juliet, Ford's sister, remembers Ford taking her as a young girl to meet Kropotkin, who impressed her greatly: '[His eyes] looked as though they could see to the end of the world and understand the tiniest thing they met, and were sorry for all the people that were unhappy'.[7]

Ford depicts in his memoirs some of the meetings of the Friends of Russian Freedom and reflects on the possible influence they had on the course of events in Russia (RY 102), but does not go into ideological details. Ford's attitude to the Russians is complex; it stems from a mixture of his personal impressions and a constant search for identity. In Return to Yesterday he says 'I suppose I have a certain proportion of Slav blood' (RY 101); but he then complicates the claim by saying that 'Conrad whose genealogical interests were deeper than my own' worked out that a branch of Ford's family had settled near Warsaw; this is offered as an explanation of the attraction Ford says he has always felt for Slavs, 'and for the cause of Poland' (RY 101). But when he remarks that 'what Slav blood [he] had was Polish rather than Russian in origin', and adds: 'I suppose it does not matter but Poles seem more romantic than Russians' (*RY* 102), he not only emphasizes aesthetic considerations again as more important than facts, but also suggests that the family stories are themselves romances that give him creative affiliations with Conrad.

Certainly Ford's attitude to Russians and Poles were profoundly affected by his friendship and literary collaborations with Conrad (even if his attitude to Russians in particular was more complex than Conrad's rejection of them). Conrad and Ford had produced two novels and a novella together, and Ford had a high view of Conrad's art. Interestingly, he considered *Under Western Eyes* to be Conrad's greatest work (*RY* 147). This novel is the exploration of Conrad's mistrust of Russians as dangerous revolutionaries. He was working on this novel while he contributed autobiographical sketches to Ford's *English Review*. Conrad was then strongly under the impressions of the traumas of his Polish past; his father was executed by the Russian authorities as a Polish nationalist activist when Conrad was a boy. This seems to have heightened Conrad's sense of dissatisfaction in collaborating with Ford on the *English Review*, a publication in which Soskice, a Russian-Jewish revolutionary and Ford's brother-in-law, was heavily involved.

In his memoirs, Ford depicts his acquaintance with the Russian exiles in more than one way. At times, he seems to see them as similar to the Victorian Greats, in their uncompromising and self-confident 'ownership' of truth. Ford was alarmed by the way the Russian exiles' emphasis on a single truth could overlook personal fates. About Stepniak he remarks that there were 'thousands of heroic young people whom his titanic conspiracies sent to die in exile' (*RY* 102).

Yet Ford also talks about his identification with the Russians' struggle for social justice. He had 'early developed a hatred for tyrants and the love for lost causes and exiles' (*RY* 61). Juliet, Ford's sister, remembers their mother as susceptible to injustice and hating tyranny, yet not interested in politics (Soskice 189-92), and Ford may have modelled his early social views on hers. In his memoirs, he comments on the poverty of the working classes, both in Britain and in Europe, as the cause for anarchist activities (*RY* 63). However, his interest in the revolutionaries was always more on the human rather than the political level, as he states himself: 'I never took any stock in politics. But political movements have always interested me' (*RY* 64).

One of the Russian revolutionary exiles, David Soskice, had become especially close to Ford. This is how Ford describes his relationship with Soskice:

> My brother-in-law, Dr Soskice, had been imprisoned without trial or charge in St Petersburg. He was sent to Siberia, escaped and found himself in Paris with badly damaged nerves. He was recommended to work in the open air. He came to Limpsfield to work in the garden of the Caerne [sic] and indeed worked in the garden of my cottage which was next door. Eventually he married my sister. My sister helped Mrs Garnett with her later translations of Dostoievsky, Mrs Garnett's eyes troubling her. Soskice played a considerable role in the political events in Russia up to the founding of the Kerensky Republic. (*RY* 102)

In an ironic tone, Ford tells the story of Soskice as an example of the close relationships between Russians and English people around the Friends of Russian Freedom: 'English left opinion heartily espoused the cause of Nihilism, supported it with funds, found houses and even wives for its more destitute exiles' (*RY* 102). Considering the fact that at the time of writing these words (1931) Ford's political sympathies were uneasy with the 'English left', this evaluation makes the Anglo-Russian relationships seem too close for Ford's comfort.

David Garnett, who knew Ford as a child, offers a more elaborate description of the acquaintance between Ford and his future brother-in-law:

> One day a family of Russian Jewish political exiles descended upon us – the man was David Soskice and with him came a French-speaking wife and a little boy called Victor, of about my age. An empty cottage was found for them at Kent Hatch, but Madame Soskice did not care for English cottages and, having decided to part with her husband, returned to Paris, taking Victor with her ... What [Soskice] liked was facts, and for some time after his arrival he was always asking questions about England and jotting the answers in a notebook. It must have contained some very peculiar information, for one of his chief sources was Ford who loved walking to and fro in front of the cottage telling Soskice about England while Soskice sat on the doorstep scribbling busily with the notebook on his knee. I can only remember two examples of the information Ford imparted to him. The first was that the biggest grain crop in Britain was rye, all of which we exported to the Continent; the second that the most prolific crop in England was a very tall cabbage, the stalks of which supplied the walking-out canes for soldiers in the British Army.[8]

Ford and Soskice, Garnett observes, never became close friends. However, Soskice and Juliet fell in love. Saunders notes that Soskice's first wife (Anna Johansen) had already begun studying medicine when they arrived in England, and then returned to Paris to resume her studies. When Juliet and Soskice met and fell in love, Soskice was able to obtain a divorce from his wife who was already living with a fellow medical student, and Soskice re-married, to Juliet, in 1902.[9]

However, already in 1898 Juliet was learning Russian, presumably under Soskice's influence. The Soskice (Lord Stow Hill) Archive at the House of Lords Record Office contains a music sheet handwritten and signed Juliet M. Hueffer, on the other side of which she had written a Russian dictation. The dictation is corrected by another hand, and serves as plausible evidence that the relationship between them dates to that time.[10]

Garnett thinks that Juliet must have seen in Soskice the antithesis of her brother, Soskice being 'a man of the strictest integrity whose every word could be relied upon' (GE 38). One may prefer to compare here not integrity but philosophy of truth. In his dealings with Soskice, Ford always showed integrity and loyalty, and what characterize their different personalities are their approaches to epistemology. Soskice, like the other Russian revolutionaries, believed in science and objectivity as the cure to the ills of prejudice and oppression. This is why he was keen to know England as a collection of facts, which can be conveniently measured, captured and written down. In his mocking 'false agricultural statistics', Ford expressed his mistrust of facts and his rejection of the seriousness of the revolutionaries.

Despite their different personalities and worldviews, Ford and Soskice later collaborated in the *English Review*, regardless of Conrad's objections to this association. In 1907 Juliet notes that Ford 'had grown so nice, so kind and serious' that she was sure her husband, Soskice, 'would not know him' (Saunders 229). Her appreciation of the change in Ford, that makes her think of Soskice's opinion, may also hint at the fact that the two men were by that time ready to work together. And indeed, Soskice became heavily involved in Ford's first literary magazine.

When the *English Review* encountered financial difficulties in 1909, Soskice offered to fund the publication (requesting some control over its political content) while keeping Ford as editor. The plan never materialized and the publication was subsequently sold to Alfred

Mond who appointed Austin Harrison as editor. However, before that happened, Soskice had been forthcoming with funds to assist the *Review* a number of times. In May 1909 Soskice made two loans of £90 and £110 to the *Review,* of which in July £100 were paid back to him. Throughout the summer and autumn of 1909 both Ford and Soskice were paid employees of the *Review*, and the fact that they were paid the same salary (first £6 then £12) may suggest that they had a similar level of involvement with the publication. In December of that year, Soskice was already receiving letters regarding the financial difficulties of the *Review*, referring to him as responsible for this aspect of the publication.[11] Beyond the financial involvement, Soskice also contributed written pieces to the *Review*. In a letter to Juliet, Ford thanks her for her story and Soskice's article, both of which he is considering for publication.[12]

As Ford notes in *Return to Yesterday*, Soskice continued to be active in Russian politics while in England. There is even evidence that he was involved in transports of guns from England to Russia during the 1905 Revolution.[13] In the aftermath of the 1905 Revolution, when an amnesty for political exiles was declared, Soskice and Juliet planned to travel to Russia (Saunders 218). Ford initially wished to join them. In a letter to his literary agent James Pinker, Ford explains his intention to write a series of articles about Russia, drawing upon his knowledge of the country which was derived from years of acquaintance with Russian political activists, to be published in a periodical and later collected in a book.[14] Unfortunately, a publisher was not found and Ford never travelled to Russia.

Soskice and Juliet travelled to Russia in 1906 as planned. It seems that the trip started as a pleasant affair. Juliet wrote to her mother on 19th March that they were staying at a famous resort on the Finnish border and eating caviar at the hotel.[15] On 10th December she wrote to say she had met a very pleasant English lady in St Petersburg, and that she and Soskice intended to return to England in January or February of the following year.[16] However, unpleasantness followed when the amnesty for political convicts was cancelled and the Russian authorities arrested Soskice, though they released him later.

However, this incident did not deter Soskice from his political activities. To the contrary, he took other journeys to Russia in following years. Proof of this fact is a postcard from Ford to his mother, sent to the address 'c/o David Soskice, Postschamskaia 6, St. Petersburg'. The postal stamp on this postcard is of 18 January 1908.[17]

Thus Soskice not only returned safely to England and back to Russia, but felt secure enough in Russia to invite his mother-in-law to visit.

In the years following the 1905 Revolution, Soskice was often consulted by the Russian Committee of the House of Commons, and was increasingly involved in Anglo-Russian trade. In 1913 Soskice travelled to Russia as a special correspondent of the *Daily Chronicle*. By 1916 he headed a Russian Law Bureau in Lincoln's Inn and founded a Russian Institute and Library in London (Hollingsworth 80-81).

Following the February Revolution in 1917, Soskice travelled to Russia in May as special correspondent of the *Manchester Guardian*. While in Russia, he became an official member of the Social Revolutionary Party in Petrograd. By August that year Soskice became the Private Secretary of Kerensky, and returned to England only after the October Revolution, in December 1917 (Hollingsworth 83 – 94).

The relationship between Ford and Soskice is, therefore, an interesting case in the history of Ford's relationship with the Russians. A political activist, firm believer in facts, a practical man, Soskice seemed to be the antithesis to Ford. When they first met, Ford began by poking fun at Soskice. Yet they ended by becoming relatives and later collaborating closely. Ford remained true to his refusal to take sides in an exclusive way, and seemed to embrace the differences between them as part of the complexity of truth in human relationships.

Ford's relationship with the Russians was an integral part of his life, and later his memoirs. Moreover, it influenced his choice of literary images. A number of Russian references in Ford's memoirs and fiction seem to have stemmed from his Russian acquaintances and his awareness of Russian culture and politics.

The novel *The New Humpty-Dumpty*, one of Ford's pseudonymous novels published under the name of 'Daniel Chaucer' in 1912, is his parody on the set of Russian and British socialists and revolutionaries he knew so well. Among fictional characters, he includes historical figures such as George Bernard Shaw and William Morris. Interestingly, the novel deals with a plan to initiate a revolution in the fictional state of Galicia, not to be confused with the real Galicia where Ford claimed his family had originated. The novel is mainly concerned with the English and the Russians, and when Ford talks about 'Galicians' they usually resemble either Russian or English characters in the novel.

The protagonist, Count Macdonald, is an aristocrat who has joined the Anarchists, like Kropotkin. Macdonald shares his name and patronymic, Sergius Mihailovich, with Stepniak. Macdonald's approach to planning a revolution is as cynical as that of the Russian embassy in Conrad's *The Secret Agent*, the plot of which is based on the Greenwich Outrage and the Anarchist scene in London, to which Ford introduced Conrad.

The novel starts as a parody of the misunderstandings between a passionate Russian (Macdonald) and a cold and practical English woman (Lady Aldington). He suggests that they 'talk about (their) sorrows to each other' and asserts that '(his) sorrows are so much greater than (hers)', while she says that he is not absolutely sane and explains that he is 'exactly like a queer and not very unpleasant nightmare'. In this conversation, Lady Aldington characterised their differences by saying: 'Only remember that I'm English as you're Russian', asserting that this is the source of their differences.[18] However, quite soon Ford abandons this tone and for the rest of the novel Macdonald is portrayed as a typical Fordian English gentleman. The Slavic context becomes purely a decorative element in Ford's political parody. However, Russian and Polish features make an appearance in the novel and testify to Ford's interest in the Slavs.

In his dedication to *Ancient Lights*, Ford uses the expression 'the heart of another is a dark forest' (*AL* xi), which is a Russian proverb (*chuzhaia dusha – potemki*). Curiously, 'The Dark Forest' was his working title for the novel *The New Humpty-Dumpty*. The epigraph to this novel is 'There be summer queens and dukes of a day, but the heart of another is a dark forest', quoting 'Tambov' as the source of the epigraph. This is another Fordian joke, as Tambov is actually a province in Russia. In the novel, Macdonald's uncle, the Grand Duke Michael Alexandrovitch, gives the actual source of the saying: 'As the Russian proverb says, "The heart of another is a dark forest"' (*NHD* 63), and Macdonald himself quotes the proverb several times during the course of the novel.

Ford's allusions to Russian literature tend to be sites of similar complexity. Take the epigraph to *Ancient Lights*: 'A hundred years went by, and what was left of his haughty and proud people full of free passions? They and all their generations had passed away' (*AL* i). Ford quotes Pushkin's 'Sardanapalus' as the source of this epigraph. However, 'Sardanapalus' is actually a poem by Byron, which does not contain these lines at all. Pushkin never translated 'Sardanapalus', although he was indeed influenced by Byron. The quotation in question comes from another poem by Pushkin, 'Poltava'.[19] Pushkin's 'Poltava', completed in 1829, was inspired by Byron's 'Mazeppa' (1819). Byron's poem, in its turn, is based on Voltaire's *History of Charles XII*.[20] Both poems reflect on the strong and fierce character of the Polish nobleman Mazeppa, who later becomes a Ukrainian *hetman*.

When Pushkin refers to the lost generations of the past, he does so with nostalgia, mourning the fact that the romantic days of great heroes are gone, never to return. Ford's *Ancient Lights*, which opens with this epigraph, shows that the Great Victorians have made the world a place too dogmatic and dispiriting. Ford is happy to be free from the great men of the past, relating their stories for the sake of historical and cultural interest, but not wishing to emulate them nor mourning their passing away as a class.

The wild goose chase on which Ford sends the reader, by mixing up his references, seems to be a conscious choice. In the dedication to *Ancient Lights*, he states: 'This book, in short, is full of inaccuracies as to facts, but its accuracy as to impressions is absolute' (*AL* xv). In obscuring the exact quotation, Ford leaves the reader with the impression of a source to the epigraph being both Byron and Pushkin. This impression puts the emphasis on Pushkin, as he is quoted as the author of the epigraph. However, the actual context of the quotation stresses not only the Russian background (Pushkin) but a Polish-Ukrainian one (Mazeppa in Byron's and Pushkin's poems). Ford, as mentioned before, claimed to have had Galician family roots, and he also said that he prefers his origins to be Polish rather than Russian. Ford's later association with Conrad would certainly support this tendency to be allied with the Polish. However, his collaboration with his brother-in-law Soskice is a Russian element in Ford's life. This all demonstrates that Ford was never a man to profess to a single truth. His loyalty was primarily to intellectual and emotional freedom, the freedom to maintain complex relationships, the freedom to forgo factual truth in the search for a personal, complex truth.

NOTES

1   Ford, *Ancient Lights and Certain New Reflections, Being the memories of a young man*, London: Chapman and Hall, 1911 – henceforth *AL*; p. xi.
2   Ford, *Parade's End*, London: Penguin Books, 2002 – hereafter *PE*; p. 10.
3   For an interesting fictional account of this venture see Helen and Olive Rossetti's novel, published in 1903 under the pseudonym Isabel Meredith, *A Girl Among the Anarchists* (now re-issued by the University of Nebraska Press in Lincoln in 1992).
4   Since the 1830s, the Russian government attempted to oppress scientific studies in universities, because such studies were perceived as dangerously related to German objectivism, the source of Hegel's and Marx's thought.
5   For more information about the Friends of Russian Freedom and their contacts with English intellectuals, see Anat Vernitski, 'Russian Revolutionaries and English Sympathizers in 1890s London: The Case of Olive Garnett and Sergei Stepniak', *Journal of European Studies* 35:3 (2005), 299–314.
6   Ford Madox Ford, *Return to Yesterday*, ed., Bill Hutchings, Manchester: Carcanet, 1999 – henceforth *RY*; p. 103.
7   Juliet Soskice, *Chapters from Childhood: Reminiscences of an Artist's Granddaughter*, London: Turtle Point Press, 1994 – henceforth 'Soskice'; p. 221.
8   David Garnett, *The Golden Echo*, London: Chatto & Windus, 1953 – henceforth *GE*; pp. 37–38.
9   Max Saunders, *Ford Madox Ford: A Dual Life*, vol. 1, Oxford: Oxford University Press, 1996 – henceforth 'Saunders'; p. 100.
10 Lord Stow Hill Archive, House of Lords Record Office, file STH/BH/3.
11 Lord Stow Hill Archive, House of Lords Record Office, file STH/BH/2/4.
12 Lord Stow Hill Archive, House of Lords Record Office, file STH/BH/1/6.
13 Barry Hollingsworth, 'David Soskice in Russia in 1917', *European Studies Review*, 6 (1976), 73-97 – henceforth 'Hollingsworth'; p. 79.
14 Richard M. Ludwig (ed.). *Letters of Ford Madox Ford*. Princeton: Princeton University Press, 1965, p. 23.
15 Lord Stow Hill Archive, House of Lords Record Office, file STH/BH/1/4.
16 Lord Stow Hill Archive, House of Lords Record Office, file STH/BH/1/4.
17 Lord Stow Hill Archive, House of Lords Record Office, file STH/BH2/2.
18 Daniel Chaucer (pseudo. of Ford Madox Ford), *The New Humpty-Dumpty*, London: John Lane, 1912 – henceforth *NHD*; pp. 24–5.
19 The Russian original is: 'Proshlo sto let – i chto zh ostalos' / Ot sil'nykh, gordykh sikh muzhei, / Stol' polnykh voleiu strastei? / Ikh pokolen'e minovalos', Alexandr Sergeevich Pushkin. *Sochineniia*, M. A. Tsiavlovskii and S. M. Petrov (eds.), Moskva: OGIS, 1949, 'Poltava', p. 286.
20 George Gordon, Lord Byron, *Complete Poetical Works*, ed. Frederick Page, Oxford: Oxford University Press, 1970, 'Mazeppa', p. 341.

MOURNING AND RUMOUR
IN FORD AND PROUST

John Coyle

> This is not a model life in every respect, but everything about it is exemplary. The outstanding literary achievement of our time is assigned a place at the heart of the impossible, at the centre – and also at the point of indifference – of all dangers, and it marks this great realization of a 'lifework' as the last for a long time. The image of Proust is the highest physiognomic expression which the irresistibly growing discrepancy between literature and life was able to assume.[1]

> There it was, then: the natural catastrophe! As when, under thunder, a dam breaks. His mind was battling with the waters. What would it pick out as the main terror? The mud, the noise, dread always at the back of the mind? Or the worry! The worry! Your eyebrows always had a slight tension to them, like eye-strain![2]

One of the finer set pieces of *It Was The Nightingale* relates how, passing through 'darkly crowded, tumultuous Paris' on the way to the solitary peace of the Mediterranean, Ford learns of the death of Proust. The city is stricken, to a man and woman; much, says Ford, as London had been when Marie Lloyd died, so that he is reminded of how intimately literature enters into French life, and how Proust embodied that intimacy.

> I shared the feeling to the full. The death of Proust came to me like the dull blow of a softened club. That statement, I am aware, will read like hypocrisy when I go on to say that I had not read a word he had written. But it is not hypocrisy. I had not read him for a very definite professional reason, but I had heard with avidity all that was to be heard of him. Thus, for a long time I had had an extremely vivid sense of his personality and of his activities . . . . And, indeed, it added to the blow, that I was to have met Proust himself on the very evening of his death.[3]

Proust has not been read or met, but only heard of; he is rumour rather than real or textual presence: death has cancelled an audience for which his books are, contrary to received expectation, scant and negligible compensation. This flies in the face not just of Derridean

promotions of writing, but also of the whole Proustian mythography
of the written, one which was inherited from Ruskin, in whose *Sesame
and Lilies* (translated by Proust) it is insisted that we wait patiently but
vainly for an audience with nonentities while the books of the great
wait silently for our attention.[4] In a further move, Ford presents
himself as the inheritor of Proust's embodiment:

> Nevertheless, it was his death that made it certain that I should again take up a
> serious pen. I think those who know my record will acquit me of the
> implication that might be read into that statement. I had no idea of occupying
> Proust's place, and even at that date I still dreaded the weaknesses in myself
> that I knew I should find if I now made my prolonged effort. I was still tired,
> and I have always been lazy.
>   I think I am incapable of any thoughts of rivalry. There is certain literary
> work to be done. As long as it is done I don't care who does it. The work that
> at that time – and now – I wanted to see done was something on an immense
> scale, a little cloudy in immediate attack, but with the salient points and the
> final impression extraordinarily clear. I wanted the novelist in fact to appear in
> his really proud position as historian of his own time. Proust being dead I
> could see no one who was doing that . . . (*IWN* 179-180)

Ford presents himself as sharing Proust's sense of the scope of fiction,
and tantalizingly offers the prospect of comparison between *Parade's
End* and *A la recherche du temps perdu*, a prospect rendered further
enticing by the fact that *Parade's End* was partly written in the
resonantly Proustian town of Guermantes. Yet it is not the work of
Proust which impels Ford so much as the image created by his death
as culmination of a 'lifework', in Benjamin's term. Ford joins the
population of Paris in mourning for the writer (with the wry
suggestion that England only mourns music hall turns), and gives
some idea of the work he is to write after Proust's example; to be the
historian of his own time who writes out of a proper intimacy with his
own country, in the way that Ford achieves with his masterpiece. Both
novels are concerned centrally with memory, and various
mnemotechnics. Both also were deemed unsatisfactory in their
resolutions: Ford notoriously and troublingly by his own pen as well
as by Graham Greene, and Proust by E. M. Forster who, in his *Aspects
of the Novel*, refused to countenance the possibility of a formal
resolution to what he saw as Proust's baggy monster. I want to
suggest how each novel offers contrasting and complementary
meditations on war, death and remembrance.

While I will be addressing ambitions and concerns common to the novels, it should be clear at the outset that they are very different in tenor and form, so that no one would want to claim that *Parade's End* was an English version of *A la recherche du temps perdu*. For all the glories of specific natural description in especially the first and last volumes of Ford, there is nothing to remind us of the great set-pieces of involuntary memory, nor of the kind of self-reflexive celebration of the transfiguring power of art which characterises Proust's novel. And crucially, rather than the super-refined voice of Proust's narrative consciousness Ford gives us a succession of unsure, and quirkily vocalic, accents, such as that of Marie-Léonie in the final volume, who introduces serious themes of tradition as memory rooted in a sense of place in spite of her seeming scattiness. Reminiscent in more than name of Marcel's Tante Léonie, she places Mark in a French tradition – the English Milor' encumbered by *spleen*.

In such differences points of interest arise. As Leo Bersani points out, common misreadings of Proust's achievement as lying principally in the area of redemptive aesthetic memory result in an undervaluing of the time in between, so that *temps perdu* becomes time wasted including the time spent reading it.[5] *A la recherche* is concerned with much more than sacramental abstraction from time. There has been a tendency in Proustian criticism, encouraged of course by Proust's own embedded rhetoric, to give almost exclusive attention to the framing instances of involuntary memory, to make the moral of the story something like Eliot's 'Ridiculous the waste sad time/Stretching before and after'.[6] Involuntary memory is, of course, pivotal in Proust's novel, but only as it is played off against other types of memory, notably mourning and rumour or scandal. *A la recherche* mourns many: the churches and villages of old France, the certainties and pleasures of the Faubourg Saint Germain and its *belle époque*, and crucially, as well as movingly and dramatically, its most memorable characters: Swann, Albertine, grandmother, Bergotte, La Berma; throughout, Marcel is heavily burdened by losses which involuntary memory seeks partly to repair. A whole section of *The Fugitive* is entitled *Grieving and Forgetting* (*Albertine disparue*, 'Le Chagrin et L'oubli'), and the First World War is a major theme of the novel, if one comparatively neglected by the critics, while death is dwelt on in terms of a universal particularity, each person's death being a bullet with their name on it.

La mort de Swann m'avait, à l'époque, bouleversé. La mort de Swann! Swann
ne joue pas dans cette phrase le rôle d'un simple génitif. J'entends par là la
mort particulière, la mort envoyée par le destin au service de Swann. Car nous
disons la mort pour simplifier, mais il y en a presqu'autant que de personnes.
Nous ne possédons pas de sens qui nous permette de voir, courant à toute
vitesse, dans toutes les directions, les morts, les morts actives dirigées par le
destin vers tel ou tel. Souvent ce sont des morts qui ne seront entièrement
libérées de leur tâche que deux, trois ans après. Elles courent vite poser un
cancer au flanc d'un Swann, puis repartent pour d'autres besognes, ne
revenant que quand l'opération des chirurgiens ayant eu lieu il faut poser le
cancer à nouveau. (*La Prisonnière*, pp. 703-704)[7]

Swann's death had deeply distressed me at the time. Swann's death! Swann's,
in this phrase, is something more than a mere genitive. I mean thereby his own
particular death, the death assigned by destiny to the service of Swann. For we
talk of 'death' for convenience, but there are almost as many deaths as there
are people. We do not possess a sense that would enable us to see, moving at
full speed in every direction, these deaths, the active deaths aimed by destiny
at this person or that. Often they are deaths that will not be entirely relieved of
their duties until two or even three years later. They come in haste to plant a
tumour in the side of a Swann, then depart to attend to other tasks, returning
only when, the surgeons having performed their operations, it is necessary to
plant the tumour there afresh. (*The Captive*, p. 223)

In *Parade's End*, though, for all that it mourns the passing of an
age and a temper, the passing of persons is little marked. This may be
partly explained by the mathematical enormity of war dead and a
resultant refusal to individuate (with the salient exception of O Nine
Morgan), partly too by Freud's suggestion that melancholia performs
the undone work of mourning at the price of an attendant disorder of
self-esteem. Rumour, on the other hand, could be said to be the
governing oppositional mode of public memory in both novels. In the
overture to *Swann's Way* we are offered the aphorism that our social
personality is the creation of other people's thoughts, and illustration
of this is given in the misprision of Swann's status arising from what
is taken to be his disastrous marriage, this being the first relation of
adult actions we meet in the novel, and one which sets the tone for the
volumes to come. Throughout the rest of the novel, from Charlus to
Morel to Rachel and Saint-Loup, there is played out a conjugation of
scandal which will be familiar to the reader of *Parade's End*: 'I am
scandalised; you behave scandalously, he spreads scandal or she is the
object of scandal'. As the laureate of complicity, Proust aims to show
us how each role here is open to all, including the reader. *Parade's
End*, as Trudi Tate has pointed out, has scandal, or gossip, as one of

its organising principles,[8] and Tietjens is as assailed by gossip as Marcel is by loss. Marcel, on the other hand, is not presented as the object of gossip: his antennae, it appears, untuned to what others may be saying about him.

The aim of the final volumes of both novels would appear to be that of restitution, but of different sorts. Marcel is remade in his own words, in terms of his visions and the book he is to write, so that in the end it is the mortality of his book which worries him more than the mortality of his body. Tietjens on the other hand, is 'in process of being reconstructed' in Ford's words; *Last Post* is built around the absence of its hero as consciousness and actor, his true and redemptive narrative being stitched together from the accounts of various voices; wives, lovers, servants and brother: what each has in common is a relative inarticulacy: none has anything like Proust's narrator's detached wit. Rather they each speak from within an individual set of limitations, but the concert of their voices has the final effect of replacing malicious talk with eulogy.

In a study which acknowledges the amnesiac tendencies of Proust's readers, Malcolm Bowie argues gracefully that jealousy, rather than being a waste of time, a distraction, is a model for heuristic practice in much the same way that paranoia is a model for plotting and interpretation.[9] Proust's novel anatomises jealousy or suspicion like no other, suspicion being of course a prime narrative mode, its hermeneutic aimed at unmasking hypocrisy, discovering secrets, dismantling reputations ill-won. *Parade's End*, relatively unusually for a novel, attends to a complementary kind of justice which operates in the reverse direction, concerned with conservation and restoration, rebuilding that which has been destroyed. Tietjens is not jealous of Sylvia, his attitude marked rather by a bitter stoicism. Rather it is Sylvia who is jealous of him. While *Parade's End* is not short of illustrations of the corrupt flourishing, Ford's main impetus seems to be to rescue the decaying reputation of the long-exiled and slandered, but resolutely incorruptible Christopher Tietjens, a man who is the object rather than the subject of jealousy.

A la recherche has its own Good Soldier in the person of Baron Robert de Saint-Loup. Idolised as the noble man of action which Marcel can never be, Saint Loup, a Guermantes, marries Marcel's childhood sweetheart Gilberte Swann, uniting the two ways of childhood, but is unfaithful to Gilberte with the loathsome Morel, violinist, deserter and cad, before dying a hero in action. A retrospective dialogue between Marcel and Gilberte memorialises Saint Loup's ideas in recognisably Fordian terms:

> « Il y a un côté de la guerre qu'il commençait, je crois, à apercevoir, lui dis-je, c'est qu'elle est humaine, se vit comme un amour ou comme une haine, pourrait être racontée comme un roman, et que par consequent, si tel ou tel va repentant que la stratégie est une science, cela ne l'aide en rien à comprendre la guerre, parce que la guerre n'est pas stratégique. L'ennemi ne connaît pas plus nos plans que nous ne savons le but poursuivi par la femme que nous aimons, et ces plans peut-être ne les savons-nous pas nous-mêmes. Les Allemands, dans l'offensive de mars 1918, avaient-ils but de prendre Amiens? Nous n'en savons rien. Peut-être ne le savaient-ils pas eux-mêmes, et c'est l'évenement, leur progression à l'ouest vers Amiens, qui determina leur projet. À supposer que la guerre soit scientifique, encore faudrait-il la peindre comme Elstir peignit la mer, par l'autre sens, et partir des illusions, des croyances, quon rectifie peu à peu, comme Dostoïevski raconterait une vie. D'ailleurs, il est trop certain que la guerre n'est point stratégique, mais plutôt médicale, comportant des accidents imprévus que le clinicien pouvait espérer d' éviter, comme la revolution russe. » (*Le Temps Retrouvé*, p. 560)

> 'There is one aspect of war,' I continued, 'which I think Robert was beginning to comprehend: war is human, it is something that is lived like a love or a hatred and could be told like the story of a novel, and consequently, if anyone goes about repeating that strategy is a science, it won't help him in the least to understand war, since war is not a matter of strategy. The enemy has no more knowledge of our plans than we have of the objective pursued by the woman whom we love, and perhaps we do not even know what these plans are ourselves. Did the Germans in their offensive of March 1918 aim at capturing Amiens? We simply do not know. Perhaps they did not know themselves, perhaps it was what happened – their advance in the west towards Amiens – that determined the nature of their plan. And even if war were scientific, it would still be right to paint it as Elstir painted the sea, by reversing the real and the apparent, starting from illusions and beliefs which one then slowly brings into line with the truth, which is the manner in which Dostoievsky tells the story of a life. Quite certainly, however, war is not strategic, it might better be described as a pathological condition, because it admits of accidents which even a skilled physician could not have foreseen, such as the Russian Revolution.' (*Time Regained*, pp. 366-7)

Some of the finest writing in *A la recherche* deals with Paris and the war, and one certain similarity between Ford and Proust is how they continue to suggest and explore parallels, connections and even equivalences between the brutal public facts of war and the continuities of the private life. It is the triumph of memory which brings *A la recherche* to its conclusion, the whole 3000 pages having re-enacted a journey from the bedroom to encompass the world and the years spent living in it. Throughout, the movement is centripetal, Proust's consciousness acting as a sort of camera obscura on which the world's impressions may be projected like a magic lantern. Such is Proustian memory, modernist memory, we may say. Ford's novel presents a visceral alternative. The Proustian model of consciousness is certainly entertained in *Nightingale* with a disturbing sense of speed and grace.

> My brain, I think, is a sort of dove-cote. The thoughts from it fly round and round, seem about to settle and circle even further than before and more and more swiftly. I try in the end to let them come home with the velocity and precision of swifts that fly at sixty miles per hour into their apertures that you would say could not let them through. I hope thus to attain a precision of effect as startling as any Frenchman who is forever on the make. Perhaps I do. (*IWN* 233-4)

And here is a similar image, but this time gone ballistic:

> The admirable trenches were perfectly efficiently fitted up with spy-holes. For himself he always disliked them. You thought of a rifle bullet coming smack through them and guided by the telescope into your right eye. (*PE* 552)

Humankind cannot bear very much reality, especially in the form of the active deaths, moving at full speed, aimed by destiny at each individual. Tietjens the memorious, the man who had learned every mistake in the *Encyclopaedia Britannica* by heart, comes to bear a wound of war every bit as real and as symbolic as that of Hemingway.

> 'What really happened to you in France? What is really the matter with your memory? Or your brain, is it?'
> He said carefully:
> 'It's half of it, an irregular piece of it, dead. Or rather pale. Without a proper blood supply . . . . So a great portion of it, in the shape of memory, has gone.'
> She said:
> 'But you! . . . without a brain!. . .' As this was not a question he did not answer. (*PE* 167-8)

Mark Tietjens, at the end, is reduced to little more than a pair of eyes and a memory. His brother Christopher, meanwhile, the subject of so many rumours, having survived oblivion and reconstructed his memory, chooses obscurity, going underground rather than admitting the light through spy-holes or camera holes.

NOTES

1   Walter Benjamin, 'The Image of Proust', in *Illuminations*, Glasgow: Fontana Press, 1992, p. 196.
2   Ford Madox Ford, *Parade's End*, Manchester: Carcanet, 1997 – henceforth *PE*; p. 477.
3   Ford Madox Ford, *It Was the Nightingale*, London: William Heinemann, 1934 – henceforth *IWN*; p. 179.
4   John Ruskin, *Sesame and Lilies*, 'Of Kings Treasuries' In *The Complete Works of John Ruskin*, edited by E. Cook and A. Wedderburn, London: George Allen, 1903-1912. Vol. 18 (Library ed.), pp. 21-192.
5   Leo Bersani, *The Culture of Redemption*, Harvard: Harvard University Press, 1990.
6   T. S. Eliot, *Four Quartets* 'Burnt Norton', Section V.
7   Marcel Proust, *A la recherche du temps perdu*. Paris: Bibliothèque de la Pléiade, 1989, Vol. 3. Translations are from *In Search of Lost Time*, Translated by C. K. Scott Moncrieff and Terence Kilmartin, revised by D. J. Enright. London: Vintage, 1996.
8   Trudi Tate, 'Rumour, Propaganda and *Parade's End*', *Essays in Criticism*, 47:4 (October 1997), 332-53.
9   Malcolm Bowie, *Freud, Proust and Lacan*, Cambridge: Cambridge University Press, 1988.

'A ROYAL PERSONAGE IN DISGUISE': A MEETING BETWEEN FORD AND JOHN COWPER POWYS

Stephen Rogers

> I felt a curious and quite especial sympathy for him [Ford Madox Ford], the
> kind of sympathy that a penetrating woman would feel for a royal personage
> in disguise, out of whose battered skull all the 'nonsense' has been knocked
> by the buffets of fate.
>
> John Cowper Powys (1934)[1]

Ford's contacts with the most eminent of the generation before his
own (James, Hardy, Conrad) have been well-documented, as have his
associations with writers of younger generations: Wyndham Lewis,
Ezra Pound, D. H. Lawrence, Ernest Hemingway, Allen Tate, Basil
Bunting, Robert Lowell and others. Yet among the inevitable and
often intriguing gaps in the lists of names occurring in Ford's memoirs
and letters are several of his exact contemporaries. One such writer of
Ford's generation was John Cowper Powys (1872-1963), who enjoyed
a career as a lecturer in America before embarking on the writing of
the novels for which he is now chiefly known.[2]

Powys may have been close in age to Ford, but the two seem to
have had little in common. Powys, although born in Derbyshire, was
brought up in Somerset, where his father was vicar of Montacute.[3] He
attended school at Sherborne, and went on from there to Corpus
Christi, Cambridge, before embarking upon his thirty years in the
United States. Nonetheless, there is a record of a meeting between the
two men that is worth recovering for the insight of Powys's
observation, because it gives us an all too rare glimpse of Ford at an
unguarded moment and because the story is told with sympathy. It is
also worth quoting for the emblematic picture it offers of Ford in New
York during the late 1920s. The meeting must have taken place
between 1928 and 1930, when Powys moved from Patchin Place to
Hillsdale in New York State, and his account of it emphasizes Ford's
disregard or carelessness for the conventions of the social world of his

time, as well as the capacity to inspire a certain openness among his contemporaries:

> As a matter of fact, the only person I've ever met, except perhaps Cousin Ralph and Cousin Warwick, whose aristocratic manner seemed to me careless and charming instead of a morbid revenge on life, was Ford Madox Ford. I had tea with him once in Patchin Place, and although he is no reader of mine and I am no reader of his, I confess I greatly 'cottoned' to his noble, stately, and altogether gallant personality. I felt a curious and quite especial sympathy for him, the kind of sympathy that a penetrating woman would feel for a royal personage in disguise, out of whose battered skull all the 'nonsense' has been knocked by the buffets of fate; and I could see that Ford Madox Ford had a real 'penchant' for America, just as I have had myself. (*Autobiography* 547)

Powys here contrasts Ford, as an 'aristocratic' type, with the general attitude of Europeans to Americans at that time, which he characterizes as 'neurotic and testy' (*Autobiography* 546). According to Powys, it would seem that Ford was different. Was it that Ford was more of the world? Hardly, one imagines. Indeed, it is the carelessness of his aristocratic manner that Powys stresses. Responding positively to Ford's personality, he emphasizes that Ford harbours no resentment against the brashness with which the emerging America of the 1920s asserts itself .

Powys was later reminded of this meeting with Ford, by his reading of Douglas Goldring's memoir, *South Lodge: Reminiscences of Violet Hunt, Ford Madox Ford and the English Review Circle* (1943). The memory was especially stimulated by the mention that Goldring made of Stephen Reynolds (1881-1919), who had been a friend of Ford's in the days of *The English Review*. Reynolds had also been the object of a passion by Powys's sister, Philippa (1886-1963), who was often known as 'Katie', and was the author of a novel and a volume of poems.[4] Reynolds had given up a promising scientific career to live with the family of a Sidmouth fisherman, an experience that resulted in his best known book, *A Poor Man's House* (1908).[5] Memories of these events had prompted John Cowper Powys to write to his sister in 1944 that:

> Phyllis & I met Ford Madox Ford in Patchin Place. We liked him & felt great respect and great honour for him. After he'd come to rather a formal tea party there I met him by chance (almost directly after) squatting on one of those high turning stools at an ice-cream counter a very shabby one too & a little one on 6th Ave somewhere but *not* the great '*Bigelows*' wh. you will doubtless recall, and *there was* he – with a very honest & extremely fashionable not

very pretty not very young girl in fact honest nice & homely enjoying himself
far more than at the rather formal literary tea-party where he had to show off
with tales about Henry James.

It made me feel such a rush of sympathy for him – that the *second* the
party was over & he had made his getaway with a good literary quip he should
bolt into a tiny drug-store and treat his girl who had *not* been at the party to an
ice-cream or one of those '*Sundays*' they eat out of Straws! and share it with
great joy – which I could not see dear old Master Henry James doing or
Conrad either![6]

It is undoubtedly difficult to see Henry James, or Conrad, perching on
a high swivel stool at an ice-cream counter! Indeed, James's
complicated and self-consciously refined response to modern New
York was explored in 'The Jolly Corner', a story that Ford published
in *The English Review* in December 1908.[7] What is clear from what
Powys records is that Ford was a participant in the recognizable
modernity of New York, and whatever his discomfort in that
environment might have been, he seems to have reacted not with
pomposity but rather with a realistic sense of the limits of the
individual to both see and understand.

Powys's enthusiasm for Dickens, Wordsworth, Milton,
Rabelais, Dostoievsky, Whitman, Cervantes, Melville and Poe, marks
out a very different temperament from Ford's. The example of Walt
Whitman is perhaps particularly instructive. Whitman was
undoubtedly one of the most cherished of Powys's literary influences,
and it is telling that he should write to Philippa, 'I think you will like
my Rabelais Book Best of all my Books for it is far the most of all
under the influence of Walt Whitman'.[8] Ford, on the other hand, was
critical of Whitman, whilst admitting that he was a great poet, stating
that he nonetheless assumed 'prophetic mantles and beards', and
chose to use 'round-mouthed rhetoric' for his poetry (*ML* 776).
Whitman may have loomed rather larger in Ford's youth. William
Michael Rossetti had been the first to introduce Whitman to England,
when he edited a selection of the poet's work in 1868, and Whitman
remained a favourite among the Pre-Raphaelites and their circle,
including Swinburne. More significantly, perhaps, is Ford's
comparison of Hardy and Whitman:

Beside him, Whitman was a hysteric. He was not wise. The essential
townsman can never be wise because he cannot see life for the buildings.
Whitman saw factories rise and was excited over the future of the race. Hardy
saw factories smudge his rural scene, and was merely depressed. He knew that
the human heart remained the essential stamping ground of the poet. (*ML* 777)

Powys had met Thomas Hardy, was influenced by him and regarded him as one of the great writers.[9] The point here is one of relative emphasis. Indeed, Powys would not have made the particular distinction that Ford made, because, steeped in a pantheistic conception of the world, owing much to the ancient landscapes of Sussex, Dorset and Somerset, he saw Whitman in essentially the same tradition. Powys was, moreover, as he stated in his *Autobiography*, 'for all my Derbyshire rusticity and Welsh "elementalism", as neurotic as D. H. Lawrence' (*Autobiography* 546). Powys's 'major phase' as a writer coincided with the end of what is generally considered to be Ford's most significant period as a novelist. Retired from the extension lecture circuit, he began writing the first of the novels for which he is now chiefly remembered, *Wolf Solent* (1929). It is tempting to speculate upon the changing cultural circumstances that might have been responsible for this shift in fortunes and aesthetic ideals. It does seem that the sense of crisis occasioned a desire in the public consciousness for prophetic and didactic literature. Powys's analysis of the qualities that he found in the works of Dorothy Richardson, perhaps were relevant in this context. He noticed her ability to 'retain her strong, fresh, exuberant, childlike zest for the old simple great things in philosophy and literature'.[10] Such a comment probably reveals as much about Powys's state of mind as about that of the author whom he is discussing and suggests the direction he was to take in his own novels.

Ford seems to have felt that the Wall Street crash of 1929 was symptomatic of what was wrong with the contemporary world, and whilst he clearly maintained his long held belief that the future of English literature was to be found in the United States of America, he became increasingly pessimistic about the nature of American business methods, especially the impact these were having on the conditions of the publication of imaginative literature.[11] Indeed, in *A History of Our Own Times*, Ford specifically places the arts in opposition to the prevailing materialism: 'The Arts have bulked always so little in the public lives of Anglo-Saxondom of either branch [the United States and England] that to mention them in any History of either of the two great materialistic peoples is almost certainly to incur a suspicion, if not a charge, of frivolity'.[12] So much of Ford's career was, in spite of this awareness, an attempt to place the arts at the centre of consciousness in a public social context, and to educate the public about the importance of aesthetics. He had criticized, in *The Critical Attitude* (1911), the old nineteenth century Goethe-inspired novel for its concern with the solitary hero:

> For, when every novel had its hero, and every picture its heroic figures, then every man was led to believe himself supported by Providence, the centre of the particular affair with which he was concerned. Such a doctrine may lead to boldness in the presence of dangers; it may confer good consciences and directness to the glance; but it takes away fortitude in the time of protracted trial.[13]

It was just such a fortitude that Ford felt was lacking in the early 1930s. It is significant that his artistic response to this worldwide depression and consequent failure of courage should be a novel like *The Rash Act* (1933), which Anthony Burgess noted, in a provocative review in 1982, was 'so patently what fictional modernism is, or was, about'.[14] Burgess's definition of fictional modernism focuses on the problems entailed by selecting a point of view and the advantages offered by the incorporation of multiple perspectives. As a novelist, John Cowper Powys was not the type of conscious craftsman that Ford famously admired, concerned with the precise techniques and fictional devices necessary for a truthful rendering of his world; rather he was a writer who recreated it in terms of his own instinctive and intelligent imagination. It is Ford's handling of subjective impressions and recollections that marks him out as an artist of the highest order. Between the wars, though, the upheavals and derangement of the European order resulted in a shift towards the grand sweep of a didactic vision, and no doubt this contributed to the sense in which Ford's record of 'how the human mind perceives the world in all its unsyntactical variety' could be described by Burgess as 'modernism, which died in 1939, along with Ford Madox Ford'.[15]

Now that modernist studies are increasingly moving away from the concern with single authors to embrace the collective collaborations of different groups within an emerging modern culture, as well as disrupting the habitual foregrounding of the acknowledged major figures,[16] it is surely time to revisit Ford's relations with some of the allegedly marginal figures of the period. Ford emphasized, in his writings and in his life, the importance of collaboration and contact, as editor and instigator, opening and maintaining lines of communication with an extraordinary number of literary figures, many of them inevitably 'minor'. It is probable that not only they but

Ford too will appear freshly enriched by a renewed examination of such associations.

NOTES

1   John Cowper Powys, *Autobiography* [1934], London: Macdonald, 1967 – henceforth *Autobiography*; p. 547.

2   Powys is best remembered for his novels, *Wolf Solent* (1929), *A Glastonbury Romance* (1932), *Weymouth Sands* (1934), *Maiden Castle* (1936), and *Owen Glendower* (1940).

3   His brother, Llewellyn Powys (1884-1939), who married Alyse Gregory (1884-1967), the editor of *The Dial* (1924-1925), had submitted some stories to the *transatlantic review* (1924), which Ford had rejected. See Max Saunders, *Ford Madox Ford: A Dual Life*, vol. 2, Oxford: Oxford University Press, 1996, p. 160.

4   Philippa Powys published the novel, *The Blackthorn Winter* (1930), and the collection of poems, *Driftwood* (1930). She lived most her life in the village Chaldon Herring in Dorset, close to a circle of writers that included another brother T. F. Powys (1875-1955), Sylvia Townsend Warner and Valentine Ackland. See Judith Stinton, *Chaldon Herring: Writers in a Dorset Landscape,* 2nd edition, Norwich: Black Dog Books, 2004.

5   Ford, in the *English Review*, noted that, 'owing apparently to some freak of his character, or to some social malaise, Mr. Reynolds seems to have abandoned suddenly his contacts with what he calls contemptuously 'The cultured classes', and to have taken up his quarters in the cottage of a Devonshire fisherman.... Such a career... should at least suffice to prove that Mr. Reynolds' nature is no ordinary one'. *The English Review*, 1:1 (December 1908), 163.

6   Letter dated Feb 4, 1944. John Cowper Powys, *The Letters of John Cowper Powys to Philippa Powys: Powys to Sea-Eagle*, ed. by Anthony Head, London: Cecil Woolf, 1996, p. 168.

7   Spencer Brydon, James's double, refers to 'the modern, the monstrous, the famous things, those he had more particularly, like thousands of ingenuous inquirers every year, come over to see, were exactly his sources of dismay'. Henry James, 'The Jolly Corner', *English Review*, 1:1 (December 1908), 6.

8   Letter dated April 8, 1944: *The Letters of John Cowper Powys to Philippa Powys*, p. 169.

9   See John Cowper Powys, *The Pleasures of Literature*, London: Cassell, 1938, which lists, among its chapters, pieces on Homer's *Odyssey*, *The Bible*, Dante, Rabelais, Cervantes, Montaigne, Shakespeare, Milton, Goethe, Wordsworth, Dickens, Matthew Arnold, Melville and Poe, Whitman, Dostoievsky, Hardy, Nietzsche, and Proust.

10 John Cowper Powys, 'An Essay on Dorothy Richardson', in *The Adelphi*, 2:3, New Series (June 1931), 236.

11 See, for instance, his novel, *When the Wicked Man* (1931).

12 Ford, *A History of Our Own Times*, Manchester: Carcanet, 1989, p. 48.

13 Ford, *The Critical Attitude*, London: Duckworth, 1911, pp. 26-7.
14 Anthony Burgess, 'Last Embers of Modernism', *The Observer*, 11 April, 1982.
15 *Ibid.*
16 See, for instance, Robert Scholes, *Paradoxy of Modernism*, New Haven and London: Yale University Press, 2006.

THE GENIUS AND THE DONKEY: THE BROTHERS HUEFFER AT HOME AND ABROAD

Joseph Wiesenfarth

We know little about Oliver Madox Hueffer (1876-1931) and a lot about Ford Madox Ford (1873-1939). We still await a biography of Oliver;[1] whereas, biographies of Ford began with his young contemporary Douglas Goldring[2] and continue to our own day. Why should this be? Their grandfather, Ford Madox Brown, called Oliver a 'mad genius'. Their father, Franz Hueffer, called Ford a 'patient but extremely stupid Ass!' And their mother, Catherine Madox Hueffer, regularly gave a portion of Ford's allowance to Oliver.[3] The early indications all point in the direction of Oliver's succeeding and Ford's not. But like many a signpost these gave the wrong direction.

We know that Ford and Oliver had some things in common. When Max Saunders writes that Oliver 'was extravagant, theatrical, charming, entertaining, and ingeniously irresponsible, particularly where facts, money, or women were concerned', he could have been writing about Ford. Each attempted divorcing their wives outside of England: Ford in Germany, Oliver in the States. Both, quoting Saunders again, 'moved in a cloud of exaggeration, rumour, and pranks'. A principal difference between the brothers is that Ford was trained in music like their father, Francis, who was intent on his elder son's becoming a composer. Oliver, for his part, admitted his total ignorance of music, though he married a professional violinist. He eventually opted for the stage where he was singularly unsuccessful. So he tried stockbroker, painter, and even valise manufacturer. 'He also considered becoming a barrister, or even a tobacco trader'. Eventually, he sat down and wrote: sometimes as a journalist – he was a war correspondent in Mexico in 1910 – sometimes as a novelist. Again, like Ford, he sometimes adopted a pseudonym. Ford became 'Daniel Chaucer' for two of his novels, Oliver was 'Jane Wardle' for five of his.

Ever possessed by projects that needed doing, Oliver conceived the idea for *the transatlantic review*, but Ford did the work of editing it. Other pertinent similarities between the brothers as writers are that both wrote books on London and New York as well as on France. And in them they agreed that New York is not America, that Paris is not France, but that, indeed, London *is* England. Each also had his say about Germany, both having served as officers in the Great War. Oliver in his novel *'Cousins German'* (1930) and Ford in *When Blood Is Their Argument* (1915) and in *Parade's End* (1924-28). Of the many books that both wrote – Ford 81 and Oliver 19 – none of Oliver's is in reprint today; whereas, there are multiple reprints of Ford's *The Good Soldier* and *Parade's End*. And Carcanet is now doing what Ford always wanted: publishing a collected edition of selected works of his poetry, fiction, and non-fiction under the heading of *The Millennium Ford*. How is it, then, that the donkey managed to do what the genius could not? A brief look at the books that they wrote about the same places may help to answer that question.

Oliver's book of 1913, *A Vagabond in New York*, is a series of snapshots. The person in the pictures is always Oliver himself. He is the vagabond who wanders from Montauk Point at the eastern tip of Long Island to the Battery at the western end of Manhattan Island. He constantly changes his clothes to fit his constantly changing jobs. The one stable figure in uniform in the book is a traffic policeman, Officer Dempsey. He manages Oliver's career by directing him to one job after another, but carefully avoids recruiting him for the police force. Consequently, *A Vagabond in New York* is a travel guide around the city and its vicinity by way of Oliver's occupations and observations. We get a doubtful relation of the apparitions of Oliver Madox Hueffer, the successful author[4] as a down-and-out, penniless tramp who advises us on which benches from the Battery to Central Park are the most comfortable for spending the night should necessity require. Just how reliable a relation we are getting is another question altogether, though Oliver insists on the truth of everything he has written.[5]

What we have then is a set of episodes centering on one character that goes on and on like any good romance until the author himself drops from exhaustion. To suggest that there is a beginning, middle, and an end would be misleading. Indeed, were one to separate the book's chapters into fascicles, toss them high into the air and gather them up in random order, it would still be the same book because the organizing principle is simply as-you-like-it. There is no logical sequence from one episode to another and thus no suspense from one episode to another. The book is like Oliver himself when he works as an elevator operator – or in his phrase, because he works in a building that houses a newspaper office – as an 'assistant-express-elevator-editor' (*VNY* 203). The book, like the elevator, has its ups and downs but never in any predictable sequence.

What *Vagabond* tells us about New York City is that it has delicatessens where the club sandwiches are to be avoided; it has beaches where lounge chairs are an important commodity; it has Coney Island where the animals are almost as exotic as the humans in the freak show. The city has bars where the bouncers reign supreme and the bartenders are decency itself; it has gambling halls where fortunes are lost, never made; it has a totally corrupt police force whose traffic officers are nevertheless surprisingly polite; it has buildings with elevators whose operators are the most obnoxious people in New York. And, obviously, it has vagabonds like Oliver who become tour guides on boats that sail the rivers round Manhattan Island and who acquire a patter to help hapless tourists digest the Big Apple.

Oliver gives us a Defoe-like introduction to all these people, places, things, and a great deal more, assuring us he has worked at every occupation he describes, slept in such places that George Washington would never have thought to doze in, on, or under, and survived New York City on empty pockets. In brief, *A Vagabond in New York* is one man's travel book on how to live in New York on five cents a day. Consequently, it is a tribute to the ingenuity of Oliver Madox Hueffer who, before coming to the city, had written books enough to enable him to afford the hotel rooms in which he claims never to have slept. And speaking of sleep, *A Vagabond in New York* is superior bedtime reading. It's a book that once you put down you can never pick up again.

Ford takes a very different attitude toward work in *The Soul of London*,[6] which appeared in 1905, eight years before his brother's book on New York. Work for Oliver is variety entertainment. Work for Ford is a necessity: 'Work is the original curse of mankind because it is the original medicine. We may go on working till we drop, occupying our minds, keeping our bodies sound – but the moment we drop work our minds decay, our bodies atrophy, it is all over with us in this world' (*SL* 78). His writing about work is therefore a philosophical meditation on the human condition and forms the central chapter of his book. It may well have been inspired by Ford Madox Brown's great painting entitled *Work*, as Ford's own painting in words suggests:

> Workers in London divide themselves, roughly, into those who sell the labour of their bodies and those who sell their attentions. You see men in the streets digging trenches, pulling stout wires out of square holes in pavements, pecking away among greasy vapours at layers of asphalte, scattering shovelfuls of crushed gravel under the hoofs of slipping horses and under the crunching tyres of wheels. If walls would fall out of offices you would see paler men and women adding up the records of money paid to these others. That, with infinite variations, is work in London.[7]

Both laborers and managers in Ford's version of work are attracted to London on a gamble. For them it is 'an immense Hamburg lottery' (*SL* 56). They leave the countryside or another country to make their fortunes in London. They see the possibility of somehow becoming Napoleons of finance. Some few do. Most simply become footsoldiers of monotonously routine work for these Napoleons. They are an army laid waste by industrial innovation and general bad taste. A new way of making cement, for instance, eliminates some two thousand jobs. A cabinet-maker with a fret saw finds a market for 'cheap Chippendales', creates a 'line' of ugly furnishings that the public loves, and rapidly becomes wealthy with the increase of bad taste. This is only one instance of the standardization of labor that kills craftsmanship, deadens personality, and puts an end to individuality: 'Unless you wish to live for posterity you cannot any more put out good work, work that is solid and lasting, leaving it alone to push its way in the world and to bring you customers paying a goodly price' (*SL* 65). One sees in this description of work why Ford believed there was no nobler job for a proper man than that of artist, musician, and writer. His impression of 'Work in London', Chapter 3 of *The Soul of London*, is the foundation of his philosophy of art and the reason why he said in *New York Is Not America* that 'If I had a son I should want him to write imaginative work; there is no better or more dignified occupation'.[8] In such intellectual and imaginative work the individual can remain himself and retain his personality. In a word, Pure Thought and the Arts are the only humanizing work in the modern world. They create the person; they nurture personality. This philosophy of work is the underpinning of Ford's *New York Is Not America* as well as of his *A Mirror to France*.

Thus all his books about places are of a piece. They are books about Pure Thought and the Arts.[9]

This makes his book on New York City decidedly different from Oliver's. Ford is interested in it as a place for writers to work. Although he recognizes that America's most promising writers are from the Middle West, he also stipulates that the narrow-mindedness of its Northern European settlers drives its writers to either New York or Paris. He also finds the city alive with an immigrant population that suggests that New York is the 'last chance of European civilisation' (*NYNA* 98), giving hope to immigrants who had none in Europe. At the same time he finds it a difficult place for writers and artists to live simply because it is expensive; crowded enough to make movement from place to place in a timely fashion difficult; full of innumerable distractions and bland food; and impossible to get help – to have someone fetch you a handkerchief while you are working away at your book, for instance. But all things considered – Ford makes many comparisons with other cities in Europe and America – he finds that New York City is 'the beginning of the world'.

> I like, at any rate, to think of it like that, and it is possible that it is true enough. For New York is Babel without confusion of tongues. A place of refuge for all races of the world from the flood of ancient sorrows; the forlorn hope of humanity that, having lived too long, seeks rebirth. And indeed, the note of New York – its gaiety, its tolerance, its carelessness – is just that of a storming party hurrying towards an unknown goal. It is the city of the Good Time – and the Good Time is there so sacred that you may be excused anything you do in searching for it. And it is an ideal so practicable! (*NYNA* 39-40).

Ford's New York opens up to writers and artists an 'immense number of human contacts' (*NYNA* 118), it does not impose a narrow-minded morality on them (*NYNA* 203), and it projects itself as 'the birthplace of humanity' (*NYNA* 123). Such conditions are ideal for the imagination of the writer and artist to thrive in even though the circumstances of everyday life in so large and dynamic a city are demanding. But *New York Is Not America* is their guidebook. It is a *vade mecum* for artists and writers, not a facile reference book for someone looking for a hotel or a restaurant.

Oliver's books are more nearly what a traveler might take in hand to find out something about England, France, and the United States. But *Some of the English*[10] and *French France*[11] are quite different from *A Vagabond in New York* in that they are more intensely focused on the English and the French character. They are similar in being books that present characteristics of a country by giving an account of particular regions and of individuals who illustrate those characteristics. So there is a predictability of method that calls on the writer's style and story-telling to sustain interest. This is especially true in *Some of the English*, which followed *French France*, its more interesting predecessor.

Oliver locates his study of the English character in a part of London that he calls Romwell, a fictitious name for an actual borough south of the Thames, which he thinks may have been the original Roman foundation of London itself. 'I am going to mention a number of real people by names which are not their own, and do not wish too closely to identify them or their homes' (*SE* 51). Now 'the folk of Romwell', Oliver says, 'are among the kindliest and the most charitable of any, which may explain why it was so often chosen as a hunting-ground by people in the last stages of poverty' (*SE* 60). Mrs. Thwaites, for instance, is an example of this Romwell-English kindness, which is especially evident in the way that she cares for down-and-out Lance-Corporal Curle, who served in the same regiment as Oliver during the Great War and who is now finding it hard to make his way in the changing economy of England in general and of Romwell in particular: 'When I saw him he was standing at a street corner, offering little home-made wooden toys for sale, carved with a penknife out of match boxes. . . . Also he was suffering from a hacking cough, so that he could scarcely reply to my questions; a cough as to the genuine deadliness of which there could be no question at all' (*SE* 59-60). Informed of the Lance-Corporal's plight, Mrs. Thwaites finds him a room to sleep in, food to nourish him, a job to give him scant funds but some funds none the less, a doctor to give him care in his illness, and a bottle of Port to initiate all these kind-nesses. Each of these interventions introduces someone connected with them and rounds out the characteristic of kindness in Romwell.

Each chapter of the book proceeds in much the same way. The Grey Mare, a pub, is the neighborhood gathering place. Religion in Romwell has just about disappeared save for the Roman Catholic Church and the Salvation Army, each insisting on its own way to thwart the obvious workings of the Devil there. As for the Church of England, Oliver 'did not meet a dozen persons, under middle age, who were in the habit of regularly attending any sort of divine worship' (*SE* 88). Religion ('Brothers' Keepers', Ch. 7) introduces a few leaders of congregations, but none of much interest compared to the people at 'The "Grey Mare"' (Ch. 6), where many gather regularly to discuss all things great and small or compared to 'Other People's Houses' (Ch. 5), where Mrs. Thwaites is benevolence itself. This, then, is the flavour of *Some of the English*. Working by illustration and juxtaposition, it treats many topics by way of many people who live their very English lives in the short stories that Oliver tells.

French France is a more interesting book because it is a schizophrenic book. The Introduction and the last three chapters deal with the problem of France as a European power in rivalry with Germany, with nationalism as a pervasive European problem, and, consequently, with the danger of another war, which Oliver sees as inevitable unless nations can form a 'United States of Europe'. Indeed, he wants more. He wants this Union of Europe to be 'but a step towards a greater, more deeply-based and all-embracing League of Continents' (*FF* 286). All the other chapters of *French France*, however, deal with the notion that Paris is not France, just as New York is not America. In them Oliver situates himself in a town just outside of Paris and from that vantage point gives us his sense of what it means to be French.

He begins with a chapter on the disposal of sewage, there being no sewer system in this town. Sewage is collected by a horse-drawn wagon that siphons it from cesspools. The proposal of a sewage system to replace this traditional way of doing things is thought to be so radical that it endangers the mayor's authority. With that we have met the conservative French mind that prevails outside Paris. With that we are introduced to the character of the French man and French woman. From sewage we make the natural transition to filthy lucre. The peasant and the farmer earn and hide their own money. The idea that it be put into a bank is simply ridiculous. There it could be identified as income and taxed. Hide it and it is tax-free. The individual is patently more important than the country as a whole. Indeed, Oliver starts with the French man and the French woman, goes on to the French family as the most important unit in society, notes that the pursuit of the sou is a matter of family pride because all the children share equally at the parents' death (there is no primogeniture); consequently, families are smaller than in England. Such limitation is acceptable because sex does not trouble the French mind as it does the English mind, the French having driven the

Puritans out a long time ago. French children tend to be healthier than their English counterparts because sports have become usual in their lives. And although the French woman doesn't have the vote, as the English woman does, the French man votes as the French woman instructs him to. She is more nearly the dominant figure in the family than he. She it is who washes the clothes, retails the gossip, and goes to Church on Sunday; he it is who does not go to Church but goes to work every day but Sunday. And both he and she are proud of what they are: they would never consider themselves as better off or better people by trying to rise in society. Worked out in the details of church and state, these basics give us French France. All this, of course, is valuable for anyone visiting France for the first time and wanting to know what he or she might find there.

The problem is that the way of life described in *French France* has little chance of surviving because Oliver sees another war as inevitable. His book, then, looks to the destruction of what he admires even though what he admires is intensely nationalistic. But it is a way of life that is hardly one that everyone would find attractive and want to survive endlessly. There is, after all, something to be said for a sewer system. His preference is obviously for life going on without any change that does not come about through the normal evolution of children growing up, learning about different ways of living, and becoming part of something larger than the town, the province, the department – indeed, something larger than France itself. So at one and the same time Oliver wants to hold tightly to the very thing that is at the heart of Nationalism when he is trying to do away with Nationalism itself. Thus my sense of a split personality in *French France*. It is a guide book to a way of life that must, alas, disappear if France is to survive in the new United Europe the book calls for.

Ford does not have this kind of problem in *A Mirror to France*.[12] He envisions a different kind of world order altogether: 'The Republic of the Arts and of Pure Thought is then the only entity that embraces all nations and all creeds and whose intimate language is universal' (*MF* 234). Everything in this book in one way or another is focused on Art and Pure Thought as the only way that the world can save itself from inevitable ruin. One reason for this is perfectly clear: 'The exact use of words', Ford insists, 'seems to me the most important thing in the world. We are, in the end, governed so much more by words than by deeds' (*MF* 40). Although Ford starts with

words in discussing the French, nothing else that bears on Pure
Thought and the Arts escapes his attention.

> Here then is presented to you a picture more than anything of how to be
> happy – of people intensely individualistic who intend to remain intensely
> individualistic; of small shopkeepers who intend to remain and only to deal
> with small shopkeepers; of people with adequate means of living who intend
> to retain adequate means of living but to leave it at that; of a people of some
> culture who get enough pleasure out of their culture to remain a people of
> some culture; of a people whose peasant families work immensely hard in
> order that one member of the family may practice an art or indulge in abstract
> thought; and of a people less represented by its governments than any other
> people that ever was. (*MF* 14)

Even in an excursion on French bureaucracy and its functionaries – an
excursion that concerns the recovery of money from a postal order
gone astray – Ford manages to show how this most wearying of
French inventions promotes his agenda: 'the Frenchman does not very
much mind, whilst the bureaucrat loves inflicting' endless delays on
him. 'Thus one person is pleased and the other not injured' (*MF* 141).
Moreover – and this is the point – all this waiting about gives one
time to think about life and imagine various outcomes of the present
event. Thus are Pure Thought and Art advanced by the most notorious
of French routines!

But France is not all bureaucrats, to be sure. Ford's France is
about Civilization and involves other pleasures than that of waiting.
'For it is of gaieties, paganisms, riches and lazinesses that civilize-
ations are born' (*MF* 122). Such are found on the Rive Gauche in
Paris and everywhere south of it to the Mediterranean, especially
Provence. 'France begins with the bookstalls on the Quai Malaquais
and ends with Marseilles. Indeed if you added to the Left Bank, Marseilles, with Toulouse and Périgord for cookery, Dijon and the Côtes
du Rhône for wines and Provence for gaiety, farces, love-making,
bull-fights and, of course garlic, you would have France' (*MF* 86).
These are the things and the places that Ford sees as saving
Civilization. They are the world of France 'pegging away at details'
that makes life so pleasant. So Ford's France varies from life 'accepted as a grey, or at best a piebald, matter' (*MF* 33) to these 'gaieties,
paganisms, riches and lazinesses'. It is where what began in Provence
continues to exist: 'All chivalry, then, all learning, all the divine
things of life came from that triangle of the world which holds the
Château d'Amour, midway between Les Baux, Arles and Avignon'

(*MF* 57). Since no other life makes sense to him, Ford, thinking back on the Great War, affirms that 'To have died for France is very nearly to have secured immortal life!' (*MF* 24).

Oliver was born Oliver Franz Hueffer and Ford was born Ford Hermann Hueffer. Today we know them as Oliver Madox Hueffer and Ford Madox Ford. Their grandfather's name was important enough for both of them to associate themselves with it. They wanted an artist who was all artist explicit in their names. Ford wrote the first biography of Madox Brown and then went on to write a critical study of Dante Gabriel Rossetti, whom Madox Brown tried, in vain, to teach the elements of painting; and a book on the Pre-Raphaelite Brotherhood, whom Madox Brown did not join, but with whom he associated. Ford's book on Holbein established him as the first of the modern painters and remains a classic today. Ford also wrote the first critical book on Henry James and a metafictional memoir of Joseph Conrad, his collaborator on three novels. With them he placed himself in the French tradition of the novel as art.

There may seem to be a donkey-like plodding in this kind of work, but Ford was no jackass. He worked harder than anyone in his generation at these tasks to learn what made an artist a good painter and what made a writer a good artist. Oliver did nothing of the kind. He moved from profession to profession to find his niche as a 'mad genius'.[13] He finally settled on the writing of fiction. But serving no apprenticeship, he never became a master. Although he would call himself 'Madox', he never understood the lesson of his grandfather's great painting. He trusted in his genius and never mastered the lesson of 'Work'. Ford for his part demonstrated – even in books like those that are the subject of this paper – that his father seriously misjudged him. Ford was never stupid even if he was endlessly patient. But like the donkey, he earned his keep by working hard. As he said to Stella Bowen when she doubted her own abilities as an artist, 'a sort of doggedness . . . is in the end what does it!'[14] Clearly he understood his grandfather's 'Work' completely. Ford's genius was Work itself.

NOTES

1   Max Saunders and Michele K. Troy have helped begin the process. Saunders wrote the entry on Oliver Madox Hueffer in the new *Oxford Dictionary of National Biography* (2004). Troy wrote the longer and earlier entry, containing summaries of some of Oliver's books, for the *Dictionary of Literary Biography*, vol. 197, *Late Victorian and Edwardian Novelists* (1998). I draw from both of these accounts for facts that I cite in my second paragraph.

2   Douglas Goldring, *South Lodge: Reminiscences of Violet Hunt, Ford Madox Ford and the English Review Circle*, London: Constable, 1943, and *The Last Pre-Raphaelite: A Record of the Life and Writings of Ford Madox Ford*, London: Macdonald, 1948.

3   Ford Madox Ford, *It Was the Nightingale*, Philadelphia and London: J. B. Lippincott, 1933, pp. 271-73.

4   Three of Oliver's previous books are advertised on the title page of *A Vagabond in New York*, London: John Lane The Bodley Head, 1913 – henceforth *VNY* – which itself was also published in New York and Toronto.

5   While saying that 'he does fully realize his own limitations' (*VNY* 13), Oliver claims that his experiences 'are one and all "founded on fact," not over and above remotely' (*VNY* 9).

6   Ford, *The Soul of London: A Survey of a Modern City*. Everyman Books, London: J. M. Dent; Vermont: Charles E. Tuttle, 1995 – henceforth *SL*.

7   *SL* 47. This passage can be compared with parts of Madox Brown's lengthy description of his painting that Ford gives completely in his *Ford Madox Brown: A Record of his Life and Work*, London, New York, Bombay: Longmans, Green, 1896, pp. 189-95.

8   Ford Madox Ford, *New York Is Not America*, London: Duckworth, 1927 – henceforth *NYNA*; p. 133.

9   See Jenny Plastow's 'Englishness and Work' in *Ford Madox Ford and Englishness*, ed. Dennis Brown and Jenny Plastow, Amsterdam and New York: Rodopi, 2006, pp. 177-94, for a wide-ranging discussion of work in Ford's philosophy of life.

10 Oliver Madox Hueffer, *Some of the English: A Study towards a Study*, New York: D. Appleton, 1930 – henceforth *SE*.

11 Oliver Madox Hueffer, *French France*, New York: D. Appleton, 1929 – henceforth *FF*.

12 Ford, *A Mirror to France*, New York: Albert & Charles Boni, 1926 – henceforth *MF*.

13 Michele K. Troy has a different sense of Oliver than I do here. She seems to find his lack of interest in becoming a classic writer more admirable than Ford's determination to become one. See her 'Double Trouble: The Hueffer Brothers and the Artistic Temperament', *Journal of Modern Literature*, 26:3/4 (Spring 2003), 28-46.

14 Joseph Wiesenfarth, *Ford Madox Ford and the Regiment of Women: Violet Hunt, Jean Rhys, Stella Bowen, Janice Biala*, Madison: University of Wisconsin Press, 2005, p. 112.

FORD MADOX FORD AND
WILLIAM CARLOS WILLIAMS:
THE COUNTRY SQUIRE AND DR. CARLOS

Christopher MacGowan

The personal and literary relationship between Ford Madox Ford and William Carlos Williams covers more than five decades, from 1913, their first appearance in print together, to Williams' recollections and praise of Ford's work in the years following the older writer's death in 1939. This relationship moved in Williams' case from a somewhat distant hostility towards what he saw Ford representing, to an ambivalent respect, and finally to viewing Ford as engaged in much the same battle against oppressive English tradition that Williams himself was fighting. Along the way Williams associated Ford first with a side of Ezra Pound that Williams felt he had to reject; then with his English father William George Williams; and finally he saw Ford as an important contrast to T. S. Eliot, the writer who, for Williams, had abandoned the United States while Ford had embraced it. One legacy of Williams' interest in Ford was that in his private library were more books by Ford than by any writer except Pound.[1]

In Ford's case the relationship between the two men saw Ford gain an increasing respect for Williams' work in the 1920s, while in the 1930s Williams became for Ford a prime example of how the industries of publishing and academe could together neglect an important writer. Taking up Williams' cause, Ford in the last months of his life made a somewhat reluctant and embarrassed Williams the center of a series of literary gatherings in New York City, and pushed to get Williams' work wider circulation in England.

In some ways this would seem a rather unlikely friendship. Williams had little in common with the circle in Tennessee of Allen Tate and Caroline Gordon, who were close to Ford in the 1930s. Ford's poetry, for all its skill, did not move far in the direction of Williams' iconoclastic poetics. Williams himself evidently was puzzled by the direction that their relationship took. Years after Ford's death Williams remarked to friend and would-be biographer John

Thirlwall, 'Someday I've got to sit down and figure out why Ford. Madox Ford liked me'. Or as Williams put it in a short 1957 essay on Ford, 'What he saw about me, an American, even though he pretended to be a poet, I could never make out'.[2]

Ford and Williams first appeared in print together in the September 1, 1913, issue of *The New Freewoman*, published in London, later to become *The Egoist*. While Ford was of course a long-established writer, this was one of Williams' earliest appearances in print. They both appeared the next year in *Des Imagistes: An Anthology* and in the years immediately following could be found together in issues of *The Egoist*, *Poetry*, and *The Little Review*. In the January 1918 issue of *The Little Review* Williams published a selection from the improvisations that would eventually appear under the title *Kora in Hell: Improvisations*, and Ford began the serial publication of his 'Women and Men'. Williams made his first reference in print to Ford in the 'Prologue' that introduced these improvisations when they appeared in book form in 1920. The reference in the 'Prologue' comes as an aside when Williams quotes a letter he had received from Wallace Stevens. Of Stevens' cautionary comments on Williams' recent work, Williams asserts: 'Wallace Stevens is a fine gentleman. . . . He is always immaculately dressed. I don't know why I should always associate him in my mind with an imaginary image I have of Ford Madox Ford'. Williams then resumes quoting the letter. Clearly the 'immaculately dressed' Stevens (and Ford) don't match Williams' view of where innovation is to be found. The second of the 'improvisations' that follow this essay looks instead for innovation to a neglected figure who is attired quite differently:

> Jacob Louslinger, white haired, stinking, dirty bearded, cross eyed, stammer tongued, broken voiced, bent backed, ball kneed, cave bellied, mucous faced – deathling, – found lying in the weeds 'up there by the cemetery'.[3]

The 'Prologue' to *Kora in Hell* is not primarily an attack upon Stevens, but an argument against international modernism generally and the work of Pound, H. D. and Pound's new 'discovery' T. S. Eliot in particular. But Williams had little patience for Stevens' interest in refreshing the Romantic legacy or his examining abstract propositions at length. For Williams, Stevens is too respectful of tradition, and the 'imaginary image' of Ford marks the older writer in Williams' mind as also tied to the past. Behind the sometimes strident tone of this essay is Williams' fear that the work of Pound, H. D. and Eliot will help shift the energies of the war-time avant-garde centered upon New York back to Europe, which of course happened. Because of the respect that Pound accorded Ford in print and in letters to Williams, Ford was for some years associated in Williams' mind with what he saw as Pound's betrayal of this nativist renaissance.

Williams dated the 'Prologue' to *Kora in Hell* September 1, 1918, and first published it, in *The Little Review*, in 1919. By 1921 he was willing to concede that Ford was innovative, at any rate alongside H. G. Wells, and even that he and Ford shared some common aims. In a 1921 'Comment' that Williams wrote for the short-lived magazine *Contact* he declared 'I prefer the man who will be influenced a trifle indiscriminately by the new, I prefer Hueffer to Wells. I prefer him to the man who is too solid. It is a common language we are seeking, a common language in which art itself is our St. Francis'.[4] But in some ambiguous remarks in Williams' improvisatory *The Great American Novel* published in 1923 he seems to include Ford among the 'fatigued', and dismisses both Wells and Ford as finally irrelevant to America's necessary search for its own culture. The rambling narrative voice in the novel muses:

> make me a radical artist in the conventional sense. Give me the intelligence of a Wells. God, Ford is so far beyond him that what Wells says really sounds sensible.
>   Must it be a civilization of fatigued spirits? Then give me Ford. My God it is too disgusting. (*Imag.* 176)

While thinking about and writing this unconventional novel, itself about writing, Williams had evidently been following – probably in the pages of *The Dial* rather than *The English Review* – the serial publication of *Thus to Revisit* and H. G. Wells' response to Ford's claims for the relative value of style and technique. (*Thus to Revisit* is one of the books by Ford that Williams owned.)

For all of Williams' aggressive nativist rhetoric in the early 1920s, at this time he could only find publishers for his longer manuscripts among the expatriates in Europe. However, this limitation again brought Williams and Ford together. *The Great American Novel* was published in France by William Bird, in collaboration with Robert McAlmon, at the same Three Mountains Press that published Ford's *Women & Men*. The two books were part of a series of six that also included Hemingway's *in our time*.

Ford and Williams first met in January 1924 at a Paris dinner party hosted by McAlmon. Almost thirty years later Williams recalled in his *Autobiography*: 'It was my first view of Ford Madox Ford, the lumbering Britisher, opening his mouth to talk, his napkin in one hand, half-stammering but enjoying the fun, a mind wonderfully attractive to me, I could see that'. Ford gets more space in this account than fellow party attendees James Joyce, Marcel Duchamp and Man Ray, but the language suggests a distance between the two writers – Ford is 'viewed' rather than met.[5]

In these early months of 1924 Ford was exploring in print his sense of the new possibilities of American literature, and in the *Paris Tribune* of February 24 he described Hemingway and Williams as two 'singularly skillful' writers whose work represented the 'two main literary trends of today' – 'raw material' and 'a pre-digested pabulum of life'. Ford's comment that, of the two, Williams' work was the more European probably did not please Williams. He may have been more satisfied with Ford calling 'The Last Words of My Grandmother' a 'typical' American study when Ford published the poem in the third issue of *the transatlantic review*. (Williams' English grandmother had died in 1920, and the poem is in some ways Williams' farewell to the English side of his family, his father having died in 1918.) Certainly Williams would have been in sympathy with Ford's observation in the *New York Evening Post* December 13, 1924, that while English literature was stagnant, 'America has developed and continues to develop an extremely vital, ebullient and extremely young literature, which is purely national and yet of great interest as an international phenomenon'. Ford too was saying his farewells to England.[6]

Williams' other major contribution to *the transatlantic review* was an account of another farewell, his 'Voyage of the Mayflower', a chapter from his prose history *In the American Grain*. This essay appeared in the issue that Hemingway edited while Ford was in the United States. But Williams also sent in – and Ford published – two unsolicited letters in support of the writing of Robert McAlmon. On the merit of McAlmon's writing Ford and Williams did not agree, Williams' assertive claims countered by Ford's sometimes more oblique dissent. For Williams, in his first letter in the May 1924 issue, the prose of McAlmon's book of stories *A Hasty Bunch* is 'profoundly invigorating' and original. The August 1924 letter goes further, praising the stories in *A Companion Volume* and *Post Adolescence* as even better, marked as they are by 'the compression of the language' which for Williams is part of their essential American quality.

Ford's views on American literature at this time indicate that while he might agree with Williams' description of characteristic American writing as compressed, he did not recognize such a quality in the work of McAlmon. Ford's editorial comments in *the transatlantic review* on Williams' first letter suggest that he is having some fun with Williams' enthusiasm. 'Dr. Carlos Williams', Ford writes, 'desires to cheer on young America [....] Dr. Williams thinks that Mr. McAlmon has been very unjustly ignored by the Reviewers of his native land; we think the same'. Ford goes on to explain that lack of 'space', 'occasion', and 'will' keeps literary reviews out of the pages of the magazine, adding: 'and, differing somewhat in approach to the merits of Mr. McAlmon's work to which we are by no means indifferent [...] we have stopped off, as the saying is, our own Critic from writing on this writer and have left the matter to Dr. Williams'. Ford then devotes space to a lengthy joke centered upon a Victorian advertisement for 'Ford's Jackets', the illustration evidently culled from an ancient issue of *Cornhill* magazine. After this diversion he returns to 'Dr. Carlos Williams' Communication' to add 'it is pretty safe to say that the influence of advertising on Literature is practically to stifle all comment on such good work as has not got a considerable advertising capital to back it. And there', Ford concludes, 'for the moment we must leave the matter'. Left unsaid is any suggestion that McAlmon's book is 'good work', or that it is more worthy of advertising, or readvertising, than Ford's Jackets.[7]

Ford is more explicit about McAlmon in the 'Literary Review' of the *New York Evening Post* a few months later, in January 1925. In this essay he again praises the work of Williams, although he declares that 'The best writer in America at this moment' is Ernest Hemingway. He goes on to argue, 'The two worst writers that I have met in Paris [...] are Waldo Frank and Robert McAlmon'. In contrast to Williams' praise of McAlmon's compression, Ford notes mischievously that 'Mr McAlmon prints his own books', while he 'pours out streams of written matter that will result in three or five volumes of the Contact Publishing Company'. McAlmon's work, for Ford, lacks any sense of organization ('the Document, compiled just anyhow') a quality that Williams, future author of the document-filled *Paterson* had commended in McAlmon's writing as 'unliterary' and the 'discarding of every literary support'.[8]

Into the 1930s, as Ford became more focused on an American market for his writing, and spent more time in the United States, he and Williams had more opportunity to see each other. One glimpse of a closer relationship comes from Williams soliciting a contribution from Ford in 1929 for an anthology he was considering putting together. Replying from New York on June 30, Ford told Williams that he had no suitable unpublished verse, but adds 'I should extremely like to see you [...] and should love it if you would give me a call on the phone saying you could go to lunch with me practically any day' – before recalling joint acquaintances Hilda Doolittle and Richard Aldington.[9]

When Williams begins to think of Ford in terms of his late father, rather than associating him with the international modernism of Ezra Pound or with even earlier European conventions, the shift is at once towards a less distant but more personally fraught relationship. This sense of the older writer might be what produces such comments as 'Someday I've got to sit down and figure out why Ford Madox Ford liked me'.

Williams makes the comparison in a letter to Pound in June 1932, responding to Ford's three poems in the collection *Profile*. He wished that he knew Ford's verse better:

> Yes, I have wanted to kick myself (as you suggest) for not realizing more about Ford Madox's verse. If he were only not so unapproachable, so gone nowadays. I want to but it is not to be done. Also he is too much like my father was – too English for me ever to be able to talk with him animal to animal.

The same comparison in a 1942 tribute adds an important qualification – Ford is both more and less than his father to him. Williams writes, 'When I first knew Ford he reminded me, every time I saw him, of my father who was an Englishman much after the same kidney. But Ford was a gifted writer'. Fifteen years later, in a 1957 essay, the comparison is similar: 'I on my part thought him admirable in a remote British sense that represented the best of England to me. He always made me think of my unfortunate father who loved me'.[10]

Although an affectionate comparison, the association with Williams' father still characterizes Ford as a figure of restraint, and suggests an ambivalence that Williams may not have fully plumbed. From early in his career Williams located his own creative and imaginative energy in the maternal, Latin, side of his family, rather than the English paternal side. In his larger cultural aesthetics it was again the Spanish rather than the English legacy that he saw as most productive for modern American poetry. In a long poem about his father titled 'Adam', from the mid-1930's, Williams describes his businessman father, who left England at the age of five but never gave up his British citizenship, as crossing South America for his New York export company, alien to the land and its culture:

> God's handyman
> going quietly into hell's mouth
> for a paper of reference –
> fetching water to posterity
> a British passport
> always in his pocket–[11]

And in a curious poem ('Death') written in 1930, a dozen years after his father's death, the doctor poet struggles to find a balanced emotional response to his father's dead body, finally solving the problem only by removing the specific references to the body as his father's for the version in his *Collected Poems* eight years later (*CPW1* 346-348, 530.)

A later poem, 'The Clouds', also began as a meditation upon his father, but shifted to become a more generalized treatment of death. Williams was apparently troubled for years by his own medical decisions in treating his father's last hours, and always remembered a dream a few nights after the death in which his father descended the stairs and peered over his son's shoulder to condemn 'all that poetry you're writing' as 'no good'.[12] Clearly any relationship that Williams compares to that with his father will have its complexities.

The two writers continued to make appearances in print together in the early 1930s. Williams published some of his most recent verse in the *Imagist Anthology 1930* for which Ford wrote an introduction and also contributed poems. In 1932 Williams was one of the authors Ford asked for a short essay on Pound's *Cantos* for the 'Testimonies' that he collected in the 1933 tribute published by Farrar and Rinehart. Williams was happy to oblige. In making the request for a contribution Ford added: 'I hope you keep writing. I come across traces of you from time to time in various sheets and always with pleasure', and invites Williams to France – 'come over here and spend a little time under this roof'.[13]

Williams could not take up this or a later invitation, but Ford's more frequent visits to the United States later in the decade brought the two writers into closer physical proximity. Williams recalled in his *Autobiography*: 'He came several times to see us in Rutherford', and that Ford tried unsuccessfully to convince Williams to buy one of Janice Biala's pictures (*Auto* 300). In *Great Trade Route* Ford describes an enjoyable outing with Williams visiting a New Jersey truck farm. And by the end of the decade Ford was thinking of ways to gain more recognition for Williams' work. (It should be recalled that Williams would not come to national prominence for another ten years, that most of his books in the 1930s had appeared in very limited editions, and that his fruitful publishing relationship with James Laughlin at New Directions was still in its early stages.) In January 1937 Ford asked Williams: 'I wish you would lend me some – or for that matter – all of your books. I want to write something about you for VOGUE. It's a pretty silly sort of paper, but it might make some publisher do his duty'. Following up on February 10, Ford declared 'I think I shall try and make a more extended piece about you than I had contemplated, though that will take longer'. (In the same letter Ford arranges a meeting for Williams with Curtis Bok, of Philadelphia's Curtis Institute of Music, probably in connection with Williams' attempts to find a composer for his George Washington opera libretto). The piece for *Vogue* never appeared, but writing in *Forum* in September Ford argued the cause of Edward Dahlberg, E. E. Cummings and Williams as three unfairly neglected yet important writers. Ford's additional efforts included trying to get Stanley Unwin to publish Williams' novel *White Mule* in England. Ford's report of Williams' reputation to Unwin is more notable for its enthusiasm than its accuracy: 'For at least a quarter of a century he has been regarded by every American and most English writers of any perception as being the best prose writer and one of the acutest minds alive'. Ford's claim in this letter to have recommended Williams' 1913 book *The Tempers* for publication to John Lane is not supported by Williams' biographer, and Ford has the wrong publisher, but as a rhetorical flourish it does tell Unwin that there is a precedent for listening to Ford's advice. Unwin was not moved. Williams did not find an English publisher until the early 1960s.[14]

Ford's most ambitious attempt to boost Williams was his organizing 'Les Amis de William Carlos Williams' in New York early in 1939. Ford intended that the Society's monthly dinners both honor Williams and promote serious creative literature generally. Participants or supporters included Sherwood Anderson, Archibald MacLeish,

Marianne Moore, Ezra Pound, Waldo Frank, Alfred Stieglitz, Charles Sheeler, James Laughlin, Marsden Hartley, Katherine Anne Porter, Allen Tate, Charles Olson, and Louis Zukofsky. The list is a tribute to Ford's literary connections in the U. S. as well as to the interest in Williams' work among his fellow writers and artists. The meetings ran from February through June of 1939, the last one taking place after Ford had sailed for France. Williams himself was embarrassed, although appreciative of the attention. An indication of his reluctant participation is a letter from Ford to Williams in May imploring Williams not to follow through on his threat to boycott the next dinner. Charles Olson's presence at the meetings may explain why Williams' most detailed account of Ford turns up in the *Black Mountain Review* in 1957, titled by way of return gesture 'Les Amis de Ford Madox Ford'. The Society did not survive its founder's death, and Williams arranged with Olivet College's President Joseph Brewer that a prize fund of $300 that had been donated to the Society by Mrs. Archibald McColl be given to Janice Biala to help her difficult financial straits.[15]

Williams saw Ford for the last time on May 25, 1939, coming in to New York to wish Ford well on his voyage back to Europe. Writing to McAlmon later the same day, Williams had a strong sense that Ford was 'toward the finish of his life'. He added that the Fords had invited the Williamses to visit them in France in August ('Damned thoughtful of them'), and Williams hoped he could manage it, although he feared that the coming war and the cost would make it impossible (*Selected* 178-179). This visit would have been only Williams' fifth crossing to Europe and his first since 1927. When he died in 1963, he had never made a fifth trip.

By October Williams was telling James Laughlin that he had written a poem about Ford, 'To Ford Madox Ford in Heaven' *(CPW2* 95-96). Although the poem appeared in a college poetry journal, Williams had tried to get the tribute a national circulation. Sending the poem to *The New Yorker*, which turned it down, he told the magazine, 'I wrote it, to be frank, for some kids up at Yale running a mag they call *Furioso*. It's a good mag but I'd like to have people think about Ford – I thought I'd aim a pot-shot at you anyway' *(CPW2* 466). Williams rarely wrote such memorial poems and when he did they were either for close friends, such as Charles Demuth ('The Crimson Cyclamen'), or writers who meant a lot to him, such as his poem on the death of D. H. Lawrence ('An Elegy for D. H. Lawrence'). By 1939 Ford was something of both for Williams.

The poem prefigures Williams' treatment of death at the close of his *Paterson IV* ten years later, and sees Ford as the dedicated recorder of a particular place, not as British but as a lover of and recorder of Provence. The role is similar to that Williams assigned to his character Dr. Paterson in his long poem on the New Jersey city. The Ford poem begins:

> Is it any better in Heaven, my friend Ford,
> than you found it in Provence?
>
> I don't think so for you made Provence a
> heaven by your praise of it

The reference is obviously to Ford's best-known poem 'On Heaven'. *Paterson IV* describes the Passaic River flowing into Newark Bay in parallel terms, transcending death through a committed, honest account of a local earthly place. And *Paterson V* was sub-titled, when one of its earliest sections appeared in print, 'The River of Heaven' (*CPW2* 238-9). 'To Ford Madox Ford in Heaven' praises Ford for not being 'delicate' and for being 'Gross as the world he has left to/ us', terms that locate Ford and his writing in the same world of 'contact' and direct engagement that Williams sought in his own work. However much this is a projection of Williams' own particular aesthetics onto Ford, the description is certainly a long way from his 'immaculately dressed' image of Ford in the 'Prologue' to *Kora in Hell*.

Williams' correspondence with Louis Zukofsky about this poem is revealing of Williams' feeling for Ford. Zukofsky played a large part in the arrangement of *The Wedge*, and he strongly advised Williams to take the poem out. Williams followed almost all of Zukofsky's editorial advice on the book, but not in this instance. 'To Ford Madox Ford in Heaven' appears as the final poem in the volume, a position that often has a thematic or summary significance in Williams' arrangements. In response to Zukofsky's comments he did remove most of the first stanza of the 1940 version for *The Wedge*, and this truncated version was reprinted in the 1949 *Selected Poems* (*CPW2* 466). But the fourteen missing lines are an important part of the poem's argument for the relation to place that Williams felt the two writers shared, and for his 1950 *Collected Later Poems* Williams returned to the earlier, fuller version.[16]

In 1942 Williams joined twenty-three other writers in paying tribute to Ford in the *New Directions Seven* annual. Williams described Ford as 'living in these later years, with such generosity and openmindedness, upon benefits made possible for others'. The nativist Williams still wants to argue for a particular American aesthetics, noting that 'Ford often spoke of France, England and the United States as one country – such feelings have their limitations but there was no offence in it from Ford. It was what he meant to imply, what he enjoyed and what he wanted to see enlarged over the world'. The qualification occurs within what is a warm and affectionate tribute, although the sometimes irascible Edward Dahlberg later termed it 'a coarse memoir' in correspondence with John Thirlwall.[17]

Editor-in-chief Harold Strauss thought of Williams when Alfred Knopf made plans to bring out *Parade's End* in 1950. Strauss invited Williams to offer 'five or ten lines on your opinion of the importance of Ford and/ or the Tietjens series'. Williams was happy to do this, was quoted in the book's publicity, and later went on to review the four novels in the *Sewanee Review*. In his letter, Strauss unknowingly gave Williams his opening for the review when he declared: 'the novel stands up for me as the revelation of the declassment of the last Tory'. Beside the last four words of this sentence on the letter Williams has scrawled: 'in favor of what?' And in opening the review he declares: 'what in God's name would Ford Madox Ford be doing writing the tale of the last Tory?' Williams goes on to read this 'prose masterpiece' by 'a major talent' as a mirror of his own central themes. For Williams, *Parade's End*, like many of Williams' poetry sequences, ends with renewal following destruction – 'Sylvia was done. Valentine up!' For Williams the novels are about 'a new *form* of love', and Tietjens and Ford bring their old values to a new situation, and out of 'a tragic confusion' the situation is 'righted'. Ford, for Williams, wants 'to lead' his British characters 'out of captivity to their rigid aristocratic ideals – to the ideals of a new aristocracy'. Sylvia is the dead past, Valentine 'is the reattachment of the word to the object... she is Persephone, the rebirth, the reassertion – from which we today are at a nadir, the lowest ebb'. Ford emerges in this review almost as a co-writer of *Kora in Hell*, even to the reference to Persephone, rather than the figure mocked along with Wallace Stevens in that book's 'Prologue'.[18]

While Williams became for Ford a late example of a neglected modernist to whose cause he could bring a career-long expertise in boosting, for Williams Ford was the first and oldest of a trio – later to include Auden, and Denise Levertov – that allowed Williams to feel that by the 1940s and 1950s the expatriate trend of the 1920s had finally been reversed, along with an excessive deference to English culture. For Williams, these writers, with Ford as pioneer, brought that 'best of England' to the place where, as Williams saw it, they recognized that their talent could most flourish and develop – the United States. Such a view is behind two of Williams' final comments on Ford. In his reply to Harold Strauss praising Ford and his work, Williams commented: 'His mind took exactly the course opposite to that of T. S. Eliot's'. And in the mid-1950s Williams took this position even further. Interviewed by Edith Heal and with a memory made faltering by strokes – Williams recalled his gratitude to Ford, and brought Ford fully home onto his own nativist side:

> [. . .] Ford Madox Ford, whom I had met in Paris in 1922 at a gay party in his studio [. . . .] For some inscrutable reason, the Englishman trained at Oxford and the country squire who knew all the names decided to become my friend [. . . .] Toward the end of his life, after he had foresworn his allegiance to the Crown of England and become an American citizen, he had the idea of founding a literary society called Les Amis de William Carlos Williams [. . . .][19]

As Williams now remembers the event, he met Ford on Ford's own territory, 'his studio', and grants Ford the Oxford education that Eliot actually received. Both details enhance Ford's status in Williams' recollection, but most importantly Ford becomes an American citizen. The inaccuracy adds to the status Ford has attained in Williams' particular mythology. So remembered, American Ford stands an ally, in sharp contrast to those two British citizens who always loomed so large as antagonists in Williams' thoughts – the expatriate Eliot, and his own father.

NOTES

1   A total of thirteen books. 'Descriptive List of Works from the Library of William Carlos Williams at Fairleigh Dickinson University', *WCWR*, 10: 2 (1984), 30-53.

2   Note by John Thirlwall dated 5/26/56, Beinecke Library, Yale University, Za
    Williams (uncat. mss.); 'Two Pieces', *The Black Mountain Review* 7 (1957), 166-8,
    see note 15 below.
3   Reprinted in Williams, *Imaginations*, New York: New Directions, 1970, pp. 15, 31;
    hereafter *Imag*. (In the 1920 version Williams wrote 'Ford Madox Hueffer'.)
4   Williams, *Selected Essays*, New York: Random House, 1954, p. 29.
5   Williams, *The Autobiography of William Carlos Williams*, New York: Random
    House, 1951, pp. 194-5. Hereafter, *Auto*.
6   *The Left Bank Revisited: Selections from the Paris* Tribune *1917-1934*, ed. Hugh
    Ford, University Park: Penn State Univ. Press, 1972, p. 259; *the transatlantic review*,
    1:3 (1924), 63; *New York Evening Post: The Literary Review*, December 3, 1924, 1.
7   *the transatlantic review* 1:5 (1924), 361-4; 2:2 (1924), 215-7; 1:5 (1924), 358-60.
8   Ford, 'From a Paris Quay (II)', *New York Evening Post: The Literary Review*, January
    3, 1925, 1-2.
9   Ford to Williams, June 29, 1930, SUNY Buffalo, Poetry Collection.
10 Williams, *The Selected Letters of William Carlos Williams*, New York: McDowell,
    Obolensky, 1957, p. 127. Hereafter, *Selected*; *New Directions Seven* (1942), 490;
    'Two Pieces', 167.
11 *The Collected Poems of William Carlos Williams: Volume I 1909-1939*, New York:
    New Directions, 1986, pp. 408-9. Hereafter *CPW1*.
12 *The Collected Poems of William Carlos Williams: Volume II, 1939-1962,* New York:
    New Directions, 1988., pp. 171-4, hereafter *CPW2*.; and see Paul Mariani, *William
    Carlos Williams: A New World Naked*, New York: McGraw-Hill, 1981, pp. 14, 156,
    566-7.
13 Ford to Williams, August 30, 1932, Beinecke Library, Yale University.
14 Ford to Williams, January 28, 1937 and February 10, 1937, SUNY Buffalo, Poetry
    Collection; *Forum*, 98 (Sept., 1937), 126-8; Ford to Unwin, January 18, 1939, *Letters
    of Ford Madox Ford*, Princeton: Princeton U.P., 1965, pp. 307-8.
15 On *Les Amis*, see Mariani pp. 424-6 and Max Saunders, *Ford Madox Ford: A Dual
    Life*, vol. 2, Oxford: OUP, 1996, pp. 537-8; Ford to Williams, May 31, 1939,
    Beinecke Library; *The Black Mountain Review* 7 (1957), 166-8; Brewer to Williams,
    July 17, 1939, Beinecke Library; Janice Biala (signed Janice Ford) to Williams,
    undated [1939], Beinecke Library.
16 Max Saunders, *A Dual Life,* vol. 2, terms the poem 'a strange tribute', but footnotes
    the truncated *Selected Poems* version, pp. 538, 666.
17 *New Directions Seven*, pp. 490-1; Dahlberg to Thirlwall, January 21, 1955, Beinecke
    Library, Yale University, Za Williams (uncat. mss.).
18 Strauss to Williams, March 16, 1950, Beinecke Library; *The Sewanee Review*, 59:1
    (Winter 1951), 154-161.
19 Harold Strauss, *Parade's End: The Story of an Old Book Newly Made*, New York:
    Alfred Knopf, 1950, p. 12; Williams, *I Wanted to Write a Poem* (1958) revised
    edition, New York: New Directions, 1967, p. 96.

THE RETURN OF THE SOLDIER
AND *PARADE'S END*:
FORD'S REWORKING OF WEST'S PASTORAL

Seamus O'Malley

In a 1918 letter to her friend Sylvia Lynd, Rebecca West wrote that 'I had a weekend with Violet [Hunt] and [Ford Madox] Ford during which Ford explained to me elaborately the imperfection of *The Return of the Soldier* compared to any of his works – a statement with which I profoundly agree but which oughtn't to be made, because it rouses emulation'.[1] Ford's remarks may have stung because *The Return of the Soldier* was her first novel – she finished it in 1918 and it was published later that year – and Ford was one of her literary idols. In a review of *The Good Soldier* she had written that 'this is a much, much better book than any of us deserve'.[2] *The Good Soldier* first appeared in the first issue of *Blast* (June 1914), alongside one of West's earliest short stories, 'Indissoluble Matrimony'. Her entry into Ford's set of writers whom he had met through the *English Review* was, according to her biographer Carl Rollyson, her '"coming out" in the literary world'.[3]

Ford and West are linked in other ways as well. Angus Wrenn's article 'The Mad Woman We Love: Ford Madox Ford, Rebecca West, and Henry James' reminds us that Ford and West were the first writers to publish full-length studies of James.[4] But the profoundest links between the two writers may concern *The Return of the Soldier* and *Parade's End*. Several critics have noted the obvious similarities: Jane Marcus's editorial comments for *The Young Rebecca* note that West's novel, 'like Ford's Tietjens novel *No More Parades*, is a study of shell shock and the effects of the First World War on the relations between the sexes'.[5] Celia Malone Kingsbury's *The Peculiar Sanity of War* includes a brief comparison of the two works and how they depict shell shock; she observes that 'Both Christopher Tietjens in *Parade's End* and Christopher Baldry in *The Return of the Soldier* lose memories of events and facts acquired prior to the war, and both memory losses are appropriate to the characters' circumstances'.[6] Max

Saunders' biography of Ford brings up West's novel, which 'illustrates how another novelist can use the idea of shell-shock to explore the psychology of war: the way the journey to France does not only alienate the soldier from his homeland, but from the land of the living, taking him into an underworld of trenches and dug-outs, or a "No-Man's Land" with the company mainly of corpses'.[7]

While critics have noted the similarities, most have stopped short of a full comparison of the two works. Wrenn's assessment is representative:

> And of course the shell-shock theme [of *The Return of the Soldier*] parallels Ford's own life in the trenches at this time and his eventual writing of *Some Do Not* [. . . .] It is not suggested that West directly influenced Ford, but what is striking is the way that both exploit shell-shock and amnesia in terms of their association with marital infidelity.[8]

I would like to argue that not only was Ford directly influenced by *The Return of the Soldier*, but that we can read *Parade's End* as a more complex and ultimately more optimistic rewriting of West's first novel. Both novels deal with shell-shock and amnesia; both depict the inseparability of the home front from the front line; both are written in a pastoral mode; and both use the offspring of the protagonists as a way of suggesting a future for society. Ford adapted many of West's techniques – and her protagonist's first name for his – but his significant reworkings speak to the heart of his novel sequence.

Saunders suggested that Ford may have been the source for West's protagonist, Christopher Baldry, but Rollyson shows that West had 'conceived the plot of her novel' by the middle of 1915, before Ford had been injured at the front.[9] *The Return of the Soldier* is remarkably prescient in several ways: it is the first novel to seriously address the issue of shell-shock, and it features one of the first fictional depictions of a psychologist in English literature.[10]

Shell-shock could manifest itself in many ways; both novels' cases result in amnesia. Baldry's selective amnesia erases his recent, traumatic memories and transports him to a safer time of his life. Tietjens' memory loss is more complex and has to do with more than an obliteration of unpleasant memories. Neither Tietjens nor Baldry remembers his actual moment of shock. But Tietjens, unlike Baldry, has retained his memories of his unpleasant domestic life. Sylvia's affairs and the possibility of a bastard son remain on his mind. Ford's personal account of amnesia may have informed this, as his temporary loss of memory did not free him from his wartime preoccupation with Violet Hunt. Thus shock does not free Tietjens from Sylvia. One of *Parade's End*'s accomplishments was to demonstrate the insepar-ability of the home front from the front line. Even before Sylvia arrives at the front in *No More Parades* we see the inescapable nature of domestic problems. But West's novel was the first to chart this aspect of modern warfare: Baldry's 'return' trip home is not an escape from his memories of war, and his 'return' to the front will be marked by his painful disillusionment.[11] Ford's treatment of this is more complex but still owes much to West's initial perceptions of the home front. *Some Do Not . . .* depicts the early, pre-war shocks that Tietjens undergoes in response to Sylvia's machinations; his wartime shell-shock is merely another shock in his life. David Trotter writes that Ford 'relativizes anxiety' in *Parade's End* by showing the similarities between domestic shock and shell-shock.[12] So Ford's novels continue West's concern with the links between front and home.

Probably the most important similarity between the two novels is their shared use of the pastoral mode. Some of the best criticism of *Parade's End* has addressed Ford's use of pastoral in the novel sequence.[13] But *The Return of the Soldier* was the first novel to use this mode to address the war and shell-shock. The novel opens with the narrator, Christopher's cousin Jenny, describing Baldry Court and the surrounding landscape; the passage bursts with imagery reminiscent of the pastoral tradition:

> The house lies on the crest of Harrowweald, and from its windows the eye drops to miles of emerald pastureland lying wet and brilliant under a westward line of sleek hills blue with distance and distant woods, while nearer it ranges the suave decorum of the lawn and the Lebanon cedar whose branches are like darkness made palpable, and the minatory gauntnesses of the topmost pines in the wood that breaks downward, its bare boughs a close texture of browns and purples, from the pond on the hill's edge.[14]

In this physical description of the estate – more detailed than any physical description of the characters – we hear echoes of lyric poets like Marvell or Wordsworth who employed color (West mentions five), distance ('miles', 'distant', 'nearer') and floral accuracy ('Lebanon cedar', 'pines'), common pastoral techniques and vocabul-ary. But also notable in this passage is the relation of the house to the rest of the landscape. It 'lies on the crest', surveying the land with 'the

eye' that is providing the impressions that form the passage. The
house is more than just a vantage point from which we can see the
estate: it is what anchors the humans who own the land.[15] West's past-
oralism is not the mode of Wordsworth, wandering lonely as a cloud
through public, anonymous landscapes. Baldry Court belongs to Chris
Baldry, whose 'eye' has the proprietary right to survey the landscape.

The similarity to Ford's novels should be clear. The two last
chapters of Part One of *Some Do Not . . .* chronicle Tietjens' and Valentine's walk through the pastoral landscape of England:

> This, Tietjens thought, is England! A man and a maid walk through Kentish
> grass fields: the grass ripe for the scythe. The man honourable, clean, upright;
> the maid virtuous, clean, vigorous; he of good birth; she of birth quite as
> good; each filled with a too good breakfast that each could yet capably digest.
> Each come just from an admirably appointed establishment: a table
> surrounded by the best people, their promenade sanctioned, as it were, by the
> Church – two clergy – the State, two Government officials; by mothers,
> friends, old maids. [16]

The passage is also rich with pastoral language, and is infused with
notions of class and power. Here the pastoral interacts with the
economic and political powers of the landed class of England. Ford
stresses the characters' good birth, genealogy being the primary means
by which wealth, mostly in the form of land, was transferred in the
still-surviving feudal order. The State and Church are there to
'sanction' not just their walk through the grass but also the hierarchies
in which Tietjens believes. This pastoral trend continues throughout
the tetralogy: *The Last Post* begins with the 'view' that 'embraced
four counties' (*PE* 677). Andrew Radford explains the political and
economic implications of their knowledge of the landscape:

> [Flowers' names] are arranged so that overlooked flora become fundamental
> to Tietjens' definition of landscape as the topography of class [. . . .] his
> account is less a vivid impression of what he sees than a linguistic exercise in
> the way a traditional vocabulary arranges itself [. . .] feudal culture has
> evolved the language of landscape, where the master-tenant relationship has
> kept Tietjens and his 'great landowning class' dominant.[17]

So their innocent walk is actually a confirmation of Tietjens' class
over the land and his family's status as landowners. Like West with
Baldry, Ford has tied Tietjens' notions of the pastoral to notions of
landowning – their idyllic language is actually a meditation on landed
power.

West and Ford use the pastoral similarly, but also for similar ends. Jenny continues: 'That day [the view's] beauty was an affront to me, because like most Englishwomen of my time I was wishing for the return of a soldier' (*ROTS* 5). This is the first appearance of the pastoral's inherent irony, as West employs bucolic imagery to invoke a very un-pastoral situation. This is not an innovation on her part: in *Pastoral and Ideology*, Annabel Patterson points out that Virgil's pastoral 'referred to something other than itself, and specifically to the historical circumstances in which it was produced – the last phases of the civil war'.[18] So suggestions of war and battle have always been implicit in the pastoral mode.

Baldry's shell-shock temporarily erases any memories he has harbored since 1901. The date is significant: it was the year of the death of Queen Victoria, closing a chapter on a period of consolidation by English landowners that left them in firm control of the countryside. Residential settlements in rural areas began in great force after 1900. The anxiety of the British countrymen concerning the incursion of the city into the country had been expressed before the war, most notably by E. M. Forster in *Howards End* (1910). As a result of his amnesia, Baldry jumps behind all these developments, nestling his mind safely in the halcyon days of late Victorianism.

Of course, Baldry has a more personal reason for his unconscious desire to return to 1901: he has reverted to a time when he was in love with young Margaret Allington, thus erasing any involvement with Kitty. His reversion displays West's awareness of the ability of the unconscious to express a desire for some 'suppressed wish' or goal:

> If madness means liability to wild error about the world, Chris was not mad. It was our peculiar shame that he had rejected us when he had attained to something saner than sanity. His very loss of memory was a triumph over the limitations of language which prevent the mass of men from making explicit statements about their spiritual relationship. (*ROTS* 65)

Sentiments that could not have been voiced before the war found their expressions in madness and dislocation. Baldry's specific shell-shock, amnesia, brings him back to a time when he was in love with Margaret and allows him to express that suppressed emotion. Similarly, Tietjens is in a sense liberated by the war, because it allows him to escape from his bad marriage and build a life with Valentine Wannop. Both West and Ford were quick to see the psychologically liberating power of war's destruction.[19]

All of Baldry's delusions, idyllic as they may appear, actually stem from some incommunicable horror. Paul Fussell writes: 'Pastoral reference, whether to literature or to actual rural localities and objects, is a way of invoking a code to hint by antithesis at the indescribable'; Cowan notes it in *The Return of the Soldier*: 'the story is really about absence – and primarily the absence which the war creates'.[20] Bucolic imagery was often used as a reminder of harsh winters to come, or devastating plagues recently experienced. In the pastoral mode, as Raymond Williams put it, 'there is almost invariably a tension with other kinds of experience: summer with winter; pleasure with loss; harvest with labour; singing with a journey; past or future with the present'.[21] Usually pastoral literature comments on these dichotomies in relation to a community or a region. West shifted this area of concern from landscape to the psyche, as Ford would later do. Baldry's renewed love for Margaret based on their shared idyllic memories only exists in the pastoral refuge of his shattered mind. The presence of this love alerts us to the shocking ordeal he has undergone and also highlights the difficult task of remembering that lies ahead. *Parade's End* also explores this relationship between landscape and the mind. In *No More Parades*, Tietjens cannot get over the death of O Nine Morgan, and he projects his feelings onto the landscape: 'The sun was glowing. The valley of the Seine was blue-grey, like a Gobelin tapestry. Over it all hung the shadow of a deceased Welsh soldier' (*PE* 378). This dynamic shows up even more noticeably in *No Enemy*:

> at that moment, the feeling of dread that those gray-blue, motionless trees under the high sky might, under heavens more lowering, feel that final humiliation – that feeling was so strong that I remember it still as a pain. [...] For of course, it would have connoted that the broad and small fields, copses, spinneys, streams, and heaths, stretching away to the quiet downs and the ultimate sea, would have felt the tread of mailed and alien heels.[22]

In both passages Ford uses grey and blue to signify memories of battle, having his protagonists view the landscapes through the lens of recent trauma.

Baldry's desire to escape into a safe past is not just a subjective response to battle; it is an absorption of a process undergone by British society in the years before the war, and that is also one of the key concerns of *Parade's End*. Williams notes that the nineteenth-century novel charts the development of various communities and the values they choose to remember: 'A valuing society, the common condition of a knowable community, belongs ideally in the past [. . . .] Value is in the past, as a general retrospective condition, and is in the present only as a particular and private sensibility, the individual moral action'.[23] In her more modernist novella, West adroitly compressed this development into Baldry's mind; he has absorbed the crises of the British landed gentry and the values that class represents. Like Tietjens, his experience in war has given him penetrating insights into society from the vantage point of a pastoral landscape.

The final scenes, in which Baldry's memories are returned, involve his dead child, and it is here that the differences with Ford's novels become most apparent. Baldry only realizes his predicament when he is reminded of the death of his young son, which occurred two years previously. The painful memories return but his shell-shock recedes. Jenny concludes that 'there is a draught that we must drink or not be fully human' (*ROTS* 87). The novel concludes with anti-pastoral images of Baldry's 'fading happiness' and predicts that he will 'go back to that flooded trench in Flanders under that sky more full of flying death than clouds, to that No Man's Land where bullets fall like rain on the rotting faces of the dead . . .' (*ROTS* 90).

West's novel was finished before the war ended, so naturally it should end with the return of the soldier to the front. In this sense we could place her work in the ranks of the first generation of war novels and memoirs, such as Henri Barbusse's *Under Fire* (1916) and Ernst Jünger's *Storm of Steel* (1919). *Parade's End* was concluded in 1928, which signaled the beginning of the classic, second generation war texts by Graves, Blunden, etc. *Parade's End* is like those works in that it tries to envision a world after the war – Tietjens' 'return' is to a new, peacetime life. The way in which the two novels handle the sons of the two Christophers signify radically different conclusions. Baldry's dead son signifies the presence of death, and his memory acts as a breaking of illusions and a return to reality and the front. Ford, however, allows Tietjens not just one but two sons – Groby is to have a legitimate heir in young Mark, and Tietjens and Valentine will have a son of their own. So both love and land are given hope in Ford's tetralogy.

This speaks to the heart of Ford's rewriting of *The Return of the Soldier*. Baldry's attempts at a different life from the one he leads are abortive; the memory of the death of his son forces him to return to his old life. Tietjens, however, experiences a rebirth in *A Man Could Stand Up* – after he is buried in mud. In his brief comparison of the two novels, Saunders notes that '*Parade's End* shows how for Ford, the soldier's return and reintegration was a form of Second Coming'.[24] The survival of Tietjens' two sons and his rebirth in the trenches signal a future for Tietjens that West does not grant to Baldry. Baldry had to confront reality and realize that his dreams could not be fulfilled, and he had to return to the front, leaving behind the pastoral idyll and his love. Tietjens, however, has a chance to build a new life for himself with his newfound awareness of both his love for Valentine and his disbelief in the old order. This may be Ford's riposte to West's war novel. With the benefit of several years of hindsight, Ford believes that war brings on not just crisis but opportunity for change. Both Christophers were faced with crises and realized what emotions they had been suppressing; only Tietjens, because of his transformation, gets what he truly desires.

The comparison with West may help shed light on the debate over the political nature of *Parade's End*. Critics on Ford differ as to his intent in employing the pastoral. Jonathan Bate and Robert Holton see it as expressing a nostalgic desire for a feudal order. Bate writes: 'The pastoral works its magic in such a way that the Tory gentleman and the suffragette come together and we glimpse an England that is worth preserving'.[25] But Bate may be underestimating the sophist-ication of the pastoral and its ability, since Virgil, to take place in a garden but be equally concerned with a battlefield. We have seen, with West's treatment of the pastoral mode, that hers is not a new, ironic use of the pastoral but rather a full and complex use of it. Ford's use is similar, and he might owe this insight to her. Tietjens and Valentine's tranquil walk imply the carnage to come, just as Baldry's love for Margaret implies recent trauma. The emphasis on the beauty and order of the landscape is an inverted image of the carnage and chaos outside of their small world. Andrzej Gasiorek addresses this: 'Both pastoral and the nostalgic longing for it are ironized in *The Last Post*, which does not show feudalism in hibernation but as a shattered ideology'.[26] I would argue that we do not have to view the pastoral mode as ironic – it already is so. As I have stressed, both Ford and West were aware of the irony inherent in the pastoral mode and utilized it to the full extent of its critical power. Their critique of an idyllic order depends upon this awareness of the critical nature of the pastoral mode.

Some Do Not . . . and *No More Parades*, like *The Return of the Soldier*, focus on the inability of the mind to forget. But in *A Man Could Stand Up* – and *The Last Post* Ford allows for the ability of the mind to incorporate and create. Tietjens' and Valentine's new life, an alternate ending to West's book, is an attempt not to blot out the war but to live with its lessons.

NOTES

1   Bonnie Kime Scott, ed., *Selected Letters of Rebecca West,* New Haven: Yale University Press, 2000, p. 40.
2   Frank MacShane, ed., *Ford Madox Ford: The Critical Heritage,* London: Routledge and Kegan Paul, 1972, p. 46.
3   Carl Rollyson, *Rebecca West: A Life,* New York: Scribner, 1996, p. 53.
4   Angus Wrenn, 'The Mad Woman We Love: Ford Madox Ford, Rebecca West, and Henry James', *Ford Madox Ford and The Republic of Letters,* Vita Fortunati and Elena Lamberti, eds., Bologna: CLUEB, 2002, pp. 168-74 (p. 168).
5   Jane Marcus, ed., *Young Rebecca: Writings of Rebecca West, 1911-17,* London: Macmillan, 1982, p. 266.
6   Celia Malone Kingsbury, *The Peculiar Sanity of War,* Lubbock: Texas Tech University Press, 2002, p. 122.
7   Max Saunders, *Ford Madox Ford: A Dual Life,* Oxford: Oxford University Press, 1996 – henceforth 'Saunders'; vol. 2, p. 256.
8   Wrenn, *op. cit.,* p. 174.
9   Saunders vol. 2, p. 29; Rollyson pp. 63, 69.
10 West may have been influenced by Ford's *A Call* (1910), one of whose leading characters, Katya Lascarides, is a psychotherapist.
11 Wyatt Bonikowski writes that 'West first draws a sharp line between the front line and the home front and then uses the figure of the returning soldier to cross that line'. See 'The Return of the Soldier Brings Death Home', *Modern Fiction Studies,* 51:3 (Fall 2005), 518. Similarly, Misha Kavka argues that one of West's goals with her novel was to show how the wartime trauma was linked to issues on the home front: 'the novel refuses a theory of trauma which remains enclosed within the context of war neurosis'. See 'Men in (Shell-)Shock: Masculinity, Trauma, and Psychoanalysis in Rebecca West's *Return of the Soldier*', *Studies in Twentieth Century Literature,* 22:1 (Winter 1998), 159
12 David Trotter, 'Hueffer's Englishness', *Agenda,* 27:4/28:1 (Winter 1989/Spring 1990), p. 52.
13 See Jonathan Bate, 'Arcadia and Armageddon: Three English Novelists and the First World War', *Etudes Anglaises: Grande-Bretagne, Etats-Unis,* 39:2 (April - June 1986), 151-62; Andrzej Gasiorek, 'The Politics of Cultural Nostalgia: History and Tradition in Ford Madox Ford's *Parade's End',* *Literature and History,* 11:2 (Autumn 2002), 52-77; Andrew Radford, 'The Gentleman's Estate

in Ford's *Parade's End'*, *Essays in Criticism,* 52:4 (Oct. 2002), 314-32; and Bruce Thornton, 'Pastoral or Georgic? Ford Madox Ford's *The Last Post'*, *English Language Notes*, 26:1 (Sept. 1988), 59-66.
14 Rebecca West, *The Return of the Soldier*, New York: Penguin, 1998 – henceforth *ROTS*; p. 4.
15 Laura Cowan's 'The Fine Frenzy of Artistic Vision' argues that the novel's 'concern with the class system is another reason [West] chose to exploit the pastoral tradition'. *The Centennial Review*, 42.2 (Spring 1998), 303.
16 Ford, *Parade's End*, Harmondsworth: Penguin Classics, 1982 – henceforth *PE*; p. 105.
17 Radford, p. 314.
18 Annabel Patterson, *Pastoral and Ideology: Virgil to Valéry*, Berkeley: University of California Press, 1987, p. 3.
19 Bonikowski's article contains an extended analysis of Freud and liberation in *ROTS*.
20 Paul Fussell, *The Great War and Modern Memory*, Oxford: Oxford UP, 2000, p. 235; Cowan, p. 287. Susan Varney writes that the novel 'bears witness to a symbolic universe struggling to come to terms with what is, in fact, an unrepresentable trauma . . . . All point to an aesthetic that bears witness to a loss that is itself unrepresentable'. See 'Oedipus and the Modernist Aesthetic: Reconceiving the Social in Rebecca West's *The Return of the Soldier'*, *Naming the Father: Legacies, Genealogies, and Explorations of Fatherhood in Modern and Contemporary Literature,* Eva Paulino Bueno, Terry Caesar, and William Hummel, eds., Oxford: Lexington Books, 2000, p. 260. See also Jane Gledhill, 'Impersonality and Amnesia: A Response to World War One in the Writings of H. D. and Rebecca West', *Women and World War One: The Written Response*, Dorothy Goldman, ed., Basingstoke: Macmillan, 1993, pp. 169-87.
21 Raymond Williams, *The Country and the City*, London: The Hogarth Press, 1985, p. 18. The pastoral mode often subtly hinted at the city as the place from which the narrator has recently escaped; it equally hints at an imminent return to the city. Similarly, the 'Return' in West's title covers both of these forces, Baldry's return to civilian life and his return to battle.
22 Ford, *No Enemy,* New York: The Ecco Press, 1984, p. 28.
23 Williams, p. 180.
24 Saunders, vol. 2, p. 256.
25 Bate, p. 156.
26 Gasiorek, p. 66.

HERBERT READ'S DILEMMA: FATHERLY ADVICE FROM FMF

By Michael Paraskos

In September 1920 Herbert Read, the man who was to become the foremost English writer on twentieth-century art, was in a state of profound spiritual turmoil. At that moment Read's interests in the visual arts were, at best, dormant, and his ambition lay in becoming a leading figure in the world of literature, not only as a critic but as a poet and novelist in his own right. The portents for this had, however, been somewhat mixed. In 1915, shortly after enlisting to fight in the First World War, Read had used his own extremely limited funds to self-publish a volume of poetry, entitled *Songs of Chaos*. Like most of his wartime verse this emulated the style of Ezra Pound, but clearly Read was dissatisfied with the result as he destroyed almost every copy within a year of its publication. At the end of the war he published two further collections of poetry, *Naked Warriors* and *Eclogues,* that were undoubtedly more successful artistically, but passed largely unnoticed in the wider world. The evidence suggests that by 1920 Read was trying to move more towards prose writing, and he submitted a short story, again based on his wartime experience, for publication in *The New Age.* The response of the editor, Alfred Orage, must have come as a shock, with Orage describing Read's effort as 'dull in every sense'.[1]

Read did, of course, have some literary successes around this time, most notably in establishing, with Frank Rutter, the literary journal *Art and Letters.* Founded in 1917, this is widely acknowledged as the forerunner to T. S. Eliot's hugely influential journal *The Criterion.*[2] Yet in 1920 this project too ran into trouble, with *Art and Letters* closing due to lack of funds. Elsewhere, Read was also finding the workload of his 'day job', as a civil servant in HM Treasury, increasingly heavy and complained that it left him little time or energy to write. In short, by 1920 Read found himself facing the real possibility that his literary ambitions were slipping away for good. It was with this in mind that in September of that year he wrote to Ford Madox Ford for advice.

The two men had met for the first time in 1918 when both were still serving in the British Army. According to Read, he came across Ford at the Tees Garrison in Redcar whilst idly looking down a list of officers attached to the base. To his 'surprise and delight' he saw Ford's name and armed only with his ambition to become a novelist introduced himself. As Read wryly noted, he became Ford's 'young and enthusiastic disciple' and Ford was 'not unwilling to adopt the rôle of mentor'.[3]

Read's description of his relationship with Ford is significant for casting light not only on how Ford saw himself as a kind of suture between the late nineteenth-century cultural world of Henry James and Joseph Conrad and the avant-garde of early British modernism, but on Read's seemingly repeated need in his early career to be guided by father-figures. Read's friendships were frequently with people who were either older or in some ways more worldly-wise than himself, and in addition to Ford the list includes Rutter, Orage, Eliot and Richard Aldington.[4] It is tempting to assume Read's motivation in seeking such guides stemmed from an unconscious desire to replace his biological father who had died in a horse-riding accident when Read was aged only eight. Read had felt the loss keenly, not only for the death of a parent, but the resulting eviction he and his brothers faced from their home in an isolated part of the rural North Riding of Yorkshire. As far as Read was concerned, his rehousing in an orphanage in the heavily industrialised West Riding town of Halifax was little short of a fall from Eden, and it was to inform his writings and political outlook for the rest of his life.[5]

Yet there is also reason to suggest that in the early stages of his writing career Read needed the support of more self-assured figures such as Ford because of a fundamental lack of confidence in his own critical opinion. Evidence for this is often circumstantial, but as an example it is worth noting the effect Eliot had on Read in the 1920s. In the 1910s Read had shown a strong and even Promethean interest in the use of psychoanalysis as a critical tool, but this was effectively banished in the face of Eliot's open hostility towards Freudianism.[6] It was to be many years before Read was self-assured enough in his own views to counter such critical opinion, and his interest in psycho-analysis was not to re-emerge until he broke free of Eliot in the early 1930s.[7] Although this might indicate the young Read was easily led by strong personalities such as Eliot, in the case of Ford there was something more gentle and open in their friendship that could be seen in Read's desire for career guidance and literary opinion from Ford.

On the surface Ford and Read could not have been more

different. Ford, the affable English bohemian, full of Edwardian bon-homie, is set against Read's northern English reticence. Indeed, Read was not widely liked by several of Ford's other friends. Katherine Mansfield claimed he was 'too serious' and 'a bore',[8] and Ezra Pound wrote to Ford to say Read was 'too bloody dull' to appear in his journal *The Little Review.*[9] Such dislike may have had an element of class-snobbery behind it, with Read's lower class and northern origins not sitting well with the bourgeois bohemia of Pound and Mansfield. This was not unique to Read,[10] although as Osbert Sitwell remarked, Read seemed deliberately to take it to an extreme. According to Sitwell, Read acted 'like a Roundhead: he is extravagant only in the lengths to which austerity carries him'.[11] Clearly Read saw the flip side of Sitwell's comment, writing to his first wife Evelyn that when he first met Osbert and his brother Sacheverell Sitwell in October 1918 he thought them enthusiastic, 'but perhaps there is a lot of pose in their revolt'.[12]

The date of Read's first meeting with the Sitwells coincided precisely with his first contact with Ford. When in London, on leave from the wartime trenches, Read had already started to engage with the world of the literary avant-garde. This had been largely the result of his involvement with Rutter and *Art and Letters*. Yet as his comments on the Sitwells indicate, he had some reservations about that world. It has been suggested that Read was attracted to the seemingly 'carefree bohemia' shown by the likes of the Sitwell brothers, Pound and Mansfield, but that he was also frightened by it.[13] Consequently, it does not seem unreasonable to presume there was something felicitous for Read in meeting Ford in Redcar as it allowed him a gentle introduction to a cultural world that could be too overwhelming, harsh and cutting for a northern working-class boy. A comparison with another working-class northern writer who was helped by Ford is instructive here. D. H. Lawrence was so shy and intimidated by London literary life that his first writings were sent to Ford *inter media,* by his girlfriend Jessie Chambers.[14] As this shows, for outsiders who were not middle class, or southern, or endowed with a superhuman self-confidence, Ford's world was an intimidating place. This means that in becoming Ford's enthusiastic disciple in the northernmost part of Yorkshire, Read was fortunate to encounter a man whose genuine desire to encourage new writers allowed him to see beyond any superficial shyness. But he was fortunate too in doing so well away from the aggressive whirligig of bohemian London. The Redcar barracks allowed time and space for a friendship to develop.

From their correspondence this was, at least for a few years, a close and warm friendship. Read was a prolific letter writer and, although relatively little of his correspondence with Ford survives, it shows an easy relationship in which gentle ribbing by Ford is coupled with fatherly advice to the young novelist that Read wanted to become. A good example of the former is the faux-outrage Ford showed in a letter written to Read in June 1920:

> Sir;
>
>> You appear to labour under a misapprehension. I can neither recall your identity nor imagine what motive can have prompted you to address to me your obscene and even blasphemous volume, 'Eclogues'!

In this letter Ford implies that Read must have shown something of the northern reticence Sitwell had seen in him by writing in a rather cold (or timid?) manner to ask whether Ford would mind commenting on *Eclogues*. As Ford went on to tell Read, 'It is unnecessary to address me as if I were an obliviscent Panjandrum with head a mile above all clouds. Of course I should be pleased to hear from you and to get your volume'.[15] Similar teasing is evident in Ford's reaction to Read gaining a job from Orage in 1921 to write a regular literary column in *The New Age*. Ford claimed, probably quite correctly, that the job had originally been offered to him. 'My dear Read', he wrote, 'Curse you! Just as in H. M. Army you mopped up that staff job over my head, so you have mopped up the New Age Lit. Page'. There is no reason to believe this was a genuine hurt on the part of Ford as the letter to Read also makes clear that Orage's offer to Ford had been made some six months earlier. In self-deprecating mode, Ford admitted he had not bothered to reply. Ford then suggested that Read visit him soon to enjoy some duckling and green peas, none of which indicates any real hurt (*LF* 133). Indeed, with such jovial banter between the two men, the worst interpretation of their relationship would be that Read's earnestness occasionally led him to mistake Ford's jokes for seriousness, no doubt much to the further amusement of Ford.

Neither the mock outrage nor the bonhomie of this correspondence should detract from the fact that Read saw in Ford a confidant to whom he could express his feelings and turn for guidance. Ford's advice was, Read stated, 'entirely reasonable and sympathetic'. In the letter previously quoted there is an indication of this with Ford writing something that at first sight seems like a *non sequitur:* 'damn the

Treasury'. Read must have written to Ford previously on his frustration at having to work as a civil servant in the Treasury. Recalling this a few years later, in his autobiography *Annals of Innocence and Experience,* Read stated that it was an often painful job:

> My mind was full of projects – projects for novels, plays and long poems which needed seclusion and ample leisure for their execution. As month after month went by with nothing accomplished, I worked myself into a desperate state of dissatisfaction and revolt, until I came near to resigning my post in the Civil Service in order to retire to some cottage in the country where I could write uninterruptedly. (*Annals* 164-5)

Read was in fact setting himself a choice that Ford could not see as necessary. Read believed that if he stayed in the civil service he would have to change his ambitions as a writer, or if he wanted to be a novelist he would have to leave the civil service and London to settle in the country where he could become a 'regional novelist'.[16] For Read in 1920 this would have meant returning to Yorkshire, and so with serious purpose, but tongue firmly in cheek, Ford attempted to dissuade Read from such drastic action. Retreating to 'the Sheeres', he told Read, and in particular Yorkshire, whose inhabitants were 'singularly lazy and singularly self-sufficient' would be a disaster. The people of Yorkshire possessed a profound dislike of the arts and a contempt for poetry that would crush Read's creative spirit. Instead, he advised Read to combine the life of a civil servant with that of a novelist (*LF* 126-7). The problem with this advice was that Ford was missing the point. Geographical location was not really the issue with Read, it was simply the problem of being able to find enough time to write. According to Read, Ford had 'an old fashioned idea of the Civil Service, as an elegant profession for gentlemen, and had no conception at all of the rationalized bureaucratic machine which it had become, within a short time and under the direction of that very department of the Treasury in which I served' (*Annals* 168-70). This lack of understanding led Ford to view Read's frustrations as a simple and arbitrary choice – stay in the civil service and be a novelist; or retreat to Yorkshire and sink into irrelevance. What Ford failed to realise was that his ideal of novelist and civil servant was unattainable for someone in Read's position, and that the options Read was exploring in his correspondence and, presumably, in their meetings were born of necessity.

    If this shows there was a difference of opinion over the civil service, it is also apparent there was disagreement over what Read should write about and in what form. Read must have made the suggestion that if he stayed in the civil service he would only be able to continue writing if he abandoned novels for shorter pieces such as literary criticism. In developing this side of his writing Read wanted to make use of his still nascent interest in psychoanalysis to create a new form of cultural criticism in which he would maintain an element of creativity. However, in the same reply in which he mocked Yorkshire, Ford admitted that he did not think he was 'the most sympathetic person to come to for one inclined to desert the practice of novel writing for the indulgence of metaphysics' (*LF* 126). As Read astutely recognised, Ford would not have minded so much his 'indulgence in metaphysics' had he decided to explore such ideas within the form of the novel. According to Read, 'Ford had such an exclusive feeling for the novel that he was willing to "ram" anything into it: the form could be inflated until it absorbed the man'. Read's view, on the other hand, was that the individual man came first and that it was 'immaterial in what particular form he expressed himself – poem, novel, essay, metaphysics or criticism – so long as he remained true to himself and to his aesthetic principles' (*Annals* 170).

Although there is a profound difference of opinion taking place in this correspondence, there is also no doubting the warmth of the exchanges. Indeed, Ford's letters to Read look to all intents and purposes like the words a father might offer a son, reading more like fatherly guidance than the simple expressions of opinion. I think that this can be seen particularly well in Ford's decidedly unbohemian suggestion that one of the reasons Read should not leave the Treasury was that he would lose his regular salary. Ford even went out of his way to reassure Read's wife, Evelyn, who was deeply suspicious of Read's literary friends, that like her he was keen Read should remain in the civil service.[17]

Although Read clearly considered himself not to have taken the advice of this surrogate father – and the fall off in his communication with Ford after 1922 might be a symptom of this – unwittingly Ford aided Read's transformation into the great art critic that he was to become. It is true that Read did effectively abandon novel writing,[18] but he did stay in the civil service, and in 1922 this allowed him to transfer to the government's museum service at the Victoria and Albert Museum.[19] At the V&A Read found himself in a new critical world discussing the visual arts rather than literature, and he had the time and space to metamorphose into a self-confident writer on art and design. Although his discussion of art made extensive use of the 'metaphysical' methods of psychoanalysis that Ford had warned him against, without Ford's advice to stay in the civil service all of this would have been an unlikely development. Indeed, Read would probably not even have met figures such as Henry Moore, with whom he was to become closely associated in the 1930s.

In some ways Ford's relationship with Read was short-lived, but even as late as 1953 Ford's name cropped up in Read's critical writings, albeit in relation to that more extended literary friendship between Ford and Pound. This was unusual, with similar figures from Read's early life, such as Orage, falling more firmly by the wayside. It was Ford whose editorship of *The English Review* 'made the years 1908-9 memorable', wrote Read, whilst also stating that Ford's 'influence on the development of English poetry was negligible'.[20] If today we might dispute that claim, to suggest that Ford's influence was subtle and indirect, I think the same might well be said of the impact Ford had on the young and at times confused Herbert Read.

NOTES

1   Although this might sound somewhat harsh comment, it was accompanied by more positive advice from Orage. See letter from Alfred Orage to Herbert Read, 9 February 1920, University of Victoria, British Columbia.

2   See Jason Harding, *The Criterion: Cultural Politics and Periodical Networks in Inter-War Britain*, Oxford: Oxford University Press, 2002, pp. 110ff.

3   Herbert Read, *Annals of Innocence and Experience,* London: Faber, 1940 – henceforth *Annals*; pp. 164-5.

4   See James King, *The Last Modern*, London: Weidenfeld and Nicholson, 1990, p. 57; and Tom Steele, *Alfred Orage and the Leeds Arts Club*, Aldershot: Scolar Press, 1990, pp. 218-31.

5   For a more complete discussion of this see Michael Paraskos, 'The Elephant and the Beetles: The Aesthetic Theory of Herbert Read' (unpublished Ph.D., Leeds: University of Leeds, 2005), pp. 202ff.

6   The result of Eliot's influence was that Read wrote a number of somewhat unconvincing pieces in which an Eliot-like classicism was promoted and psychoanalysis slated. For examples see Herbert Read, *Julien Benda and the New Humanism*, Seattle: University of Washington, 1930. See also Herbert Read, 'Review of Irving Babbitt's *Democracy and Leadership*', in *The Criterion, 3:9* (1924), 129.

7   Read was well aware of the dominance Eliot had over him at this time and later wrote an allegorical poem to explore his feelings towards Eliot, entitled *Lu Yün's Lament*. In this, Lu Yün, the younger brother of the celebrated Chinese poet Lu

Chi, bemoans being born 'in the shadow of a mighty oak'. Herbert Read, *Moon's Farm and Other Poems*, London: Faber, 1955, p. 27.

8   Letter from Katherine Mansfield to Sydney Schiff, 3 November, 1920, reproduced in Katherine Mansfield, *The Collected Letters: Volume IV*, ed. Vincent O'Sullivan, Oxford: Oxford University Press, 1996, p. 99.

9   Pound to Ford, 11 May 1921: *Pound/Ford*, ed. Brita Lindberg-Seyersted, London: Faber, 1982, p. 57.

10 It was in fact a common complaint by the southern cultural elite of their northern counterparts. See Michael Saler, *The Avant-Garde in Interwar England*, New York: Oxford University Press, 1999, pp. 22-3.

11 Osbert Sitwell, *Laughter in the Next Room*, London: Macmillan, 1949, p. 30.

12 Quoted in King, *Last Modern*, p. 61.

13 *Ibid*, p. 60.

14 See John Worthen, *D. H. Lawrence: The Early Years 1885-1912*, Cambridge: Cambridge University Press, 1991, pp. 214-7.

15 *Letters of Ford Madox Ford*, ed. Richard M. Ludwig, Princeton: Princeton University Press, 1965 – henceforth *LF*; pp. 102-3.

16 The phrase is Read's. See Read, *Annals of Innocence*, p. 168n.

17 See King, *Last Modern*, p. 57; and Steele, *Alfred Orage*, pp. 66-7.

18 The notable exception to this is Read's novel *The Green Child*. However this novel owes as much to the influence of his artist friends in the 1930s as Ford's influence in the 1920s.

19 Until the 1960s curators at most of London's main museums and galleries were considered civil servants and employed as such.

20 Herbert Read, *The True Voice of Feeling*, London: Faber, 1953, pp. 116ff.

ALL AT SEA WITH PETRONELLA: A FORD MADOX FORD BIOGRAPHICAL MYSTERY

Brian Ibbotson Groth

> To the remotest verges of the sea,
> Unto ends of night following day
> There shall no refuge be for you and me
> Who haste away.
>
> Beyond the furthest stretches of the foam
> Beyond the last horizon of the sky
> For you and me: for you and me, no home
> Waits, quietly.
>
> But in the deep remoteness of the heart,
> In the deep secret chambers of the mind,
> Hidden, unchanging, secret, set apart –
> Beyond the whitest surges of the foam,
> Beyond the limitless verges of the wind,
> In the deep, tender, quiet places of the heart:
> Lo! you, enshrined.[1]

Ford Madox Ford's beautiful poem 'To Petronella at Sea' can arguably be read as being about a secret love affair and given its frequent references to the sea, perhaps even a love affair connected with a journey by sea.

I find my evidence for the secret nature of the relationship in the last stanza of the poem especially. Phrases such as 'deep remoteness of the heart', 'deep secret chambers of the mind', 'hidden, unchanging, secret, set apart' and 'deep, tender, quiet places of the heart' all indicate clearly that this was an relationship of an intensely private nature. The word 'secret' appears in consecutive lines, while 'deep' (used twice), 'remoteness' and 'hidden' are thesaurus synonyms for 'secret' and 'secrecy'.

That it is has also been a romantic relationship is strongly suggested by the repetition of the word 'heart' in the sixth line of the last stanza after it was used in the first, as does the last line, 'Lo! you, enshrined' linked as it is to the poet's 'heart' and 'mind'. However 'enshrined', employed climactically to end the poem, is as enigmatic as 'Petronella' herself has proved to be. It could simply mean that the 'you' is 'treasured' or 'cherished' in the writer's heart and mind and therefore loved. But 'enshrined' can also denote distance and inaccessibility; even loss, as with dead loved ones. The word also conjures up sacred associations with revered saints. Perhaps then by ending his poem the way he does Ford the poet and perhaps Ford the person is telling us that while he still loves Petronella and reveres her, they can no longer be together.

Of course it might be only Ford the poet speaking here with the poem being a piece of literature that merely imagines contact. Did Ford literally dream up 'Petronella' as he lounged in his deck chair staring at the Atlantic waves? Or has he seen a fellow passenger whom he does not know and fantasized about a romantic relationship, even giving her an imagined name? In the thrice-uttered phrase 'for you and me', is only the 'me' real and the 'you' fictitious? Are the poem's 'deep secret chambers of the mind' only in Ford's mind? If this is what happened we have yet more evidence that for Ford 'literary contacts' were not only matters of reading books, or socializing with other writers, but contacts real or imagined that he transfigured into literature.

However, if the poem does refer to a love affair, a recent purchase of mine, the American first edition of *A Mirror to France* published in August 1926 and still in its dust wrapper,[2] may provide evidence – indeed perhaps the only evidence – that this affair was more than a figment of Ford's poetic imagination. I say this because the book has the dedication 'For Petronella with whom I came from France, Ford Madox Ford. New York, Nov. MCMXXVI'.

The date of the dedication is interesting and a clue in the mystery since the 'Petronella' poem appears for the first time in *New Poems*, which Ford's bibliographer David Harvey thinks was probably published in January 1927. The proximity of the November and January dates would seem to indicate the dedicatee and the 'Petronella' of the poem were one and the same person. The question which then comes immediately to mind is obviously who was this 'Petronella' with whom Ford 'came from France'?

Max Saunders does not mention a 'Petronella' in his biography (nor does any other Ford biographer) but writes that Ford travelled from France in October 1926 on the *Savoie*: 'He had a noisy crossing [...] and slept badly. But he enjoyed it none the less'.[3] Thus Ford is placed 'at sea' in the month before the book is dedicated and presumably around the same time as 'Petronella' was written.

But who was 'Petronella'? Not an especially common name in the English-speaking world but still quite widely used in the Low Countries and Germany and usually shortened to Petra in speech. Could it somehow be linked to Jean Rhys with whom Ford had been having an affair around this time? After all Rhys' original name was Ella. Moreover we know that Petronella was the second name of Jean Rhys' then mother-in-law, Johanna Lenglet who was Dutch (Saunders vol. 2, 611).

We also know that Rhys wrote a short story called 'Till September, Petronella' which was first published in the 1960s though Diana Athill states in her introduction to *The Collected Short Stories* of Jean Rhys that some of these later stories may have been begun a good deal earlier.[4] Though the short story's narrator and protagonist Petronella Gray could arguably be Rhys, there is no one in the piece that reminds us of Ford. However other major characters in 'Till September Petronella' have been linked to real people by Rhys' biographer Carole Angier, most notably Peter Warlock, the pseudonym of Philip Heseltine, a composer and music critic.[5]

The time in which the story is set also counts against there being a Ford connection. Rhys and Ford first met in 1924 but the September in the short story's title is shown to be the year 1914 when Petronella looks at a calendar in a tea shop and sees the date is July 28th, 1914 (Rhys 140). September is first mentioned a little further on in the story when both her lover – whom she scorns – and later a stranger who picks her up at a taxi rank both arrange to see her two months later. The fact that the First World War with all its carnage will break out in August is nowhere indicated in 'Till September Petronella' but the reader is still left wondering if Petronella will ever see the two young men again – in September or at any other time.

But the strongest case to be made against 'Petronella' the ship's passenger being Rhys, or her mother-in-law for that matter, is that there is no biographical evidence in Angier or Saunders that either woman travelled from France to the United States by boat in the autumn of 1926. Indeed Angier claims – somewhat confusingly – that the affair ended in 'August and September 1926' (Angier 157). Furthermore Rhys is reported as sending a letter to Ford from France in November 1926. It was forwarded by Ford's *de facto* wife at the time Stella Bowen. Rhys maintained it was merely about her agent but

Bowen was sure it contained 'a good deal besides' (Saunders vol. 2, 303). When Max Saunders was recently made aware of the 'Petronella' dedication he was to write 'a new biographical mystery opens up: if is not Jean Rhys, who else is it?'[6]

Who else indeed? Given the poem and the dedication I am tempted to speculate that whatever her real name, 'Petronella' was someone Ford met on the *Savoie* and with whom he had some sort of romantic affair. Perhaps that is why he enjoyed the voyage despite his lack of sleep! After all, it was widely believed that such affairs were pretty much *de rigeur* on transatlantic crossings. If her real name were not 'Petronella' we will probably never know why he gave her that name in the poem and book dedication.[7] A derivation check doesn't appear to help. 'Petronella' is supposed to be derived from the Latin for 'stone' but, for me at least, this provides no clue. Who knows? Ford may even have given her that name using the black and white seabird, the petrel, as a basis.

However if Ford did have some sort of one-trip stand, as it were, this would hardly surprise my compatriot Clive James. Writing in *The Listener* in 1972 about Arthur Mizener's biography of Ford he says:

> The women succeed each other sensationally throughout the book. Even at his youngest and trimmest Ford looked like an earless Bugs Bunny on stilts, and by his own admission he was more interested in chat than sex: nevertheless the Grade A crumpet came at him like kamikazes, crashing through his upper decks in gaudy cataracts of fire.[8]

Never did James's phrase 'crashing through his upper decks' appear more apt than in this nautical setting on board the *Savoie*!

If Ford did succumb to or initiate a romantic adventure during his October 1926 voyage it would surely have not surprised Janice Biala, his third and final *de facto* wife from 1930 until his death in 1939. Interviewed by Max Saunders in 1990 she said that Ford was an intensely lonely man during the period 1926-1927. Saunders goes on to note that Ford 'desired the effect of stirring a new love' and tellingly sees him as 'a passion looking for a new object' (Saunders vol. 2, 309). Perhaps this desire and passion found their target in 'Petronella' as she and Ford steamed westwards to the New World.

Once there we have clear evidence that Ford was not slow to display a frequent 'readiness for romance'.[9] Whatever may have happened to 'Petronella' (now possessed one presumes of her crisp new dedication copy of *A Mirror to France* still in its dust wrapper), there is no doubt that once in New York Ford soon found other objects for his love if not his passion. Jeanne Foster, an old acquaintance now living in New York quickly became a companion and a correspondent. Although Ford wrote to Stella Bowen in Paris that he and Jeanne were not lovers, his letters to Foster are very intimate. Max Saunders supports Ford about the couple not being lovers but goes on to add that Ford's Christmas letter to Foster in 1926 is very like a love-letter (Saunders vol. 2, 308).

If Christmas 1926 was for Jeanne, New Year's Eve was for another old acquaintance, Rene Wright, a woman he had first met in 1906 and who now attended a New Year's party held in a speakeasy where Ford was also present. Rene's marriage was foundering and she was alone in New York that winter. A 'passion target' if ever there was one. Unsurprisingly Ford fell in love with her immediately (Saunders vol. 2, 309). But it seems as if here too they were not lovers in the sexual sense.[10] Rene and 'Petronella', however, are forever linked. This is because in *New Poems*, the piece immediately following 'To Petronella at Sea' and the last poem in the book , 'Winter Night-Song' is generally accepted as being addressed to Rene Wright. It is also widely seen as one of the worst poems Ford ever wrote. 'To Petronella at Sea', on the other hand, is often rated as one of his better ones. Viewed from this angle at least our unknown lady could depart the Ford scene in New York with her head held high.

In conclusion let me return directly to our biographical mystery with its nautical connection. For one fleeting moment recently it seemed as if I could present an Agatha Christie ending to the 'Petronella' case where all would be revealed and the mystery solved. This occurred as I was sitting in front of a computer near the conclusion of my researches. More in hope than anticipation I made one last Google trawl and got an exciting bite on the 'Ford and Petronella' search hook. Up popped the name of an English actress called Petronella Ford. A love child from the good ship *Savoie*, one dared to hope, honoured with the names of her mother and father. What a story she might be able to tell! Alas no! A quick scroll down the screen revealed that Miss Ford was born in 1947.

NOTES

1   Ford Madox Ford, *Selected Poems*, edited by Max Saunders, Manchester: Carcanet, 1997, p. 141. The poem is reprinted in its entirety here with the kind permission of Michael Schmidt.

2   The presence of a dust wrapper often indicates that a book has had few owners (possibly only one or two with regard to a book published in 1926). Thus the identity of 'Petronella' could conceivably be traced through the bookseller if he or she had records of where *A Mirror to France* had been purchased. Frustratingly, however, this trail remains cold for, not realizing the biographical significance of the dedication, I did not keep a record of who sold me the book which was purchased over the Internet.

3   Max Saunders, *Ford Madox Ford: A Dual Life*, 2 volumes, Oxford: Oxford University Press, 1996 – hereafter cited as 'Saunders'; vol. 2, p. 300.

4   Jean Rhys, *The Collected Short Stories*, New York : W. W. Norton & Company, 1987 – hereafter cited as 'Rhys'; p. vii.

5   Carole Angier, *Jean Rhys*, London: Penguin Books Ltd. , 1992 – hereafter cited as 'Angier'; p. 92.

6   Max Saunders to Brian Groth, email, 7 February 2007.

7   Ford's biographer Alan Judd would presumably be the first to caution against the use of the word 'never' in this context. He thought he had 'got' all Ford's women when he published his biography *Ford Madox Ford* in England in 1990. Shortly after publication, however, sixty-three letters, telegrams, postcards and notes turned up sent by Ford to a Miss Elizabeth Cheatham spanning the years 1927-29 and 1938-1939. Fortunately Judd was able to include this information in a postscript to the American edition of the book and to the English paperback edition. Inevitably Ford was in love with the lady though once again it appears as if the liaison was never consummated. But, as Max Saunders makes clear, romance there was, and yet again on board a ship and yet again en route to America. This sense of *déjà-vu* is reinforced by the fact that Ford wrote poems to Elizabeth every day of the voyage (except one when he wrote to her friend instead!): Saunders, vol. 2, p. 336.

8   Clive James, 'Ford Madox Ford: The Last Amateur' reprinted from *The Listener*, 1972 on James' website:
Clivejames.com: http://www.clivejames.com/pieces/metropolitan/madox-ford

9   A paraphrase of the description the narrator Nick Carraway gives of the hero Jay Gatsby in F. Scott Fitzgerald's *The Great Gatsby*. Like Ford, Jay Gatsby too was in love in New York in the 1920s though he limited himself to one woman.

10 Alan Judd, *Ford Madox Ford*, Cambridge, Massachusetts: Harvard University Press, 1991, p. 451.

IMAGES OF THE FIRST WORLD WAR: FORD'S 'IN OCTOBER 1914' READ IN THE CONTEXT OF CONTEMPORARY GERMAN WRITERS

Jörg W. Rademacher

'An image that shall take long to pass'
'In October 1914' ['Antwerp'][1]

Like T. S. Eliot and Aldous Huxley, Ford Madox Ford spent some time at Marburg, though not as a student at the university but while doing research for what became *The Fifth Queen Trilogy* and *The Good Soldier*. This is one reason why Ford rendered many images originally recorded in Germany when he started writing prose pieces, two propaganda books, and his most acclaimed war poem – all triggered by what happened in Belgium from 4th August 1914.

Ford didn't witness the outbreak of war on the continent, nor was he in Germany in July like T. S. Eliot who left his Marburg hosts and the country as soon as possible, fearing that, though an American citizen, he might soon be interned. No, Ford the close observer must have absorbed multiple images only to release them in a rare choice of words, intricately rhymed with subtle rhythms, when the appropriate moment had arrived.

Two months into the Great War, at a crucial moment for any writer of poetry, however, Ford remains the craftsman who echoes both the event he's dealing with and the poetical movements of the day.[2] Moreover, he elaborately connects a series of images – taken from the ongoing war and from all wars that ever were – to the only image he witnessed himself: of Charing Cross Station in London, that is, and of the women of Flanders, a forlorn crowd waiting in vain for their lost loved ones.

Thus endowed with a powerful imagination fed by visual material both historical and witnessed *in personam*, Ford condensed his impressions of the moment into a highly dramatic poem, not unlike a six-part dance suite such as Claude Debussy (1862-1918), Richard Strauss (1864-1949), or Igor Stravinsky (1882-1971) might have composed.

Recited in German at Münster/Westphalia, Ford's 'In October 1914' was coupled with a 'Minuet' by the eight-year-old Mozart, written for the piano in London in 1764/1765, and the popular air of 'Tom Dooley'. The two pieces were played *in toto* after the first and second parts of 'In October 1914' respectively, later to be partially echoed or varied in alternation. The impression created was one of mixed feelings consisting of sombre melancholy and musical serenity which chimes with what contemporary German poets achieved once they had grasped the unprecedented aspects of the Great War.[3]

Since 'In October 1914' was first presented as part of a mixed English, German, and French reading at Münster on 26th June 2004 to commemorate the 65th anniversary of Ford's death, it has several times been juxtaposed with poetry and prose by German writers all of whom share a special relationship to the city of Ford's German ancestors. What is striking is how these war writings by Hermann Löns (1866-1914), August Stramm (1874-1915), and Clara Ratzka (1872-1928) surprisingly read today as if their authors had been comparing notes with Ford. There is no evidence for his having had any personal contact with them, nor that he read their work. Instead, this essay is an exercise in 'literary contact' in that it puts their work in touch; and it does so on the grounds that all four writers were in contact with the same milieu just before the War, and that their work shares its impress.[4]

As an impressionist rather than a theorist, Ford nevertheless provides us with an idea of why it is that these writers rather than better known ones such as Theodor Fontane (1819-1898) or Thomas Mann (1875-1955) have chosen a furrow similar to his own. A small sample of intertexts may help to connect the English modernist with his German contemporaries.

Fontane and Mann were not only Protestant Prussians but the irony running through their novels of manners had at least in Fontane's case not yet crossed the linguistic barrier, for to Ford the Berlin novelist of French Huguenot descent was

> forced by the exigencies of [his] career[.] and by what in the eyes of the Prussian educational authorities appear to be national and imperial necessities into wasting an unreasonable amount of time in patriotic and semi-militarist orations and writings.[5]

Ford alludes to Fontane's four-volume history on the battles of the Franco-Prussian war in 1870/1871 which precedes his emergence as a novelist.[6] Nonetheless, Ford is basically right in pointing out that Fontane, along with the academic historians Leopold von Ranke (1795-1886), Nobel laureate Theodor Mommsen (1817-1903), and Heinrich von Treitschke (1834-1896) 'ha[s] formed, at any rate until August 1914, the ordinary reading of a normally cultured man'.[7]

As a man of letters, not a professor, Fontane was an outsider to the society he later came to write his novels about, some of which like *Effi Briest* (1895) or his last *Der Stechlin* (1898) Ford may have appreciated for their clear conception of the very caste system that he evokes in his first propaganda book:

> The society in the town with which I was at the time most acquainted divided itself into rather rigid sections. There was, for instance, the professorial society, the jurists' society, the military society, the manufacturers' society, each forming a little ring more or less rigidly separated from all the other rings. An officer could hardly know a manufacturer, a professor could hardly know an officer. In some cases this will be a matter of law, in others it was merely a matter of custom. Thus, in a German university, when a new professor takes up his residence, the *doyen* or dean will provide him with a list of families upon whom he must call, and he will almost certainly get into bad odour if he calls upon any one else. And this system of espionage extends even to the students.
> As a result social life in Germany is singularly stereotyped and singularly wanting in incident. (*WBTA* 181-182)

In this context, Ford clearly doesn't describe the city and university of Münster but he may also have applied his analysis to the Westphalian city where at the *alma mater*, re-established during the rule of the *Kaiser* as Westfälische Wilhelms-Universität in 1902, the Prussian Kultusmin-isterium ruled supreme and was to do so until 1933.[8]

It is at Münster, however, that Hermann Löns and Clara Ratzka spent formative years and where August Stramm was born. While a controversially received history of German literature has recently confirmed my view that there is something in Ford's thesis about a bifurcation of German culture following the Catholic-Protestant divide, it will still take a long time to become received knowledge that it is precisely because the likes of Löns, Ratzka, and Stramm are somehow connected with the 'other' Germany that they managed to write as they did: following supra-national rather than national trends. In a comparative European perspective this means that in the 19th century

> the [German] intelligentsia in its addiction to reality is preoccupied with the conquest of the world at once by economic, technological, scientific means and by military enterprises. Deemed unproductive the production in art,

music, and literature is therefore handed over to people living on the margins: to women in England, to the Bohème in France, finally to the Southern Catholics and the Austrian Jews in Germany.[9]

First, Ratzka, to apply the last sentence to the German writers discussed in this chapter, was a divorced single mother living in Berlin before marrying a portrait painter of Hungarian descent who enabled her to take a doctorate in national economy at Tübingen University in 1912 and to travel around Europe as a full-time writer.

Second, Löns, born and bred a Catholic, a journalist as well as a poet infatuated with nature, a scientific naturalist with a poetic vein and a conservationist *avant la lettre*, was also a convert to Protestantism before he volunteered as a private for war-service in August 1914, posing as a Wildean dandy. In summarizing their posthumous reception one should mention that, unlike Ratzka, Löns remained well-known since his writings were exploited by Nazi ideologues, which still makes it difficult to discuss him, though he died before anyone knew of Adolf Hitler.

While Ratzka is read in relation to Münster, our third author, Stramm, has been canonized internationally as a German Expressionist, and his small œuvre, like Ford's two master novels, never fell into oblivion. [10] Stramm was a Jewish soldier's son who took a doctorate with a thesis on globally standardised postage before he started a second career as a poet and dramatist in 1912 which crunched to a halt when he was drafted on 2nd August 1914 writing as late as 30th June 1915, three months before his death, that a German poet mustn't desert.[11]

Like Ford in England, the three German writers were outsiders to the literary establishment. Löns and Stramm died on the Western and Eastern front respectively while Ratzka and Ford continued to write after the Great War. So the poems and diary entries written by Löns and Stramm convey images from the trenches while Ford's 'In October 1914' and the excerpt from Ratzka's novel *Familie Brake* (1919) convey images from the home front both before and after mobilisation. In what follows I shall try to juxtapose and analyse these images providing the German quotations in the endnotes.

To begin with, Löns had written his 'Engellandlied', 'Song of England', that is, in 1910, glorifying war. He asks his sweetheart not to cry for him, since it was for the fatherland that he was to shed his blood, and, most importantly, that he was going to fight England across the North Sea. This mood still holds in August 1914 when Löns notes that 'Lo, life is so beautiful, now, that it's worth my while to die'.[12] Half-way through the war journal he kept from 3rd to 26th September 1914, he evokes an image of the trenches: 'Eyes full of dirt, nose, face, hands full of scabbed wounds. A pig's life'. As a naturalist, he compares his existence with a pig digging for food in the field, using the North-German dialect adjective 'borkig' to highlight the look of the wounds nobody tends in the trenches.[13] He both watches the fighting and talks to his sergeant-major about 'Staphyliniden'. An expert on plants and insects, Löns sees whole what others, survivors, that is, would have kept apart. On 16th September, he writes:

> Insects humming and buzzing around the red, blue, yellow, white stubble flowers with a dreadful duel going on between our and the Fr. artillery [. . . .] Their bullets buzzing like bumble-bees or like dung beetles which suddenly land in the grass.[14]

Dreadful though it is, the war in the trenches doesn't blind Löns's eyes to the fields where the corn must have been mowed before the fighting began, and since he lives and 'writes to the moment', he links the bullets to creatures closer to his heart: bumble-bees or dung beetles he observes while hearing two armies firing away.[15]

Unlike Ford in London, Löns in France saw action in September 1914, but he missed the effect the conflagration had on the loved ones at home, which Ford captures in the final part of his poem:

> This is Charing Cross;
> It is midnight;
> There is a great crowd
> And no light.
> A great crowd, all black that hardly whispers aloud.
> Surely, that is a dead woman – a dead mother! (*Selected Poems* 84)

While there's the summer's light and colour plus the noise and sounds of war and nature in Löns' journal, Ford first sees only a mass of people – 'all black' – producing hardly any sound before he singles out – privileging visual impressions – a woman, whom he imagines, in a way Löns couldn't, as an uncanny example of the living dead.[16]

Löns's attitude isn't singular in German accounts of the Great War, for Clara Ratzka in the final chapter of her novel *Familie Brake* (1919), written from hindsight, shows a kind of enthusiasm unimaginable a few months later.

The scene is set in the country. A large Münster family is celebrating its 'Familientag', an annual gathering organised in turns by different branches. Ratzka's prose appears to be smooth and without barbs, and only after repeatedly listening to the text being read out aloud did minute passages emerge evoking a tense atmosphere:

> Dietrich Brake, the young captain, whose uniform fitted his elegant body like a glove, sat at a larger table surrounded by as many young girls as possible.
>   Wedlock – o God – how difficult! There were still, and everywhere, so many charming girls!
>   No, not yet.
>   He told tales, in a lively manner, and all laughed.
>   Elsewhere, however, you saw quite a few shaded faces. Hidden among the heightened *Lebenslust* of the young and the collectedness and safety of the older generation, there was a deep-seated excitement, an extreme feeling of tension.[17]

Once the news of mobilisation had shaken the family members, all the men had to leave immediately: on foot, by car, and

> In the last carriage Stefan Brake stood, raised to his full height.
>   He waved his hat all round and shouted in a resonant, jubilant voice: 'Die Heimat'.[18]

So Löns and Ratzka provide complementary images of Germany before and after mobilisation, writing to the moment or after the fact, with Löns the former journalist more expressive of the imminent danger. Ratzka, however, seeks to serve both the readers avid for nostalgia and those clairvoyant ones, who, like her, see that in summer 1914 an era had run its course irrevocably.

It's not the personal Apocalypse that Löns faced ten days after the diary entry last quoted, nor yet that which Ford's mothers faced waiting in vain for the return of their loved ones, but the fore-knowledge of a greater catastrophe that Ratzka suggests after the Armistice of 11th November 1918. It needs a more radical imagin-ation-*cum*-idiolect like that conceived by August Stramm to face the full reality of the Great War. By contrast to the three male writers, it was only Ratzka who lived among the high society from which she originated, so that unlike Ford in *Parade's End* she couldn't depict the stratum she came from as a completely disinterested observer.

Similarly, Stramm, from a petty bourgeois background, didn't achieve in 'his own personal life' what René Radrizzani calls the 'renewal of man, the realisation of a fulfilled essential existence':

instead he makes them happen in his art, his language, in his poetry above all. Here you can perceive in fact what Stramm's characters on stage only dream of: the bold liberation from convention, the restriction to what is essential, fulfillment, truth, presence. Any words which are not absolutely necessary as well as prefixes or suffixes are omitted: at any moment language is as much as possible fulfilled presence. Moreover, both feeling and the drive for truth assert themselves against conventionality.[19]

A late parallel to Ford's description of German civil society, this passage conveys an impression of the rigidity and rigour Stramm and other German writers were up against. He survived 'over seventy battles and engagements' (Stramm II 79) on both Western and Eastern Fronts and wrote poems on his everyday life:

Patrol
The stones hostile are
Window treason grins
Branches strangle
Mountains bushes flake off rustling
Piercing
Death. (Stramm II 70)[20]

Guard
The night weighs down the lids
Fatigue flickers and teases
The enemy snuggles up
The pipe smoulders
Is lost
And
All spaces
Shiver
Shrinking
Small. (Stramm II 70)[21]

While Ford records sense impressions, Stramm expresses them without neglecting the mnemotechnic dimension. It's a breathtaking exercise following his imagination and relating it to the reality of war he reflected on whereas Löns merely juxtaposes them in his diary:

All are one: Battle and need and death and nightingale. One! And fight and sleep and dream and action: all are one. There's no separation! All is one and blurs and shimmers like sun and abyss. It is only that once one thing prevails, then the other. Thus we fight starve die and sing. All do! Soldier and leader! Night and day. Corpses and flowers. And above it all it seems there is a hand! I swim above all. Am all! I[22]

Nature & war, life & death, officer & subordinate: Stramm sees his life whole just as Ford, still in London in October 1914, imagines battles past & present, mothers & wives present and sons & husbands absent. At the Western Front, Stramm had even connected his solitary position with his day and age, showing a keen sense of belonging to his precarious existence:

> I'm sitting in a hole in the earth, a so-called shelter! fantastic! Candle, heater, armchair, table. All conforming to the Modern Age. The culture of the 20th century. And there's no end of shots above! Clack! Clack! Sht.summ! That's the ethics of the 20th century. And beside me some earthworms wind out the wall. That's the aesthetics of the 20th century. (Stramm I 183-184)[23]

Here Löns' and Stramm's visions finally converge with Ford's whose personalized view of the war resembles what they saw on the spot, with Stramm an angry, middle-aged officer prepared to hang up a war reporter for a few hours to make him see the world differently (7th/8th March 1915; Stramm II 186). This question concerns him, the German expressionist, as much as Ford and his Modernist *confrères*, *les Imagistes*, but, of course, it took a long time until Stramm became a household word in German literature, with Löns and Ratzka even now hovering on the margins.[24]

NOTES

1   Ford, *Selected Poems*, ed. Max Saunders, Manchester: Carcanet, 1997 – henceforth *Selected Poems*; pp. 82-85 (p. 83). The poem first appeared as 'In October 1914' in *Outlook*, 34 (24 Oct 1914), 523-24, but was re-titled 'Antwerp'.
2   Unlike his more hermetic Modernist colleagues, Ford sustained an interest in contemporary writing. He was aware of Imagism and its insistence on the clarity of verbal imagery. See my *James Joyce's Own Image. Über die allmähliche Verfertigung der Begriffe 'image' und 'imagination' beim Schreiben in 'A Portrait' and 'Ulysses'*, Münster: Waxmann, 1993, pp. 26-28. On the memorial aspect see Gene M. Moore, 'Ford and Germany: The Question of Allegiance', in: *Modernism and the Individual Talent. Re-Canonizing Ford Madox Ford (Hueffer)*, ed. Jörg W. Rademacher, Münster: Lit, 2002, pp. 148-155 (pp. 148-9).
3   The recital took place at Café arte, Domplatz, on 27th and 28th October 2006.
4   The translation by Cristoforo Schweeger of 'In October 1914' is part of the volume *Vater und Sohn. Franz Hüffer und Ford Madox Ford (Hüffer)*, ed., tr., and with commentary by Jörg W. Rademacher, Münster: Lit, 2003, pp. 93-97 – henceforth *Vater und Sohn*. Unless otherwise stated, all translations from the

German are mine. As far as I know it can safely be maintained that Ford cannot have encountered August Stramm or Clara Ratzka before 1914, for the former began writing in 1912 and the latter published prose fiction from 1916. For more biographical details on these writers see Jörg W. Rademacher and Christian Steinhagen, *Gelehrtes Münster und rundum. 88 Schriftsteller, Philosophen und Theologen*, preface Götz Alsmann, Berlin & Weimar: Jena 1800, 2005 – henceforth *Gelehrtes Münster*.

5 *When Blood is Their Argument*, New York & London: Hodder and Stoughton, 1915 – henceforth *WBTA*; pp. xvii.

6 The late Gordon A. Craig appreciated both Ford's and Fontane's historiographical achievement. He prefaced *Der Krieg gegen Frankreich 1870-1871*, four volumes, Zürich: Manesse, (1985) 1988, and Ford's *A History of our own Times*, ed. Solon Beinfeld and Sondra J. Stang, Manchester: Carcanet, 1988 – henceforth *History*. Like Fontane and Ford, Craig visited Münster, receiving the *Historikerpreis der Stadt Münster*, but while failing to connect the two writers, he calls Ford's history 'a very readable book' (*History*, p. xi), and he praises Fontane for his impartiality and objectivity as well as his unquenchable thirst for finding all pertinent sources. Craig's judgment of Fontane's work as a historian culminates in the statement that the latter surpassed Heinrich von Treitschke in terms of historiographical expertise. See *Heinrich von Treitschke's History of Germany in the Nineteenth Century*, ed. Gordon A. Craig, Chicago 1975, p. xi-xxv. With hindsight, Ford's judgment of Treitschke, stated in 1915, is proved right.

7 *Between St. Dennis and St. George: A Sketch of Three Civilisations*, London: Hodder and Stoughton, 1915, p. 33 – henceforth *BSDSG. –* The caveat concerning Ford the Impressionist relates to the copies of books sold by Fontane in his life-time. Indeed, most of his late novels, apart from *Effi Briest*, were unsuccessful,.

8 For the rigid protocol involving the holder of a new chair at Münster University in the late 1920s see the entry on Heinrich Behnke (1898-1979), a mathematician, in *Gelehrtes Münster*, pp. 13-15 (p. 13).

9 Heinz Schlaffer, *Die kurze Geschichte der deutschen Literatur*, München: dtv, 2003, pp. 135-136 (p. 135).

10 See *Gelehrtes Münster*, pp. 43-45; pp. 56-58; pp. 73-74.

11 'Und ein deutscher Dichter darf auch nicht fahnenflüchtig werden'. Letter to Nell and Herwarth Walden, 30th June 1915, in: August Stramm, *Gedichte, Dramen, Prosa, Briefe*, ed. Jörg Drews, Stuttgart: Reclam, 1997 – henceforth 'Stramm I'; p. 196.

12 'Mensch, das Leben ist so schön, jetzt, daß es sich lohnt zu sterben'. Hermann Löns quoted in: Thomas Dupke, *Hermann Löns. Mythos und Wirklichkeit*, Hildesheim: Claassen, 1994 – henceforth 'Dupke'; p. 166.

13 'Augen voll Dreck, Nase, Gesicht, Hände voller borkiger Wunden. Ein Schweineleben'. Löns, quoted in Dupke, p. 170.

14 'Insektengesumme um die roten, blauen, gelben, weißen Stoppelblüten und furchtbares Duell zwischen unserer und der frz. Artillerie [...] Ihre Kugeln summen wie Hummeln oder auch wie Mistkäfer, die sich plötzlich ins Gras setzen'. Löns quoted in Dupke, p. 171.

15 Applying a phrase relative to writers in English voicing dissent to German Catholic writers is all but ironical. See Tom Paulin, *Writing to the Moment. Selected Critical Essays 1980-1996*, London: Faber and Faber (1996) 1998, p.

xiii, and his *Crusoe's Secret. The Aesthetics of Dissent*, London: Faber and Faber, 2005, p. xix.

16 'Hier ist Charing Cross;/Es ist Mitternacht;/Da ist eine Menschenmenge,/Die im Dunkel wacht./Eine Menschenmenge, schwarz, und kaum ein Flüstern im Gedränge./Wahrhaftig, da ist eine tote Frau – eine tote Mutter!' *Vater und Sohn* 96.

17 'Dietrich Brake, der junge Hauptmann, dem die Uniform wie ein Handschuh auf dem eleganten Körper saß, hatte an einem größeren Tisch so viele junge Mädchen um sich versammelt, wie nur möglich./Heiraten – o Gott – wie schwer! Es wimmelte ja immer noch, und überall von reizenden Mädchen!//Nein, noch nicht.//Er erzählte, lebhaft, und alle lachten.//Sonst sah man aber manches beschattete Gesicht. Unter der erhöhten Lebenslust der Jugend und dem Gesammelten, Sicheren der älteren Generation verbarg sich tiefe Erregtheit, ein Gespanntsein bis zum Äußersten'. Clara Ratzka, *Familie Brake*, Münster: agenda, 2000, p. 316 – henceforth *Familie Brake*.

18 'Im letzten Wagen stand Stefan Brake, hoch aufgerichtet.//Er schwenkte seinen Hut in die Runde und rief mit tönender, jauchzender Stimme'. 'Die Heimat'. *Familie Brake*, p. 319.

19 René Radrizzani, 'Nachwort', in: August Stramm, *Dramen und Gedichte*, selection and afterword by René Radrizzani, Stuttgart: Reclam, 1979, pp. 76-86, here pp. 82-83 – henceforth 'Stramm II'.

20 'Patrouille//Die Steine feinden/Fenster grinst Verrat/Äste würgen/Berge Sträucher blättern raschlig/Gellen/Tod' (Stramm II 70).

21 'Wacht//Die Nacht wiegt auf den Lidern/Müdigkeit flackt und neckt/Der Feind verschmiegt/Die Pfeife schmurgt/Verloren/Und/Alle Räume/Frösteln/Schrumpfig/Klein' (Stramm II 70).

22 'Schlacht und Not und Tod und Nachtigall alles ist eins. Eins! Und Kampf und Schlaf und Traum und Handeln alles ist eins! Es gibt keine Trennung! Es geht alles in eins und verschwimmt und erschimmert wie Sonne und Abgrund. Nur mal herrscht das vor, mal das. So kämpfen hungern sterben singen wir. Alle! Soldat und Führer! Nacht und Tag. Leichen und Blühten. Und über mir scheint eine Hand! Ich schwimme durch alles. Bin alles! Ich!' Letter to Nell and Herwarth Walden, 27th May 1915 (Stramm I 195-196).

23 'Ich sitze in einem Erdloch, genannt Unterstand! famos! Eine Kerze, Ofen, Sessel, Tisch. Alles Konform der Neuzeit. Die Kultur des 20. Jahrhunderts. Und oben drauf klatscht es ununterbrochen. Klack! Klack! Scht.summ! Das ist die Ethik des 20. Jahrhunderts. Und neben mir aus der Wand ringeln sich einige Regenwürmer. Das ist die Ästhetik des 20[.] Jahrhunderts'. Letter to Nell and Herwarth Walden, 5th March 1915 (Stramm I 183-184).

24 For reasons of space, the Wildean *fin-de-siècle* undercurrents linking all these writers to the discussion of ethics and aesthetics in the early 1900s can only be mentioned rather than discussed here. I'd like to acknowledge the help given me by Gerhard Rademacher (Unna/Westphalia), Antje Rademacher (Leer/East Frisia), and Gregor Bohnensack (Münster/Westphalia).

'THUS TO REVISIT OR THUS TO REVISE-IT': ERNEST HEMINGWAY, DEFIANT DISCIPLE

Susan Swartzlander

Ford Madox Ford described the young Ernest Hemingway as a devotee: 'he comes and sits at my feet and praises me. It makes me nervous'.[1] Ford need not have worried about such devotion for long. In short order, this literary disciple would become a thankless detractor.

The well-documented history of their relationship shows the brash youth taking aim as soon as Ford gave him an opportunity to edit the *transatlantic review*.[2] Perhaps the seeds for animosity were sown even earlier, as Ezra Pound and Hemingway corresponded about the new magazine, prompting Hemingway to consider what he might contribute to the periodical:

> Glad Hueffer . . . laid hold of Magazine . . . . What Mag. is it or a new One. Will try and get some of Oh Canada in shape for him. Feel that I am so full of hate and so damned, bitchingly, sickeningly tired that anything I do will be of little value. Still the diseased oyster shits the finest pearl as the palmist says.[3]

Although 'Oh Canada' never emerged as a fine enough 'pearl' to grace the pages of the *transatlantic review*, or any review for that matter, Hemingway did quit the *Toronto Star* job that left him too exhausted for literary pursuits. He jumped at Pound's offer to edit Ford's *review*. On November 9th, Hemingway wrote Gertrude Stein and Alice B. Toklas asking if they had seen the magazine, announcing that he had been 'invited to come home and direct its policy etc'. He does wonder, however, if Pound's 'invitation has been exaggerated'.[4] On January 19, 1924, the Hemingways boarded the Cunard ship *Antonia*, bound for Paris and a new attempt to live the literary life.

Within weeks of his arrival, Hemingway began to disparage Ford and the magazine to their mutual friends, taking issue with everything from Ford's preference for more established, conservative writers over the American upstarts to Ford's penchant for adopting the persona of the country squire, the English gentleman, as well as frequently invoking his wartime experiences. In a letter to Pound, Hemingway dubbed the magazine, with its motto 'Fluctuat' from the Paris city seal, the *Transportation Review*, as if it were as exciting as a staid industry's publication.[5] He explained, 'Ford is running the whole damn thing as a compromise', seeking safety and mediocrity when he could publish what mainstream magazines would not consider: 'he hasn't any advertizers to offend or any subscribers to discontinue why not shoot the moon'.[6]

Presenting himself as an antidote to what he perceived as Ford's conservatism, Hemingway described selling Ford on Stein's *The Making of Americans*: 'I made it clear it was a remarkable scoop for his magazine obtained only through my obtaining genius'. He then went on to instruct Stein about the proper care and feeding of her long-time friend Ford, 'treat him high, wide, and handsome', as if she is in the driver's seat, 'it is really a scoop for them you know'. Hemingway describes, in a conspiratorial tone, how he let Ford believe that Stein received 'big prices when you consent to publish'. As the magazine's finances deteriorated, Hemingway sought new backing and pushed Ford to make good on the magazine's debt to Stein. By the fall Hemingway found Ford so frustrating that he declared, 'I am sick of Ford and his megalomaniac blundering'. He proclaimed Ford 'an absolute liar and crook always motivated by the finest synthetic English gentility'.[7]

Undoubtedly, Hemingway did feel frustrated that Ford, rather than himself, directed the *review*'s policy, and Hemingway believed his contributions were thwarted by Ford's decisions. If editorial policy rankled Hemingway, editorial practice enraged him, particularly when he found it applied to his own writing. Hemingway could not stand Ford's blue pencil: 'I wrote him on 1 hour's notice quite a funny N.Y. Paris letter. He changes it, revises it, cuts it, makes it not have sense, etc. What the hell'. Hemingway's usual bluster gives way as he suggests he would prefer Pound as mentor: 'I am writing some damn good stories. I wish you were here to tell me so, so I would believe it or else what is the matter with them. You are the only guy that knows a god damn thing about writing'. Playing on a title of Ford's reminiscences about his own literary masters, Hemingway complains to Pound that Ford 'can explain stuff i.e. Thus to Revisit or Thus to Revise-it but in private life he is so goddam involved in being the dregs of an English country gentleman that you get no good out of him'.[8] Hemingway yearns for a mentor like Ford 'to explain stuff', such as how to revise manuscripts, yet he cannot resist taking aim at the master. Hemingway's pun on 'revise it' and 'revisit' reveals his perception of Ford as an unreliable and untrustworthy source, one who frequently revisits the past, particularly in order to revise it; ironically, a charge frequently applied to Hemingway as well. Hemingway thinks of Ford not as the avante garde leader of this new generation, but as a product of a placid, bygone era, 'the dregs'. It is little surprise that the upstart who could even conceive of the metaphor of the execratory oyster to represent writing would clash with his more gentle and genteel elder.

In a classic reaction to his own anxiety of influence, Hemingway jokes, 'The thing to do with Ford is kill him. I am fond of Ford. This ain't personal. It's literary'. However, Hemingway could not dispatch Ford so easily. The letters reveal his desperation to remain on good terms, at the same time he excoriates Ford. Hemingway implores his correspondents to withhold his negative comments from Ford, saying over and over again that he does not want a 'row' with Ford. In the month before he began writing *The Sun Also Rises*, Hemingway indicated that the strain was mutual: 'I don't want a row with Ford just now. He dislikes me enough as it is'.[9] When Ernest Walsh, editor of *This Quarter*, asked Hemingway for a contributor's note to include with his 'Big Two-Hearted River', Hemingway initially said he 'tried to keep Transatlantic Review alive . . . Failed'. The very next day Hemingway prevailed upon Walsh to suppress this note as 'it was a lot of crap'.[10] Clearly Hemingway had mixed feelings about Ford, and at some level knew he owed Ford a great deal. Hemingway could not just dismiss Ford out of hand or ignore his large presence, physically or psychologically. If we revisit those Paris years, we see that Ford permeated Hemingway's work; in fact, Hemingway worked quite deliberately to revisit and revise Ford's texts, perhaps in an attempt to 'kill off Ford' symbolically by appropriating him for his own ends.[11]

In those early years, Hemingway played on his mentor's titles, adopting them and adapting them for his own purposes. For example, the first book published in William Bird's Three Mountains Press series edited by Pound was Ford's *Women & Men*, a collection of stories that included what Pound called Ford's 'peasant biographies' of individuals he knew near his home in the English countryside (some of this material appeared earlier in *The Heart of the Country*).[12] Hemingway counters Ford's *Women & Men* with his own 1927 collection *Men Without Women*, despite the presence of a few women in the stories, which would seem to suggest another choice would be better. Ford's subtitle for *The Good Soldier*, 'A Tale of Passion', finds its way into Hemingway's unpublished, and *inaccroachable*, text 'A Lack of Passion', the story of a young bullfighter who cowers before a bull, is impotent with a waitress who carries a glass of milk to his room, and feels homoerotic attraction for the handsome man who carries his long swords.[13] Gavira is neither a eunuch, nor 'a raging stallion forever neighing after his neighbors' womenkind', as Ford's narrator Dowell so indelicately puts it.

Hemingway adopts Ford's practice of using an old French poetic device, 'L'Envoi' (a separate verse or conclusion emphasizing a poem's moral point). The last section of Ford's poem 'Antwerp' bears the heading 'L'Envoi'. Ford also employed the device in prose, as in the conclusion to *Joseph Conrad: A Remembrance*. 'L'Envoi' serves as the title, as well, for the concluding vignette in Hemingway's collection *in our time*.

Not only are Ford's titles transformed by Hemingway's touch, but two of Ford's literary icons appear in *The Sun Also Rises* in a rather diminished capacity. Henry James, whom Ford dubbed 'the great master of all us novelists today',[14] appears only as a vehicle for a sexual joke, the repetition of a rumor that a bicycle accident rendered him impotent. Ford called W. H. Hudson the 'unapproached master of the English tongue',[15] yet Jake declares Hudson a fit read only for adolescents, '"The Purple Land" is a very sinister book if read too late in life. It recounts splendid imaginary amorous adventures of a perfect English gentleman in an intensely romantic land' (*SAR* 16).[16]

What is Hemingway up to with such gratuitous borrowing and recasting? He could be trying intentionally to get Ford's goat. Curiously, Ford's brother Oliver Hueffer indulged in a similar practice to which Ford imputed an unkind motive: he would 'deliberately take one of my own subjects – to show that he was more brilliant than I'.[17] Michelle Troy details this sibling rivalry noting, 'one has but to scan the titles of the brothers' books' to find evidence Ford was right.[18] Perhaps Hemingway knew the practice irritated Ford. In any event, to embed Ford's titles in his own work invests it with an interesting duality, as much acknowledgement as repudiation, a contrast that mirrors their complicated relationship.

Nowhere do we see the Ford influence more clearly than in Hemingway's first novel.[19] Perhaps taking a cue from Ford who had

begun *The Good Soldier* on a birthday, Hemingway said he started
The Sun Also Rises on his birthday. He set out to create a novel of
modern life, what Ford said he wanted to see in poetry: 'I want the
poetry of cafés, of automobiles, of kisses, and of absinthe'.[20]
Hemingway's novel of cafés and kisses begins with two epigraphs,
one associated with Gertrude Stein ('you are all a lost generation') and
the second, a passage from Ecclesiastes that Hemingway must have
associated with his other mentor Ford:

> One generation passeth away, and another generation cometh; but the earth
> abideth forever . . . The sun also ariseth, and the sun goeth down, and hasteth
> to the place where he arose . . . The wind goeth toward the south and turneth
> about unto the north; it whirleth about continually, and the wind returneth
> again according to his circuits. . . . All the rivers run into the sea; yet the sea
> is not full; unto the place from whence the rivers come, thither they return
> again. (Ecclesiastes 1:4-1:7)

Ford returned frequently to Ecclesiastes. As a teenager he compiled a
notebook of quotations, including the line 'What profit hath a man of
all his labour which he taketh under the sun?'[21] Echoes of the Biblical
passage reverberate through a number of Ford's works, but of these,
Ford's Great War poem 'Antwerp' best illustrates the influence Ford
exerted on Hemingway.[22] Featuring a line from Ecclesiastes 1:9, Ford
describes the siege of Antwerp, the violation of Belgian neutrality that
precipitated the war, as an often told tale, 'For there is no new thing
under the sun, / Only this uncomely man with a smoking gun/ In the
gloom...' The poem invokes the ghosts of heroes past, as they all
mingle on the battlefield:

> Well, there have been scars
> Won in many wars . . .
> Punic,
> Lacedæmonian, wars of Napoleon, wars for faith, wars for
>   honour, for love, for possession,
>
>   * * *
>   III
> For the white-limbed heroes of Hellas ride by upon their horses
> Forever through our brains.
> The heroes of Cressy ride by upon their stallions;
> And battalions and battalions and battalions –
> The Old Guard, the Young Guard, the men of Minden
>   and of Waterloo,
> Pass, for ever staunch,

> Stand, for ever true;
> And the small man with the large paunch,
> And the gray coat, and the large hat, and the hands behind
>   the back,
> Watches them pass
> In our minds for ever . . .

In *The Sun Also Rises*, 'the Old Guard, the Young Guard' of battles past appear in the public monuments (such as Marshall Ney's near the Closerie des Lilas) and in the street names. From Jake's struggle with his faith to various male characters' battles for Brett, even in the appearance of a little stuffed dog in a taxidermist's shop window, we can read in miniature these 'eternal wars', the 'wars for faith, wars for honour, [wars] for love, [wars] for possession'. Although Hemingway converts these battles into the material of internal conflict, or the petty engagements between characters, the ghosts of the Great War certainly pervade the text as well. Hemingway's novel is also an answer of sorts to the questions Ford poses in 'Antwerp' when he asks why did the Belgians not agree to neutrality, make a deal with Germany, rather than continue fighting against all odds:

> And what in the world did they bear it for?
> I don't know.
> And what in the world did they dare it for?
> Perhaps that is not for the likes of me to understand.
> They could very well have watched a hundred legions go
> Over their fields and between their cities
> Down into more southerly regions.
> They could very well have let the legions pass through their woods,
>
> And have kept their lives and their wives and their children and cattle
> and goods.
> I don't understand.
> Was it just love of their land?
> Oh, poor dears!
> Can any man so love his land?

'Can any man so love his land?' The land matters so much to Hemingway that in November 1926, he asked Maxwell Perkins to cut some of the Ecclesiastes epigraph precisely to put even more emphasis on the land: 'The point of the book was to me that the earth abideth forever – having a great deal of fondness and admiration for the earth and not a hell of a lot for my generation'.[23] *The Sun Also Rises* then provides Hemingway's direct answer, and a sort of challenge, to

Ford's seemingly rhetorical question. For Hemingway, Ford's preoccupation with the war, his sense of himself as a gentleman, and his connection to the countryside were all interconnected. Ford, he wrote,

> has never recovered in a literary way from the mirricale, or however you spell it, mirricle maybe, of his having been a soldier. Down with gentlemen. They're hell on themselves in literature. DeMaupassant, Balzac, the Chartreuse de Parme guy [Stendhal], they all made the war, or didnt they? In any event they just learned from it. They didn't always go on under the social spell of it. I'm going to start denying I was in the war for fear I will get like Ford to myself about it.[24]

During his apprenticeship with Ford, Hemingway began to conceive of his writing as an attempt to 'do country so you don't remember the words after you read it but actually have the Country'. Of course, Ford himself had been 'doing country' long before Hemingway set sail for Paris, but often doing it in a way that Hemingway would invariably find inauthentic. He says specifically that such rendering of the landscape is difficult because 'you have to see the country all complete all the time you write and not just have a romantic feeling about it'.[25] In contrast, Ford's landscapes not only were often quite romantic, at times they seemed fairyscapes with a spirit of their own. The small farmer's monologue in 'From the Soil' describes such an enchanted, but ominous, landscape:

> I wonder why we toiled upon the earth
> From sunrise until sunset, dug and delved,
> Crook-backed, cramp-fingered, making little marks
> On the unmoving bosoms of the hills,
> And nothing came of it. And other men
> In the same places dug and delved and ended
> As we have done; and other men just there
> Shall do the self same things until the end.
> I wonder why we did it. . . Underneath
> The grass that fed my sheep, I often thought
> Something lay hidden, some sinister thing
> Lay looking up at us as if it looked
> Upwards thro' quiet waters; that it saw
> Us futile toilers scratching little lines
> And doing nothing. And maybe it smiled
> Because it knew we must come to this. . .[26]

Ford sometimes treated landscape as mere setting. In the dedication to his novel about Henry Hudson, *The 'Half Moon'*, Ford wrote: 'it is not the seas, but the men who cross them; not the hills, but the men who live on them, and in time mold their surfaces; not the rivers, but the hearts of the men who sail on them, that are the subjects of interest'.[27]

Especially in his early work, Ford seemed to know little of the country Hemingway wanted to render in prose. After the war, Ford began to express a more rich and complex view of the country: acknowledging its redemptive power for those broken by war, experimenting with the narrative possibilities of having landscape reflect a character's psyche, and ultimately, proclaiming the country as a metaphor for humanity. As he recovered from the war in a Sussex 'labourer's' cottage, watering 'martially arranged' corn and feeding prize-winning pigs, Ford wrote *No Enemy*, the story of poet Gringoire's coming to terms with his war-time experiences and their effect on his psyche.[28] Originally entitled *English Country*, the work presents Gringoire's visions of the four times he recalled actually noticing landscapes 'for themselves'. These 'four moments in four years' are rendered as epiphanies, 'intermissions of the spirit, exactly like gazing through rifts in the mist' (*NE* 14). Gringoire longs for 'the country that is just country', not the romanticized 'heaths, moors, crags, forests, passes, named rivers, or famous views' (*NE* 63). 'Just country' is the land that endures when generations have passed, what Gringoire sees as an immense expanse which dwarfs the individual:

> Quite suddenly, I felt that, for thousands and thousands of miles, on the green fields and in the woodlands, stretching away under the high skies, in the August sunlight, millions, millions, millions of my fellow men were moving – like the tumultuous mites in a cheese . . . all across a broad world to where the sun was setting and to where the sun was rising. (*NE* 64-5)

This vision of the land is quite different from the one in Ford's poem 'Antwerp', written just as the war began. In fact, it seems Ford revisited the earlier poem in light of his recent experience; he thought quite consciously about this new understanding, at one time considering entitling the book with a line from 'Antwerp', *For Love of Their Land*. Instead, he uses as an epigraph for the novel a poem that echoes 'Antwerp':

> What is love of one's land?. . . .
> 　　　　　　　　　　　　I don't know very well.
> It is something that sleeps
> For a year, for a day,

> For a month – something that keeps
> Very hidden and quiet and still
> And then takes
> The quiet heart like a wave,
> The quiet brain like a spell,
> The quiet will
> Like a tornado – and that shakes
> The whole of the soul.

Throughout the time Hemingway worked on the *transatlantic review*, Ford continued to think about the implications of landscape that 'shakes the soul', particularly in the changing context of post-war life. In a column called 'Stocktaking', Ford concludes that writers are remembered not for their political or moral statements but for their powers of observation, their work as 'naturalists' or 'minute observers': 'the fields remain. That is not only a profound political truth – the profoundest political truth of all but a metaphor useful to ourselves' (*CE* 260).[29] This metaphor is one Hemingway would eagerly take up for his own work.

We know Hemingway had Ford in mind when he began *The Sun Also Rises* because the Ford character (Henry Braddocks) figured so prominently early on in the draft (Fitzgerald convinced Hemingway to cut much of this material, but the uncharitable sketch resurfaces as 'Ford Madox Ford and the Devil's Disciple', in the posthumous volume *A Moveable Feast*). In the handwritten draft of *The Sun Also Rises*, Hemingway's narrator is as grudging toward Braddocks as Hemingway could be toward Ford himself: 'I would avoid if it were possible putting him in this story except that he was a great friend of Cohn and Cohn is the hero'.[30]

Hemingway's names for the protagonist Jake Barnes and his antagonist Henry Braddocks underscore this rivalry with his mentor, especially in the matter of how best to 'do the country'. Starting with the end of the Braddocks name, docks are weeds, as in Shakespeare's *Henry V*, V. ii.: 'Hatefull Docks, rough Thistles, Keksyes, Burres'. Common docks are also sometimes called burdocks (a word that sounds similar to Braddocks). Dock and burdock appear in Ford's 1924 novel *Some Do Not . . .*: Tietjens cleans his pipe with a surgical needle and then wipes that off 'methodically with a great Dock leaf'. In the dissertation on fauna and flora that follows, Ford lists among the flowers the weeds 'burr, burdock' and then recounts the old farmers' saying about keeping the weeds at bay: 'farmer that thy wife may thrive, but no burr and burdock wive!' (*PE* 104-105). (This is from Part One of the novel, which was serialized in the *transatlantic*. When left in charge during Ford's American tour, Hemingway dropped the instalment slated for the August 1924 issue.) In addition to the weedy associations, the *Oxford English Dictionary* traces, from the Renaissance period, the use of dock to mean 'the rump or buttocks'.[31] In fact, Braddocks sounds suspiciously like buttocks.

Why is Ford's character named Braddocks instead of just Burdocks? Not only does Braddocks rhyme with Madox, but Hemingway trumps, alas at Ford's expense, what is already a tour de force worthy of James Joyce. A brad is slang for a half penny, or money in general, pointing to Ford's preoccupation with finances. In the draft of *The Sun Also Rises*, this side of Ford/Braddocks emerges when he encounters 'Jake' and Dos Passos drinking whiskey, and exclaims, 'You must be rich!'[32] Hemingway's portmanteau name for Ford is also packed with 'brady' which means slow, as in a bradypod, a slow footed mammal such as the sloth, an effective association given Hemingway's unflattering description of the heavy, wheezing Ford as someone who looked like an 'upended hogshead' (another rustic image connecting Ford to the countryside). In addition, a brad, the small headless finishing nail, undoubtedly plays on that sturdier fastener, the dowel, recalling the name of Ford's narrator in *The Good Soldier*.

Jake Barnes has quite the country appellation, fitting for his self deprecating humor: 'A rustic lout or simpleton: usually country jake'. In this down and dirty battle over who is closest to the country, Jake with its additional associations of privy, and excrement or filth, reveals here no sham squire, putting on country airs.[33] In this case Jake's given name is reinforced by the last name as well, invoking that timeless rural structure the barn. As if that weren't enough, the French use a version of Jake, Jacques, to refer to a French peasant. Twenties slang would also endow Jake with the meaning that everything is 'Excellent, admirable, fine, "O.K."', as in 'it is all jake'. Characters even discuss Jake's name with him. Georgette, the prostitute Jake has picked up, associates his name with the Flemish, perhaps a subtle allusion to Ford's 'Antwerp', a center of Flemish culture in Belgium. When she finds out he is American, Georgette says, 'Good, I detest Flamands' (*SAR* 21-22).

In addition to these connections, the men's names allude to a potential power struggle. Jake is short for Jacob, a point Brett makes

when she says, 'I've promised to dance this with Jacob . . . you've a
hell of a Biblical name Jake' (SAR 27). Jacob means 'supplanter';
Braddocks' first name, Henry, is Germanic: 'From . . . Heimerich
which meant "home ruler," composed of the elements heim "home"
and ric "power, ruler."'[34] The French Jacques also carries echoes of
revolt: in 1358, 'When the peasants complained, and asked who was
to redress their grievances, they were told in scorn Jacques Bonhomme
. . . i.e. no one. At length a leader appeared, called himself Jacques
Bonhomme, and declared war to the death against every gentleman in
France'. A jacquerie is a bloody peasant revolt.[35] When Stella Bowen
wrote to Ford saying she did not care for her portrayal as Mrs.
Braddocks, and 'even you don't quite escape', she did not realize the
half of it.[36]

If Hemingway could not confront Ford directly, he would at
turns imitate and parody the master in print. We even see Hemingway
take up some of Ford's more intriguing statements about the artist's
role in society. For example, Ford wrote that 'great works of art . . .
put their fingers upon the disease spots of nations or describe the
diseases of civilisations'.[37] In a reflection on their post-war world,
Jake and Georgette discuss his problem, a malady Georgette, despite
her professional skills, does not discern, 'What's the matter? You
sick?' When Jake answers 'yes', Georgette of the bad teeth proclaims,
'Everybody's sick. I'm sick too' (SAR 21). In a 1914 essay on
impressionism, Ford compared the writer's skills to a prostitute's:

> To him [your audience] you will address your picture, your poem, your prose
> story, or your argument. You will seek to capture his interest; you will seek to
> hold his interest. You will do this by methods of surprise, of fatigue, by
> passages of sweetness in your language, by passages suggesting the sudden
> and brutal shock of suicide. You will give him passages of dulness, so that
> your bright effects may seem more bright; you will alternate, you will dwell
> for a long time upon an intimate point; you will seek to exasperate so that you
> may the better enchant. You will, in short, employ all the devices of the
> prostitute.[38]

As Mrs. Braddocks puzzles over the identity of the prostitute Jake
falsely introduced as his fianceé, we see Hemingway's inside joke that
'it takes one to know one' when Braddocks readily agrees, 'Of course,
darling. Mademoiselle Hobin, I have known her for a very long time'
(SAR 24).

Hemingway declared 'he knew F. M. Ford (Hueffer) for a long
time and too bloody well'. He claimed to have 'learned nothing from

old Ford except mistakes not to make that he had made'. Yet, he asked Fitzgerald, 'Didn't Ford say I was the greatest writer of English?'[39] Although Ford did not appreciate that 'everyone I ever helped kicked me in the teeth', he understood the writer's need to find a 'master' and the compulsion subsequently to cast him off. In a lecture on the literary life, Ford advises aspiring artists to find a great master to analyze, meticulously observe everything, 'compare precepts with practices'. You may not learn anything from this person, but this study will 'give you a standard by which you will work or one from which you will merely jump off'. He goes on to warn that frequently a young person matures to find 'the great masters of their adolescence appear stupid, vulgar, or negligible. That is all right'. These 'cycles of taste' are to be expected: 'To-day it is to me, to-morrow to thee – but in a thousand years' time the wheel may come round to me again'.[40]

NOTES

1   Quoted in Max Saunders, *Ford Madox Ford: A Dual Life*, vol. 2, Oxford: Oxford University Press, 1996 – henceforth 'Saunders'; p. 149.

2   For details of Hemingway's *transatlantic* transgressions, see Bernard J. Poli, *Ford Madox Ford and the Transatlantic Review*, Syracuse, New York: Syracuse University Press, 1967.

3   13 October 1923, Hemingway to Pound in Ernest Hemingway, *Ernest Hemingway: Selected Letters, 1917-1961*, ed. Carlos Baker, New York: Charles Scribner's Sons, 1981, p. 96. Subsequent references will be abbreviated as *HSL*.

4   9 November 1923, Hemingway to Stein and Toklas: *HSL* 102.

5   17 March 1924, Hemingway to Pound: *HSL* 112.

6   2 May 1924, Hemingway to Pound: *HSL* 116.

7   14 September 1924, Hemingway to Stein and Toklas: *HSL* 125 and 10 October 1924: *HSL* 127.

8   2 May 1924, Hemingway to Pound: *HSL* 116 and 17 March 1924: *HSL* 113.

9   21 June 1925, Hemingway to Horace Liveright: *HSL* 163.

10 Michael Reynolds, *Hemingway: The Paris Years*, New York: W. W. Norton and Co., 1989, p. 266.

11 Reynolds notes that in some ways 'the two were curiously well matched': they both embellished their stories, particularly their war experiences, and both could be imperious, p. 171.

12 Saunders, 93-5.

13 Hemingway intended to publish this story in his collection *Men Without Women*. For more information, see Susan Beegel, '"A Lack of Passion": Its background, sources, and composition history', *Hemingway Review*, 9:2 (Spring 1990), 50-56;

see also in the same issue, Ernest Hemingway, 'A Lack of Passion', 57-68, and Beegel, 'The "Lack of Passion" Papers', 69-94.
14 Frank MacShane, ed. *Critical Writings of Ford Madox Ford*, Lincoln: University of Nebraska, 1964, p. 54.
15 Ford, *Thus to Revisit: Some Reminiscences*, New York: Octagon Books, Inc., 1966, p. 69.
16 Ernest Hemingway, *The Sun Also Rises*, New York: Scribner's Sons, 1926. Cited parenthetically as *SAR*.
17 Ford, *It Was the Nightingale*, Philadelphia: J. B. Lippincott, 1933. p. 274.
18 Michelle Troy, 'Double Trouble: The Hueffer Brothers and the Artistic Temperament', *Journal of Modern Literature* 26:3/4 (Spring 2003), 28-46.
19 Charles L. Ross analyzes language use and characterization to draw parallels between *The Sun Also Rises* and *The Good Soldier*. '"The Saddest Story" Part Two: *The Good Soldier* and *The Sun Also Rises*', *The Hemingway Review* 12:1 (Fall 1992), 26-34.
20 Ford, 'Mr. Sturge Moore and "The Sea is Kind."' 'Literary Portraits 33', *Outlook* 25 (April 1914), 560; quoted in Joseph Wiesenfarth, 'The Ashbucket at Dawn: Ford's Art of Poetry', *Contemporary Literature* 30:2 (Summer 1989), 245.
21 Ecclesiastes 1:3. This manuscript is discussed by Ashley Chantler, 'Against Oblivion', *Ford Madox Ford Society Newsletter* 11 (26 June 2004).
22 Ford, 'Antwerp', *Selected Poems* ed. Basil Bunting, Cambridge, Massachusetts: Pym-Randall Press, 1971, pp. 26-30.
23 19 November 1926, Hemingway to Perkins: *HSL* 229.
24 17 March 1924, Hemingway to Pound: *HSL* 113.
25 12 September 1924, Hemingway to Edward J. O'Brien: *HSL* 123.
26 Ford, 'From the Soil', *Selected Poems* ed. Basil Bunting, pp. 99-100.
27 Quoted in 'Hudson and His Times in Fiction', *New York Times* July 24, 1909, BR451.
28 Ford Madox Ford, *No Enemy* (1929) ed. Paul Skinner, Manchester: Carcanet, 2002 – henceforth *NE*. Although Ford published the book in 1929, he wrote most of it in 1919. According to Paul Skinner, in August and September of 1919, Ford published three essays in *The New Statesman*; these 'formed the basis of Part One' of *No Enemy* (*NE* xi).
29 Ford repeats this revelation several times in *Parade's End*. I thank Paul Skinner for bringing the *transatlantic* essay to my attention.
30 Ernest Hemingway, *The Sun Also Rises: A Facsimile Edition*, ed. Matthew J. Bruccoli (Detroit: Omnigraphics, Inc., 1990), pp. 63-4. For an astute analysis of Hemingway's changes, see Frederic J. Svoboda, *Hemingway and 'The Sun Also Rises': The Crafting of a Style*. Lawrence, Kansas: University Press of Kansas, 1983.
31 All definitions are from the *Oxford English Dictionary* online database version of the 2nd edition, Oxford University Press, 1989.
32 Ernest Hemingway, *The Sun Also Rises: A Facsimile Edition*, p. 61.
33 In addition to Hemingway's metaphor of 'the diseased oyster [which] shits the finest pearl', the connection of artist and excrement may owe something to James Joyce's 'Shem the Penman' episode of *Finnegans Wake*, drafted in 1924 (Richard Ellmann, *James Joyce,* Oxford: Oxford University Press, 1982, p. 794). In addition, Hemingway, annoyed that Ford's partner Stella frequently recounted her

50-hour labor during dinner, said he was tempted to interrupt with his own creation story, a 'Homeric physical exploit' of the 'time I plugged the can in Kansas City' (2 May 1924, Hemingway to Pound: *HSL* 115).

34 See http://www.behindthename.com and similar dictionaries of name etymology.

35 E. Cobham Brewer. *Dictionary of Phrase and Fable* (1898). See: http://www.bartleby.com/81/9089.html
    In her 1928 novel *Quartet* (*Postures*), Jean Rhys names her Ford figure H. J. Heidler because Ford so admired Henry James. Perhaps Hemingway uses the name Henry for Braddocks in a similar way.

36 Sondra Strang and Karen Cochran, eds. *The Correspondence of Ford Madox Ford and Stella Bowen*, Bloomington: Indiana University Press, 1993, p. 316.

37 Ford, 'The Nigger', *The Outlook* (24 July 1915), 110-11, quoted in Joseph Wiesenfarth, 'Ford's *Joseph Conrad, A Personal Remembrance* as Metafiction', *Renascence* 53:1 (Fall 2000), 43.

38 MacShane, *Critical Writings of Ford Madox Ford*, p. 54.

39 29 July 1952, Hemingway to Charles A. Fenton: *HSL* 776; 3 April 1933, Hemingway to Arnold Gingrich: *HSL* 384; 20 May 1926, Hemingway to F. Scott Fitzgerald: *HSL* 204.

40 Joseph Wiesenfarth, 'The Literary Life: A Lecture Delivered by Ford Madox Ford', *Contemporary Literature,* 30:2 (Summer 1989), 170-182.

RICHARD HUGHES: FORD'S 'SECRET SHARER'

Corwin Baden

In the summer of 1929, amidst a great prelude to historical disaster, Ford Madox Ford might have done a double-take, even imagining that he was seeing a ghost that walked on water. A financial hurricane was about to level Wall Street, the world was plunging into the Great Depression, and Richard Hughes was coming off his transatlantic success, *A High Wind in Jamaica*. The prolific Ford, for his part, had just completed his last Tietjens novel (1928), had produced his less-than-successful Napoleonic romance *A Little Less Than Gods* (1928), had successfully analyzed *The English Novel* (1929) in what Saul Bellow considered 'a straightforward little book',[1] and had, in that same year, published a set of fictionalized 'war memoirs' (*No Enemy*). His own review of Hughes's book lauds it as 'sheer magic', a 'lithograph come to life', yet he is struck by Hughes's 'horrible' depiction of children become monsters at sea.[2] The book's great success prompted Hughes's publishers to keep him 'in the public eye' (Graves 183), and it was there that Ford was able to get a good look at him. The meeting of these two minds most likely began in one of those New York minutes, a crossing of paths in Times Square or a chance meeting in an avant-garde salon; perhaps they even met like ships in the night, yet it was a night that both prophetically recognized would be filled with shattered glass and long knives. Certainly, the young Hughes made a lasting impression on the aging Ford. As with most of his perceived protégés, Ford was instinctively effusive, praising Hughes in his December 1929 letter to Hugh Walpole:

> By the bye, there is an English writer I saw a good deal of in N. Y. C. this summer, called Richard Hughes author of INNOCENT VOYAGE, or HIGH WIND IN JAMAICA who I think is really a fine writer and a keen intelligence – as good as any American *jeune* [. . . .] (*LF* 191)

Yet his qualifying remarks reveal his natural tendencies as an encourager of all the young writers with whom he came into contact:

except Hemingway or Elizabeth Madox Roberts [. . . .] But I could tell you
forty others who are of the same order in New York alone, let alone
Chattanooga, Pike's Peak and Rockford, Ill. Not that I mean to deprecate
Hughes. But how can one poor swallow make a summer all by itself? (*LF*
191)

As has been well documented,[3] Ford made a habit of tossing literary
crumbs to fledgling writers. Ford's reference to Hughes as a 'poor
swallow' in typical idiomatic style signifies his general good will even
as it betrays a certain awareness of his own extravagance. But
underlying the belief he had formed in the 1920s that the best modern
writing was coming from America, was the view to which his entire
life testifies: that writers work best in community, whether in Rye or
Concord, Paris or New York.

By the time of Ford's and Hughes's first meeting in 1929, Ford
recognized the divide between himself and the newer generation of
Modernists. Stang writes that '[w]hen, upset by Conrad's sudden
death in 1924, Ford began to plan a memorial issue of the [*Transatlantic*] *Review*, he had trouble finding anyone for whom Conrad was
not an old fossil' (*Presence* 205). Not only was Ford looking for those
who knew Conrad, he was also looking for the *next* Conrad. In this
sense Hughes represents a Fordian fantasy, a Conradian doppelgänger.
Hughes, whose picture for a 1966 TIME-LIFE Books edition of *In
Hazard* prompts a second glance from any informed reader, was the
spitting image of Conrad, and it really is not such a stretch to suggest
that, in the mind of Ford, his image conjured the second coming of
Conrad, a literary metempsychosis.

By 1938, the summer in which Ford had seen a 'good deal' of
Hughes was a distant memory. Hughes had published no novels since
that time, and Ford was at the end of his writing career, only months
from his deathbed. The two had met again when Ford spent three
months in London in the spring of 1934.[4] But it is in 1938 that we
have the first recorded correspondence between the two writers, and in
it Ford once again calls up Conrad, using Hughes's new novel to
elevate the young author even as he pays homage to his old friend. In
short, Ford calls Hughes's *In Hazard* 'a masterpiece' that 'demands
[…] coherent comment', explains that his wife has been continuously
singing its praises 'for the last thirty-six hours', and declares that 'the
best thing to say about it' is that it 'is the greatest and most amazing
novel ever written' (*LF* 306). Here is the people's Ford, gushing praise
from a critical leak:

Your gift is so individual [...] I certainly know of no other book – or temperament – in the least like it. It is rather as if the book itself were a ship in a hurricane and the hurricane be overtones of which I have just written. (*LF* 306)

A rhetorical question used to demonstrate italics in the *MHRA Style Guide* asks, 'Where is a storm more brilliantly portrayed than in Conrad's *Typhoon*?';[5] Ford's unequivocal rejoinder would seem, then, to be: 'In *In Hazard*!' Ford's final assessment of Hughes's work is stunning when taken at face value: 'You stand really quite apart from any other writer known to me – I mean, any other writer in the whole history of Literature' – this from a man who has 'known' everyone from Confucius to Conrad. At the same time, Ford is clearly concerned with Conrad's legacy; even amidst the accolades, Ford cannot bring himself to lift Hughes above the man whose work he has elevated as the pinnacle of English fiction, and his justification is almost mystical: '[*In Hazard*] isn't, of course, better than *Typhoon*. *Typhoon* was written by a great writer who was a man. *In Hazard* is written by someone inhuman – and consummate in the expression of inhumanities' (*LF* 306). Joseph Wiesenfarth sees this distinction as Ford's acknowledgement of Conrad's humanity, 'his own human failings';[6] perhaps, for Ford, Conrad was more 'human' because of their shared intimacy, while Hughes remained for him a name on a book, an apparition from his cluttered past.

The face of Ford's estranged friend and mentor is ever before him. As Ford tries to put his finger on the key ingredient to the Welshman Hughes's success, he drifts toward visions of the immigrant Conrad: '[Your uniqueness] comes, perhaps, from your foreignness from things Anglo-Saxon. The little dark persistent race might see better where you get it from but they couldn't admire more' (*LF* 306). This assessment addresses not only Hughes's status as Other, even among his own countrymen, but also the author's insertion of a significant body of non-Western Chinese myth and history into the narrative (a Communist Chinese sailor encounters the seaman's protector-goddess T'ien Fei/Matzu on board the battered ship).

Certainly, Ford himself was familiar with the outsider's role. Apparently treated as a sort of tag-along by the Rye gang of his youth, Stephen Crane included,[7] Ford found himself particularly attuned to the attention that a young writer's psyche craves. Goldring's analysis of Ford's relationship with James is telling (considering Goldring's own positive experience as Ford's sub-editor and as the beneficiary of Ford's mentoring while working on the *English Review*): 'With James [...] Ford always comported himself as "*le jeune homme modeste*", so much so that, probably to Ford's secret annoyance, James never seems to have taken him seriously, as an author in his own right. Modesty has its drawbacks',[8] and it appears that Ford learned from this experience.

Beyond their scant correspondence, we are left to imagine on our own the conversations that Ford had with Hughes. Did they discuss Conrad? This is most certain, considering that Hughes's first novel would have inspired comparisons with Conrad's *Heart of Darkness* just as it has since drawn comparisons with Golding's *Lord of the Flies*. More interesting is a second line of questioning: Did they discuss Freud or Jung? Were any of Hughes's memories of Robert Graves (Hughes co-edited a volume of poetry with Graves at Oxford) and his theories (the ones which later would create such a stir in *The White Goddess* and *King Jesus*) recollected over coffee or a glass of port? Unfortunately, their sharing will remain forever secret.

In fact, these two authors are rarely mentioned in the same breath – that is, when they are mentioned at all. Yet The Modern Library's much-discussed '100 Best Novels' of the twentieth century list (1998) bears them both, as in a literary lifeboat, preserving for posterity at least some irreplaceable novels that lack popularity.[9] Fortunately for our study, the similarities do not end here. Both men were eclectic. They wrote poetry, criticism, and even children's stories. (While Ford began his career with a trio of fairy-tales – *The Brown Owl*, *The Feather*, and *The Queen Who Flew* – Hughes ended his career with a book for children called *The Wonder Dog*.) As Modernists, they would appear to have little claim on anything beyond the demolition of 'the old Lie'. Nevertheless, both Ford and Hughes found solace in spirituality, even if they embraced it on their own terms. Both had daughters who were prepared to enter what Hilary Mantel calls 'contemplative communit[ies]'.[10] In all of these elements, there is common ground. Even if these two were not intimate, as Conrad and Ford had been, they confronted the same general period of global upheaval, albeit at different stages, as fellow pilgrims in the grimmest of worlds. While Ford was gassed in the trenches of the Great War, Hughes felt the effects of the Second World War even at home in Wales. In fact, Hughes writes of his role as 'therapist' for child evacuees from London, 'taxed to his utmost' to provide them stories that might reconcile them 'to the awful wrench from Home and Mother'.[11] Ford also understands the potentially therapeutic effects both of fantasy (in his telling of *The Brown Owl* for Juliet) and of Dowell's brand of cathartic soul-baring. Both authors were, above all, story-tellers. And of course, they always had Conrad in common.

Wiesenfarth reminds readers that Conrad's *The Secret Sharer* can be read as a transcript of the relationship between the author and Ford:

> that story could be read as an allegory of the Ford/Conrad collaboration, which ended only shortly before 'The Secret Sharer' was composed in August and September 1910. Ford and Conrad, like Leggatt and the young captain, parted company after having each given the other skills to navigate the lonesome waters of their respective literary enterprises. Neither the young captain nor Leggatt, however, like Conrad and Ford themselves, were without limitations.[12]

Similarly, in the relationship that I am attempting to reconstruct, neither Hughes nor Ford were without limitations. The former was an inveterate perfectionist while the latter was a loquaciously prolific grandstander. Both authors remain underappreciated in our day.

Hughes, influenced by both Freud and Jung as well as his old friend Graves, later came to understand his own work in terms of archetypal and mythic patterns. His interest in visionariness and the unconscious is something else he shares with Ford.[13] In a new introduction for *In Hazard* he explains Graves's view that:

> the writing of poetry does for the poet what dreaming does for Tom, Dick, and Harry: it allows a safe outlet for conflicts and tensions too painful for his conscious mind to face, disguised so impenetrably in symbol that the poet himself has no inkling of what his poem is really 'about' – just as the dreamer has none till his analyst tells him. The tension both determines the symbol and generates the compulsive force.[14]

At the same time, Graves

> downright den[ies] the same to be true of prose, that the roots of a prose piece ever run right down 'under the threshold' as poetry does. But why? If an imaginative prose work has also insisted on being written – in its humbler way yet still just as irresistibly as a hen's egg insists on being laid – why must the novelist's compulsion be assumed to differ in kind from the poet's? (*IH* xviii)

Hughes is here formulating his own brand of psychological criticism. He goes on to explain how his novel, while never constructed as a conscious allegory, is a representation of archetypes which produced in him an imaginative figure similar to Keats's *La Belle Dame sans Merci.* He explains,

> I should probably be the last to know even today what private neuroses of my own saw themselves reflected in these twin symbols of ship and hurricane [. . . .] But tensions can also derive from the situation of a whole society. (*IH* xix)

In comparing Hughes's work to Ford's, it is interesting to note Ford's use of the same metaphor of the egg to explain the origins of what he called his 'great auk's egg', *The Good Soldier*:

> I was astounded at the work I must have put into the construction of the book, at the intricate tangle of references and cross-references. Nor is that to be wondered at for, though I wrote it with comparative rapidity, I had it hatching within myself for fully another decade.[15]

Both Ford and Hughes were creating consciously based on their shadowy understanding of the unconscious. Thus attuned, their fiction has an uncanny predictive power that seems to flow from latent tensions such as the world had never experienced. Just as Ford remarkably identified 4 August as a day to remember in *The Good Soldier* (*GS* xxxiii-xxxiv) and writes presciently about the collapse of Edwardian society, Hughes relates that 'the fading smell of remembered death in Britain was just beginning to be replaced by a new stench that was death prefigured' (*IH* xix). In their tapping of the unconscious, both authors essentially predicted Hitler and his human holocaust, long before the rest of the world was conscious of this monster and his mission. Goldring affirms that

> Passages in the dedicatory letter to his autobiographical novel *It Was the Nightingale*, begun in Paris in January 1933, and completed at Cap Brun six months later, indicate his growing awareness of the world situation and his immediate grasp of the significance of Hitler. In this he was several years in advance of many of even the most politically intelligent of his contemporaries. (Goldring 264)

If Richard Hughes was indeed Ford's secret sharer, it is a pity that we have only one letter by which to document their relationship; there is no memorial – only a passing hat tossed by these literary Leggatts to mark, if not a close communion, then at least a Conradian conjunction. Ford closes his 1938 letter, '[W]hen is a third book coming? And what is it? I'd appreciate it if you would keep us from time to time posted as to your activities and vicissitudes' (*LF* 307). One is even tempted to wonder whether one of Hughes's '26 wheelbarrowsful' (*IH* vii) of unpublished manuscripts, a secret story we will never see, might have been in Ford's hands when the older man was on his deathbed. Goldring writes of Ford that:

> He was constantly surrounded by young and unknown writers on whom he spent endless time and trouble. He worked with them on their MSS. and tried to find them publishers. He had about two hundred MSS. in his possession at the time of his death and his last energies were spent on them. (Goldring 276-7)

It is worth a little of *our* energy, then, to try to unearth the last remnants of what was, at the very least, a warm acquaintance. Even now, in remembering Hughes's remark that '[t]he days of Conrad's *"Typhoon"* are passed' (*IH* 26), we recognize that the days of Ford's *Parade's End* and Hughes's *In Hazard*, times of tumult, are sadly far from over. Therefore, the work of these two authors (and their regard for one another) is still relevant. Since Ford and Hughes are both frequently neglected, picking up their pieces is the work of pilgrims. Edwin Frank refers to literary contributions like Hughes's *In Hazard* and Ford's *Parade's End* when he says:

> It has survived, as books will do, whether on the shelves of libraries, private and public, or in boxes in attics or on tables at yard sales, on the crammed shelves of second-hand shops, or in the messiest storehouse of all, memory, until picked up again by a curious child or an idle adult and given a chance to reexert their charm and reestablish their command.[16]

I found my own copy of *In Hazard* in just such a place – a public library discard pile – and already it has become an old friend. And old friends – even secret ones – can suddenly re-exert charm and re-establish command; it just takes a secret hearer to listen in.

NOTES

1   Saul Bellow, 'LITERATURE: The Next Chapter', *The National Review*, 52 (2000), 34.

2   Richard Perceval Graves, *Richard Hughes: A Biography*, London: André Deutsch, 1994 – henceforth 'Graves'; pp. 182-3.

3   See the description of Ford's 'essential kindness, his boundless generosity, a quality frequently imposed upon by the selfish and unscrupulous' in Douglas Goldring, *Trained for Genius: The Life and Writings of Ford Madox Ford*, New York: E. P. Dutton, 1949 – henceforth 'Goldring'; p. 253 and Ann Barr Snitow, *Ford Madox Ford and the Voice of Uncertainty*, Baton Rouge: Louisiana State UP, 1984, pp. 5 and 205.

4   Frank MacShane, *The Life and Work of Ford Madox Ford*, New York: Horizon Press, 1965, p. 229.

5   *MHRA Style Guide: A Handbook for Authors, Editors, and Writers of Theses*, London: MHRA, 2002, p. 21.

6   Joseph Wiesenfarth, 'Ford's *Joseph Conrad: A Personal Remembrance* as Metafiction; or, How Conrad Became an Elizabethan Poet', *Renascence*, 53 (2000), 43-60 (p. 53).

7   See Nicholas Delbanco, *Group Portrait*, New York: William Morrow, 1982, regarding a notable Christmas party at which a play by James, Conrad, Crane, Wells, and numerous others was performed. Ford's name is noticeably missing from this collaborative work. Afterwards, 'when Ford came to call, on January 2, Crane [...] seems to have mistaken Ford for the bailiff' (p. 48).

8   Goldring, p. 93.

9   '100 Best Novels', *The Modern Library*, http://www.randomhouse.com/modernlibrary/100bestnovels.html [accessed 4 January 2007].

10 Hilary Mantel, 'Introduction', *The Wooden Shepherdess*, London: Chatto & Windus, 1973; reprinted New York: New York Review Books, 2000, p. xi.

11 Richard Hughes, 'Foreword', *The Wonder Dog: The Collected Children's Stories of Richard Hughes*, New York: Greenwillow, 1977, p. 10.

12 Wiesenfarth, p. 53.

13 My argument here is indebted to another neglected author; a 'secret sharer' of Hughes' name, the literary critic Richard E. Hughes, whose *The Lively Image: 4 Myths in Literature*, Cambridge, MA: Winthrop, 1975, relies heavily on both *Heart of Darkness* and 'The Secret Sharer'.

14 Richard. Hughes, *In Hazard*, TIME Reading Program special ed., New York: Harper & Row, 1938; reprinted New York: TIME, 1966 – henceforth *IH*; p. xviii.

15 Ford Madox Ford, *The Good Soldier*, Oxford World's Classics edition, ed. Thomas C. Moser, Oxford: OUP, 1990 – henceforth *GS*; p. 2.

16 *Unknown Masterpieces*, ed. by Edwin Frank, New York: New York Review Books, 2003, pp. viii-ix; Frank is here referring to Hughes's *A High Wind in Jamaica*.

FORD AND GRAHAM GREENE

Bernard Bergonzi

In his second volume of autobiography, *Ways of Escape* (1980), Graham Greene wrote of his early novel *It's a Battlefield* (1934): 'If the reception of this book, which added to my failure in the eyes of my publishers, did not discourage me, it was for three reasons: the best review I had yet earned came from V. S. Pritchett, a kind phrase from Ezra Pound, and some words of praise from Ford Madox Ford'.[1] Greene had sent a fan-letter to Ford, stating his admiration for Ford's work and mentioning that he himself was a novelist. In his reply Ford invited the young writer to let him see something he had written, and Greene sent him the recently published *It's a Battlefield*. He was overwhelmed by Ford's response, which called it 'a truly admirable work, construction impeccable; writing very good indeed & atmosphere extraordinarily impressive [. . . .] I would not have believed that such writing cd. come out of England'.[2] In reply Greene wrote, 'I can't tell you the pleasure your letter gave me. I have for so long admired you as so incomparably the finest living English novelist that your praise goes to my head. I had thought the book would probably be followed by a tactful silence…. I wish I could convey to you the excitement and joy your letter gave me'.[3]

Greene did what he could to repay Ford, whose reputation was at a low ebb in England at that time. In reviews he referred in passing to Ford's 'admirable book on the English novel' and to his 'brilliant and short-lived *Transatlantic Review*'.[4] In 1936, Ford, who was living in France, visited England; he and Greene met for lunch, and Ford signed and inscribed his admirer's copy of *The Good Soldier*. Greene's admiration persisted, but his tone in writing about Ford became more detached. Reviewing *Provence* in 1938, he remarked: 'He is an author who, like his old friend Henry James, has a personality which calls for both respect and mockery. A fine writer with traces of a most engaging charlatan…'.[5] Ford died the following year, and in a memorial article Greene mythologized him as the last survivor of the era of James and Conrad: 'The death of Ford Madox Ford was like the obscure death of a veteran – an impossibly

Napoleonic veteran, say, whose immense memory spanned the period
from Jena to Sedan: he belonged to the heroic age of English fiction
and outlived it – yet he was only sixty-six'. Greene refers with respect
to Ford's whole literary oeuvre, but gives the highest praise to *The
Good Soldier* and the Tietjens sequence. He concludes that Ford, after
a life full of difficulties, 'had come through – with his humour intact,
his stock of unreliable anecdotes, the kind of enemies a man ought to
have, and a half-belief in a posterity which would care for good
writing'.[6]

Greene continued to hold Ford in high regard, but his attitudes
developed beyond personal gratitude and general admiration to an
interest in Ford's narrative devices. In the late 1940s Greene was
moving on from the dominant modes of his earlier fiction, which
combined poetry and melodrama, and drew eclectically on Jacobean
drama, boys' adventure stories and the contemporary thriller. He
started to aspire towards a novel which would be a serious and
psychologically realistic study of human passion. He was becoming
attracted by first-person narrative, which he had not employed before,
and he admired the ease with which Dickens used it in *David
Copperfield*. This new direction resulted in *The End of the Affair*
(1951), one of Greene's most admired and accomplished novels. He
remarked of it in *Ways of Escape*, 'I had learned something from my
continual rereadings of that remarkable novel, *The Good Soldier* by
Ford Madox Ford'.[7] Ford's novel had shown Greene how a story
could be told by a character who is sometimes deluded, and how
chronology might be loosened and rearranged. *The Good Soldier* is
subtitled 'A Tale of Passion', and was described by John Rodker as
'the finest French novel in the English language';[8] one of Greene's
best critics, Roger Sharrock, has called *The End of the Affair* 'a natural
history of love concentrating on the psychology of passion in a
manner that is more French than English'.[9]

In the 1960s Greene repaid his debt to Ford by editing *The
Bodley Head Ford Madox Ford*, a selection of his writings in four
volumes (1962-3). This enterprise is an *hommage* comparable to those
studies by nineteenth century novelists of a distinguished forerunner,
like James's book on Hawthorne, or Gissing's on Dickens. In his
introduction Greene writes with affection and admiration of Ford and
his career, and discusses *The Good Soldier* in some detail:
'Technically the story is undoubtedly Ford's masterpiece...' The
Bodley Head edition was originally intended to consist of only two

volumes; the first contained *The Good Soldier* and a selection from Ford's memoirs and some poems; the second was taken up by *The Fifth Queen,* his Tudor trilogy, first published between 1906 and 1908. In his introduction Greene regrets the exclusion of the novels comprising what he called 'the Tietjens Saga', but remarks, 'remarkable though they are, they do not stand up to the erosion of time so satisfactorily as *The Good Soldier'*.[10] Nevertheless, there was a change of policy by the Bodley Head – perhaps because of pressure from Greene – and two further volumes came out, devoted to *Parade's End*: the third contained *Some Do Not . . .*, and the fourth *No More Parades* and *A Man Could Stand Up* –. In the introduction to these two volumes Greene has overcome his earlier reservations about *Parade's End*, though he is still uneasy about 'the sentimentality which sometimes lurked in the shadow of Christopher Tietjens', and expresses his satisfaction that the Bodley Head Ford has added *Parade's End* to *The Fifth Queen* and *The Good Soldier*: 'three great novels, a little scarred, stained here and there and chipped perhaps, but how massive and resistant compared with most of the work of his successors'.[11]

As Greene acknowledges, his approach to *Parade's End* is controversial, since he omits *Last Post* (called *The Last Post* in the U. S.), generally regarded as the final volume of a tetralogy published between 1924 and 1928. Greene rejects it because he thinks it is a failure: 'it was a disaster, a disaster which has delayed a full critical appreciation of *Parade's End'*. He supports his decision by saying that Ford himself wanted to suppress the novel, quoting from his letter to a literary agent in 1930, concerning a proposed new edition of the sequence. Ford wrote then, 'I strongly wish to omit the *Last Post* from the edition. I do not like the book and have never liked it and always intended the series to end with *A Man Could Stand Up'*.[12] That is an emphatic statement, but as Max Saunders makes clear in his biography, Ford never finally made his mind up about *Last Post,* and in the years following its publication he made contradictory suggestions about its relation to *Parade's End*. Writers are entitled to second thoughts, and the fact that Ford had wanted to exclude *Last Post* in 1930 was, in Greene's judgment, a sufficient reason for him to do so; indeed, he had done something similar himself with his second and third novels, *The Name of Action* (1930) and *Rumour at Nightfall* (1931), which he decided were inferior work; he never allowed them to be reprinted, and the prohibition has been continued by Greene's estate, so that these two early books will be unavailable for many years to come. But other readers are less ready to give absolute weight to incidental authorial statements. Ford's American admirer, Robie Macauley, who had known him in the 1930s, had no hesitation about including *Last Post* in the one-volume edition of *Parade's End* that he edited for Knopf in 1950. He wrote in his introduction, 'Without *The Last Post* the novel would have been sadly truncated and though it could never "turn out" as an ordinary novel must turn out, the recapitulation and final statement of *The Last Post* is indispensable'.[13] More recently Max Saunders has defended *Last Post* against Greene's dismissal, remarking, '*Last Post* concludes *Parade's End* in a masterly achievement of a highly precarious tone and form and one which is profoundly expressive of Ford's temperament'.[14] But another Fordian, Thomas Moser, disagrees: 'Surely Ford and Graham Greene are right that that novel is superfluous to the whole scheme'.[15] He believes that *Last Post* is a great aesthetic falling off from the preceding volume, *A Man Could Stand Up –*.

This is a disagreement that is not likely to be resolved. To speak for myself, I tend to see *Parade's End* in the way that Greene and Moser do. But some time ago I reread *Last Post* for the first time in many years, and found it absorbing in its own terms. It shows the earlier volumes in a different light, and is certainly not a 'disaster', as Greene claimed. That is not to say, though, that it is an essential part of *Parade's End*, even if one disregards Ford's own uncertain view of the novel. One perhaps needs to be more tentative about questions of definition; we could then read *Parade's End* either as Greene's trilogy or Macauley's tetralogy, which would be significantly different works, rather like the Quarto and First Folio texts of some Shakespeare plays. Or one could regard *Last Post* as a sequel or a coda to the three-volume version, or even as a different novel linked by a Balzacian continuity of characters to the earlier work. Without intending to, Greene opened up an area of controversy that involves bibliography, editorial method and literary theory.

NOTES

1   Graham Greene, *Ways of Escape*, Harmondsworth: Penguin, 1981, p. 28.
2   Greene to Ford, 18 December [1934], quoted by Max Saunders, *Ford Madox Ford: A Dual Life*, Oxford: Oxford University Press, 1996, vol. 2, p. 476.
3   Frank MacShane, *The Life and Work of Ford Madox Ford*, London : Routledge, 1965, p. 256.
4   Ian Thomson, editor, *Articles of Faith: The Collected 'Tablet' Journalism of Graham Greene*, Oxford: Signal Books, 2006, pp. 88, 91.
5   Greene, 'The Good Life', *London Mercury* (December 1938), 217-8.
6   Greene, 'Ford Madox Ford', *Spectator*, 113, (7 July 1939), 11; reprinted in Frank MacShane, editor, *Ford Madox Ford: The Critical Heritage*, London: Routledge, 1972, pp. 212, 215.
7   Greene, *Ways of Escape*, p. 107.
8   MacShane, *The Life and Work of Ford Madox Ford*, p. 119.
9   Roger Sharrock, *Saints, Sinners and Comedians: The Novels of Graham Greene*, Tunbridge Wells: Burns and Oates, 1984, p. 161.
10 Greene, *The Bodley Head Ford Madox Ford: Volume One*, London: The Bodley Head, 1962, pp. 11, 7.
11 Greene, *The Bodley Head Ford Madox Ford: Volume Three*, London: The Bodley Head, 1963, p. 5.
12 Richard M. Ludwig, editor, *Letters of Ford Madox Ford*, Princeton: Princeton University Press, 1965, p. 197.
13 Macauley, 'Introduction' to *Parade's End*, New York: Vintage Books, 1979, p. xxi.
14 Saunders, Vol. 2, p. 253.
15 Thomas C. Moser, *The Life in the Fiction of Ford Madox Ford*, Princeton: Princeton University Press, 1980, p. 231.

HUEFFER/FORD AND WILSON/BURGESS

William Mill

Anthony Burgess's admiration for Ford Madox Ford is less familiar than that for Joyce, Lawrence or Shakespeare. Yet he regularly argued for Ford's eminence amongst Modernists.[1] And Ford is certainly another writer to whom he keeps returning and referring. There's an acknowledgement of Ford's experiments with the narrative 'time shift' near the start of the first of his two volumes of autobiography, *Little Wilson and Big God*, for instance, when Burgess writes: 'The years become confused, obedient to Proust or Ford Madox Ford. Real time emerges with a vague chronology'.[2] Grouping Ford with Proust may sound casual to those less familiar with Ford. But the basis for it is made more explicit in the long essay Burgess wrote as the entry for 'the novel' in the *Encyclopedia Britannica* in 1970. It is in the section on 'Impressionism' that he gives closest attention to Ford:

> The desire to present life with frank objectivity led certain early 20th-century novelists to question the validity of long-accepted narrative conventions. If truth was the novelist's aim, then the tradition of the omniscient narrator would have to go, to be replaced by one in which a fallible, partially ignorant character – one involved in the story and hence himself subject to the objective or naturalistic approach – recounted what he saw and heard. But the Impressionist painters of late 19th-century France had proclaimed a revision of the whole seeing process: they distinguished between what the observer assumed he was observing and what he actually observed. That cerebral editing which turned visual data into objects of geometric solidity had no place in Impressionist painting; the visible world became less definite, more fluid, resolving into light and colour.[3]

Burgess notes that the German novelists Thomas Mann and Hermann Hesse were proclaimed 'Impressionist' as they moved away from realism's exterior notations. 'But in England', he continues:

> Ford Madox Ford went much further in breaking down the imagined rigidities of the space-time continuum, liquidating step-by-step temporal progression and making the visual world shimmer, dissolve, reconstitute itself. In Ford's tetralogy *Parade's End* (1924-28), the reader moves freely within the time continuum, as if it were spatial, and the total picture is perceived through an

accumulation of fragmentary impressions. Ford's masterpiece, *The Good Soldier*, pushes the technique to its limit: the narrator tells his story with no special dispensation to see or understand more than a fallible being can, and, in his reminiscences, he fragments whole sequences of events as he ranges freely through time[.]

Where most critics have confined claims for Ford's significant Modernist innovation to *The Good Soldier*, and possibly *Parade's End*, Burgess is attuned to linguistic experiment in some of his earliest work, arguing that in the 'approach to dialogue' in *The Inheritors* (written mainly by Ford, with some collaborative input from Conrad; 1901), 'a particular aspect of literary impressionism may be seen whose suggestiveness has been ignored by other modern novelists':

> As the brain imposes its own logical patterns on the phenomena of the visual world, so it is given to editing into clarity and conciseness the halting utterances of real-life speech; the characters of most novels are impossibly articulate. Ford and Conrad attempted to present speech as it is actually spoken, with many of the meaningful solidities implied rather than stated. The result is sometimes exasperating, but only as real-life conversation frequently is. The interior monologue, which similarly resists editing, may be regarded as a development of this technique.

For Burgess, then, Modernism's interior monologues and streams of consciousness begin with the literary Impressionism of Ford's era: 'To show pre-articulatory thought, feeling, and sensuous perception unordered into a rational or "literary" sequence is an impressionistic device', he argues. Like Joyce, he traces the technique back to 'Édouard Dujardin's minor novel *Les Lauriers sont coupés* (1888; *We'll to the Woods No More*)'.[4] But Ford is thus seen by Burgess as a crucial transitional figure: importing continental developments away from realism to Impressionism, but also taking them further, to the point where they anticipate the stream-of-consciousness techniques later used by Modernist writers in English such as 'Dorothy Richardson, Joyce, and Virginia Woolf to William Faulkner and Samuel Beckett'. This essay for the *Encyclopaedia* is one of Burgess's most important pieces of criticism; not only for its shrewd and original juxtapositions of national traditions, but also for what it says about the view of art incarnated in his own novels.

What Burgess says in this essay about the modern English novel is excellent too. Again Ford is mentioned, this time as one of the 'major English-born novelists' (along with Forster and Woolf) influenced by James and Conrad, two foreigners who changed the course of British fiction. The way Burgess develops the argument suggests another ground for his interest in Ford:

> Early 20th-century British fiction needed the impact of an alien tradition to jolt it out of bourgeois empiricism, and perhaps the two major influences were both foreigners who had elected to write fiction in England – Joseph Conrad (1857-1924), Polish-born, to whom English was a second language, and Henry James (1843-1916), an American who had drunk deeply at French fountains and brought to the exercise of his craft a scrupulousness and a concern with aesthetic values that was almost obsessive and, it may be said, very un-English.[5]

He goes on to discuss Graham Greene immediately after Ford, not only as another Catholic convert indebted to Conrad and James, but also because, as Burgess well knew, Greene owed a debt to Ford too (as Bernard Bergonzi shows in this volume). Greene sought to repay it when he introduced the Bodley Head editions of Ford's greatest novels, *The Good Soldier* and *Parade's End*. But Burgess never forgave him for omitting the fourth and final volume of the *Parade's End* series, *Last Post*, from that edition.[6]

Burgess especially admired *Parade's End*, writing about it:

> The best novel produced by a British writer (and *British* has everything to do with culture, nothing to do with blood) is the tetralogy by Ford Madox Ford (previously named Ford Madox Hueffer) called *Parade's End*. It is also the finest novel about the First World War. It is also the finest novel about the nature of British society. Ford is neglected. The finest editor of his time, he not only encouraged Joyce and Lawrence but actually wrote a good deal of Joseph Conrad's fiction for him. If this judgment on the supremacy of *Parade's End* be cavilled at, I am prepared to yield and to submit Ford's *The Good Soldier* as the best novel ever produced in England. [7]

Where the Encylopaedia entry is more formalist in its emphases, here it is clear that Burgess also values *Parade's End* for the subjects it takes on: the war; British society. Like Greene, who said the Tietjens novels were 'almost the only adult novels dealing with the sexual life that have been written in English. They are our answer to Flaubert',[8] Burgess also valued Ford for the inventiveness with which he brings language into relations with sexuality. Which allies him with the other Modernists of Burgess's pantheon, Lawrence and Joyce. He didn't write a book on Ford, as he had on Joyce and Lawrence; but that says more about what publishers wanted to commission, than about what Burgess wanted to write. As Andrew Biswell has shown, he continued to present Ford as a central figure in the development of modern literature, and on the grounds of his ability to present the power of human sexuality.[9]

This is evident from another reference to Ford in Burgess's autobiography, again indicating how Ford's writing represents a kind of touchstone for both sexual and technical intensity. In *Little Wilson and Big God* he explains how the novel *The Right to an Answer* was based on a story his wife Lynne told about two wife-swapping couples: 'For a writer like Ford Madox Ford it might have provided material for another *The Good Soldier*; for me it was almost, but not quite, the stuff of comedy' (*LWBG* 438).

Burgess's other references to Ford in his autobiographies suggest a rather different point of contact, however. They are themselves the stuff of comedy: in particular, comedy turning on Ford's names. When Lynne was transferred to London in 1943, Burgess explains:

> When I went on my first weekend leave (signed Ford Madox Ford, Capt for Lt Col), I saw that I would have to be more careful than in easy-going Manchester. For in London there was a larger ration of military police, who would waylay guilty-looking soldiers at the top or bottom of Underground escalators and perhaps be experts in pass forgery. A name like Ford Madox Ford would arouse suspicion because of its implausibility. (*LWBG* 286)

The joke is that Ford Madox Ford was a real name, and legally valid, however implausible.

In his second volume of autobiography, *You've Had Your Time*, Burgess recalls how in one of his early novels he had played differently with Ford's names. He explains the conception of *One Hand Clapping* (1961) as follows:

> How far did I understand women? I would find out by turning myself into a woman, or rather a girl of the direct, unsubtle, uneducable kind whose womanly qualities would not be obfuscated by books or introspection. I would write a first-person narrative about a girl working in a supermarket, pretty, cheerful, optimistic, married to a rather gloomy young man who suspects that the world is going to pot but is too uneducated to know why.[10]

Television quiz shows are made to bear much of the responsibility for the world's decline. Burgess said he 'hated' the popular quiz show host Hughie Green, and decided to put him into the novel at a crucial scene. The gloomy husband, who has no knowledge of books, but a photographic mind, memorises facts from an encyclopedia and enters the quiz show, answering all the questions and accumulating a large prize:

> But when the thousand-pound question comes – who wrote *The Good Soldier?* – he gives, according to the quizmaster's rubric, the wrong answer: Ford Madox Hueffer. The right answer is Ford Madox Ford.[11]

Why does this episode matter? The point is as much the nod towards *The Good Soldier*, Ford's masterly first-person narrative told by a gloomy man whose world has gone to pot, as towards Ford's names. Yet there is a point about names too. Burgess, who was John Burgess Wilson before he was Anthony Burgess, published *One Hand Clapping* under the pseudonym Joseph Kell. Burgess's reinvention of his names gave him some sympathy with Ford, who himself used other pseudonyms occasionally. One of the things such changes of name suggest is how fiction writers need to inhabit multiple identities; both in the using of two names, but also in the choosing of a forename (Ford) or middle name (Burgess) as a pen-surname.[12] Ford, I think, was peculiarly conscious of how the writer's life was subject to this sense of multiplicity, especially when involved in fictionalising its own autobiography.

And perhaps Ford is a significant figure to Burgess not only for his novels, but also for his prolific autobiographical writing; especially his two-volume autobiography about the writing-life: *Return to Yesterday* (1931) and *It was the Nightingale* (1933). Burgess certainly knew *Return to Yesterday*, in which Ford writes about his pre-war literary contacts, especially with James and Conrad, and recounts his life up to the time he was writing *The Good Soldier*.[13] He's very likely also to have known *It was the Nightingale*, which is mostly concerned with the postwar expatriate Paris Modernism of Hemingway, Pound and Joyce, and the conception of *Parade's End*. Ford presents his life as divided by the First World War. His experience, during the battle of the Somme, of being concussed into amnesia by a shell-burst, felt like a near-death. He gives his war experience to Christopher Tietjens in *Parade's End*, and doesn't cover most of it in his autobiography. The war occupies the no-man's-land between the two autobiographical books. In the second paragraph of *It was the Nightingale* he describes his leaving the army in 1919 as a form of rebirth: 'Naked came I from my mother's womb. On that day I was nearly as denuded of possessions'.[14] And it was after the war that Ford Madox Hueffer began publishing under his new name, Ford Madox Ford. Burgess also splits his autobiography into two volumes, and like Ford, presents his life as divided at the point where he thought it was going to end: when in 1959 he was told he had only a year to live; when he began his career as a novelist under this – as it turned out, fictional – death-sentence; and under a new name.[15]

A full discussion of Ford, Burgess and Autobiography would be a different essay, and one which has been written already.[16] Instead, I'll conclude with Burgess's *tour de force* novel *Earthly Powers* (1980): a fictional autobiography narrated by a character in his eighties, Kenneth Toomey, whose life spans the two *milieux* of *Return to Yesterday* and *It was the Nightingale*. *Earthly Powers* confronts the questions, germane to all imaginative writers, of the ethical status of fiction and its claims to truth; the ways in which fiction draws upon autobiographical experience; and the ways in which autobiography may turn into fiction. It isn't just that these questions have bedevilled Ford's reputation. Toomey's remark that 'We lie for a living' perhaps suggests Burgess's awareness of how novelist-autobiographers like Ford and Conrad are particularly susceptible to accusations of untruthfulness (*EP* 17). It is also that Ford appears, with a hallucinatory exuberance that seems straight out of his account of literary contacts in *It Was the Nightingale*, as a character in Burgess's novel, in chapter 30. 'Benedicent numen my arse', says Ford, according to Toomey, as he rejects Toomey's queer narrative for the magazine he's just starting, the *transatlantic review*: 'Your act of buggery here smells of unfrocked priests. Or untrousered, if you like' (*EP* 188-90). In his bitterness Toomey accuses him of having 'a dirty mind'; but Burgess shows that it's the style he objects to, which tries to spiritualize and sacralize homosexuality with its Latinate pseudo-liturgical phrasing. It's a fictional literary contact, as Burgess inserts imaginary Toomey into Ford's real coterie. But through it, Burgess effects another form of literary contact, between his art and Ford's.

NOTES

1 This essay is a revised and excerpted version of one in *Anthony Burgess and Modernity*, ed. Alan Roughley, Manchester: Manchester University Press, forthcoming, 2007 – henceforth *ABM*; and is printed here with the kind permission of the editor.

    In addition to Burgess's accounts of Ford quoted in this essay, see: 'Last embers of modernism', *Observer* Review (11 April 1982), 31, on *The Rash Act*; 'Mad about Writing', *Observer* (13 March 1983), 33, reviewing *Pound/Ford*, ed. Brita Lindberg-Seyersted, London: Faber, 1982; and 'Catherine Howard et Henri VIII', *Le Monde* (24 February 1984), 13, reviewing Claudine Stora's translation of *The Fifth Queen*, *La Cinquieme reine*, Paris: Acropole, 1984.

2 Burgess, *Little Wilson and Big God*, London: Heinemann, 1987 – henceforth *LWBG*; p. 32.

3 *The New Encyclopaedia Britannica*. 15th edition, Chicago, Encyclopaedia Britannica Inc, 1995, vol. 23, pp. 123-4.

4 See Frank Budgen, *James Joyce and the Making of 'Ulysses' and Other Writings*, London: Oxford University Press, 1972, p. 94.

5 Burgess, 'The Novel in English', *The New Encyclopaedia Britannica*, *op. cit.*, p. 130.

6 See Burgess, Contribution to Symposium: 'Reputations Revisited', *T. L. S.* (21 Jan 1977), 66-68 (p. 67); and Graham Greene's response, '*Parade's End*', Letter to the editor, *T. L. S.* (4 Feb 1977), 130. In Burgess's 'Introduction' to Richard Aldington, *The Colonel's Daughter*, London: The Hogarth Press, 1986, pp. [i]-[ix], Green's 'editorial misguidedness' is berated on p. [iv], which also states: 'The finest war novel ever to come out of England is undoubtedly Ford's *Parade's End*, whose philosophical distinction lies in its capacity to see the First World War as a symptom rather than a cause of the breakdown of European society'.

7 Anthony Burgess, in *The Best of Everything*, ed. William Davis, London: Weidenfeld and Nicolson, 1980, p. 97.

8 Quoted on the jacket flap to vol. 3 of *The Bodley Head Ford Madox Ford*, London: Bodley Head, 1963.

9 See Andrew Biswell, 'Anthony Burgeons: Expanding the Burgess Canon', *ABM*, for a discussion of Burgess's unpublished 1992 book proposal 'Modernism and Modern Man'.

10 Burgess, *You've Had Your Time*, London: Heinemann, 1990, p. 27.

11 *Ibid.*, p. 28.

12 It should be acknowledged here that Burgess's *Earthly Powers*, Harmondsworth: Penguin, 1981 – henceforth *EP*; p. 54, offers a different motivation for Ford's name-change: 'A man called Hueffer, Ford rather – he changed his name because of the war'. Toomey is remembering a conversation he had with Father Frobisher in late 1916. Historically this is wrong. Ford changed his name in 1919, having kept his German surname throughout the war. The change was motivated more by personal reasons: making a new start with a new partner. It is tempting to attribute the error to the novel's unreliable narrator (and thus make it an oblique homage to *The Good Soldier*'s unreliable narration), especially given Toomey's own doubts about the accuracy of his memory. However, Burgess makes the same mistake in

They Wrote in English (see note 13), this time placing the name-change even earlier, saying that Ford's name was 'prudently changed when the British began to fight the Germans': vol. 1, p. 63.

13 Burgess included an excerpt from it in his anthology *They Wrote in English: A Survey of British and American Literature*. 2 vols, Bresso (Milan): Tramontana editore, 1979. Vol. 2: *L'Antologia: I campioni*. The excerpt from *Return to Yesterday* (pp. 561-3) is on Henry James. Burgess also includes excerpts from Ford's *Parade's End* (pp. 556-61). I'm grateful to Andrew Biswell for drawing my attention to these volumes.

14 Ford, *It was the Nightingale*, London: Heinemann, 1934, p. 3.

15 See the scrupulous discussion of this episode in Andrew Biswell's excellent biography, *The Real Life of Anthony Burgess*, London: Picador, 2005, pp. 205-13.

16 See Max Saunders, 'Burgess, Joyce, and Ford: Modernity, Sexuality, and Confession', *ABM.*

'LONG LETTERS ABOUT FORD MADOX FORD': FORD'S AFTERLIFE IN THE WORK OF HAROLD PINTER

Angus Wrenn

At first glance Ford Madox Ford and Harold Pinter would appear to have little in common. Ford is known chiefly for his prose fiction and, although he produced a significant body of poetry, made only a handful of sorties into writing for the stage, all equally devoid of success. Pinter did write an early novel, *The Dwarfs*, long withheld from publication, but has built his international reputation, recognized in 2005 by the award of the Nobel Prize for Literature, as one of the greatest playwrights of his age. Ford died only nine years after Pinter's birth and belonged, at least in terms of his upbringing, to the nineteenth century, a contemporary of Conrad and James, scion of the Rossettis and the Pre-Raphaelites. Pinter, born in 1930, grew up as the grandson of Jewish immigrants from Poland in London's East End, although he subsequently abandoned religion. Ford became a Catholic in his adolescence and makes Catholicism a prominent theme of his work. Ford's most famous fiction – *The Good Soldier* and the *Parade's End* tetralogy – is predicated upon a pre-First World War social order, although the latter work certainly shows it, after 1918, undergoing transformation. That social system is characterized by rigid hierarchy. The Kilsyte case is able to occur because Edward Ashburnham, who should be travelling first, is actually, owing to Leonora's economies, travelling third class. The centre of gravity is unquestionably the employing classes, indeed in *The Good Soldier* the leisured, continental spa-haunting classes. Tietjens' wife Sylvia has aristocratic connexions, albeit Valentine Wannop offers a vision of a more modern woman. Pinter's most celebrated plays, the plays which gave the word 'Pinteresque' to the language, belong by contrast to a much more proletarian world. *The Birthday Party* (1957) is set among tenants of a bottom-of-the-range seaside boarding house on the South Coast of England. *The Caretaker* (1960) goes a stage further, including in its cast the central figure of Davies, who is a homeless tramp, the very bottom of the social hierarchy, and a level to which Ford never descended in his fiction. *The Room* (1957) is set among tenants of a mysterious, sinister and absent landlord. The setting here and in some of the other early plays is surely Hackney, where Pinter grew up. Ford refers to the experience of Pinter's family in the generations before the playwright's birth in *The Soul of London*: 'A Polish Jew changes into an English Hebrew and then into a Londoner without any legislative enactments, without knowing anything about it',[1] but in Ford's fiction this East End world does not figure. Ford's politics are emphatically Tory, albeit he espoused feminism, where Pinter has been a lifelong adherent of the Left. Ford volunteered for military service in the First World War at the advanced age of 41, whereas Pinter was a conscientious objector to National Service in the 1940s and as recently as 2003 took an active part in protests against the Allied invasion of Iraq.

And yet, for all this long litany of their differences, in certain regards surprising parallels can be drawn between both authors' work, and this is nowhere better demonstrated than in Pinter's 1978 play *Betrayal*. This play, subsequently filmed, and revived in the West End four years ago, is of a quite different character from the plays of the late 1950s and early 1960s mentioned above. The working-class world of Pinter's early plays may be in some limited measure an expression of kindred spirit with contemporary plays of the so-called 'kitchen sink' school produced by Arnold Wesker and John Osborne. They are also, as betokened by the tramp in *The Caretaker*, indebted in at least as great a degree to Beckett's plays, first performed in Britain only five years before. But even from as early as 1963[2] another strand was emerging in Pinter's drama, in the one act play *The Lover*, originally broadcast on independent television. This play involves a married couple and is set in an affluent Home Counties suburb, from which the husband commutes into the City of London each day to work. They have, as far as we can tell, no children. (Perhaps – if they do exist – they are safely off the scene at a boarding school.) Each afternoon, in the husband's absence, the wife entertains her lover. With similar frequency, up in town, the husband visits a prostitute. The wife is what might be termed a 'trophy wife' – she does not seem to need to pursue a career for financial reasons – although perhaps in 1963, still twelve years before the Equal Opportunities legislation of the mid 1970s, she is a less unusual figure than she would certainly appear today. The part of the wife's lover is taken by the same actor who plays the husband, the doubling of roles serving to emphasize the calling into question of the artificial conventions alike of drama and of society beyond the stage. The play is by no means straightforward realism, for the husband reveals that he is privy to his wife's liaison, at which she bats not an eyelid, while she is fully aware that he visits his prostitute. The play is an early foretaste of a quite different genre of drama which came increasingly to make its mark in Pinter's later output. This would appear, at least on the surface, to bear uncanny parallels with the so-called well-made play and the society drawing room drama of the Inter-War period and of the 1940s (practised above all by Terence Rattigan). Indeed here Pinter's world is not so far from the employing classes of novels of Ford's such as *A Call*, *The Good Soldier* and *Parade's End*. In *The Lover*, *The Collection*, and the later *No Man's Land* and *Betrayal*, Beckett's tramps and Wesker's kitchen sink (or Osborne's *Look Back in Anger* ironing board) are nowhere to be found. Instead the setting is usually a smart, civilized drawing-room equipped with coffee table and a well-stocked cocktail cabinet. The denizens of this world are educated and socially and materially privileged. If they do not have aristocratic titles neither do they speak in the accents of Hackney and the East End where Pinter grew up in the 1930s.

Betrayal, Pinter's play first performed in 1978, is a full evening in the theatre but employs a cast scarcely larger than that of the one-act *The Lover*. Where that play was a two-hander, with the emphatic doubling of parts, *Betrayal* runs to a cast of four, although one of these is the relatively perfunctory part of a waiter in a restaurant for a solitary scene out of the nine which make up the play. The three main parts in *Betrayal* are those of Robert, aged 40 in 1977, his wife Emma, aged 38, and Robert's close friend Jerry, also 40 in 1977. Robert is a successful publisher, Emma runs an art gallery, and Jerry, a literary agent, who has known Robert since undergraduate days, was best man at their wedding. The play's nine scenes cover the period from 1968 to 1977 (a year before the play's National Theatre premiere). The social milieu of literary London might make the play seem like a hark-back to the world of Rattigan or even Coward, and the setting of one scene in Venice does nothing to counter this sense of a materially privileged world. However, where the play goes against the canons of the well-made play is rather in its theatrical technique. For the play starts in 1977 but finishes in 1968.

The summary given so far does not suggest any emphatic link with the work of Ford, and perhaps nothing further might be thought of any connexion between the two authors, were it not that Pinter has the publisher, Robert, say to Emma in Scene Five:

> He used to write to me at one time. Long letters about Ford Madox Ford. I used to write to him too, come to think of it. Long letters about ... oh, W. B. Yeats, I suppose. That was the time when we were both editors of poetry magazines. Him at Cambridge, me at Oxford. Did you know that? We were bright young men. And close friends. Well, we still are close friends. All that was long before I met you. Long before he met you. I've been trying to remember when I introduced him to you. I simply can't remember. I take it I did introduce him to you? Yes. But when? Can you remember?[3]

Why these writers should be mentioned at this juncture in the play (or indeed anywhere else in it) is far from immediately apparent. It might be considered simply plausible realistic detail, to flesh out the characters of the two men, both of whom work in the literary world. Ford and Yeats (perhaps above all Ford, as the more recherché of the two) are precisely the kinds of author it would be expected that such men might discuss. Ford was in the past and even today remains, *pace* the Ford Society's mission, a writer probably more mentioned and discussed (in the same breath as Pound, Conrad, Joyce and other canonical writers of the early twentieth century) than actually read by most of Pinter's audience.

Little has been written on the links with Pinter in the context of Ford studies, and among Pinter studies scarcely more has been made of this allusion in *Betrayal*. Most Pinter scholars prefer to concentrate on the references to Yeats, since Yeats is mentioned elsewhere in the play, and perhaps because he himself was a dramatist of significance. William Dohmen says :

> It is no coincidence that both men in *Betrayal* are fond of reading William Butler Yeats, whose belief in the wheels and gyres of history underlies his numerous poetic and dramatic portrayals of the recurrence of the past. In fact *Betrayal*'s structure invites comparison with Yeats's concept of 'Dreaming Back' e.g., as experienced by the Old Man in *Purgatory*.[4]

Anthony Roche mentions the importance of the letters which Robert and Jerry wrote to each other as undergraduates and budding literati.[5] Penelope Prentice is alone in going beyond the importance of Ford as a synecdoche for literary connoisseurship, to suggest a possible parallel with *The Good Soldier* in particular:

Robert's allusion to Ford Madox Ford, recalling *The Good Soldier* with its brilliant ambiguities, its searing yet restrained passion, and its heartbreakingly revealed betrayal, suggests one source in the play's inspiration, just as Emma's name suggests another (82). Whereas many of Pinter's earlier central women characters carry Biblical names – Ruth, Jesse, Sarah – the central woman in this play invites a Western audience's comparison with Emma Bovary, who like her nineteenth century counterparts, Anna Karenina and Tess of the D'U[r]bevilles, must pay with her life for infidelity. Pinter does not kill off his twentieth-century heroine. Although Emma may privately suffer diminished circumstances in the end she does so almost equally with the two men in her life, and all remain publicly successful.[6]

However, more can surely be said about the 'brilliant ambiguities' of *The Good Soldier* and the way they might be said to inform *Betrayal*. In the play Pinter's dramatic technique can be seen as corresponding to Ford's narrative method in *The Good Soldier*, which famously employs in the figure of Dowell an unreliable narrator. Unreliability is the very essence of *Betrayal*, and extends not only to the unreliability of communications between characters but also to the unreliability of a character's own memory of his or her own past. It is often said that *Betrayal* is technically radical because it tells its story chronologically in reverse: 'the play was technically original in its arrangement of the scenes in reverse chronological order'.[7] While this may be true overall – the opening scene takes place in 1977 and the final scene in 1968 – in fact the movement between each of the play's nine scenes is not consistently in a single direction. If it were that would make it a foreshadowing of another postmodern work, Martin Amis's novel *Time's Arrow*, of 1992, where the whole life story of the Nazi war criminal Tod is told backwards from the moment of his 'appearance' at death through to his 'disappearance' at birth. A close examination of Pinter's play, however, reveals that its action is presented in an order less consistently linear (albeit in reverse) and closer to the 'intricate tangle'[8] which Ford felt he had achieved in *The Good Soldier*. Thus the play's scenes actually go in normal chronological order, from 'Spring 1977' to 'later Spring 1977', then backwards until Scene 5 (Summer 1975) before going forwards again between Scene 5 (Summer 1973) and Scene 7 (Later Summer 1977). Between Scenes 7 and 9 the movement is again backwards, from 1977 by way of 1971 to 1968.

In another sense the action of *Betrayal* may be said to take a further cue from *The Good Soldier*. Clearly the two works share the theme of marital infidelity and betrayal, but it is not simply the act of adultery which constitutes betrayal in either case. Edward Ashburnham does indeed betray his wife in the most basic and conventional sense of the word, but Leonora also betrays Edward by throwing Nancy Rufford upon him in order perversely 'to keep him'. In *Betrayal* Jerry certainly betrays his best friend Robert by conducting a seven year affair with his wife, but she and her husband then betray Jerry by not revealing for four years that Robert now knows about the affair.

A more controversial area in which the two works may be said to share common ground involves the relationships between Robert and Jerry in the play and Dowell and Ashburnham in the novel. At least since Mizener's biography there has been a school of thought in Ford criticism which sees a (perhaps repressed) homosexual component to their friendship. 'I loved Edward Ashburnham – and [...] I love him because he was just myself' (*GS* 161).

In the play Jerry and Robert's friendship, going back to undergraduate days at Oxford and Cambridge respectively, predates Robert's marriage to Emma. (Indeed, crucially, it is perhaps because he remembers the letters Jerry used to write to him about Ford that Robert recognizes the hand in which the intercepted letter to Emma at the hotel in Venice has been addressed.) Pinter makes a great deal of the much-discussed all-male ritual of the game of squash between Jerry and Robert, from which they pointedly exclude Emma. At one point Robert tells Emma: 'I've always liked Jerry. To be honest, I've always liked him more than I've liked you. Maybe I should have had an affair with him myself'.[9]

A still more controversial area, where another parallel may perhaps be identified, concerns the issue of paternity. Saunders, in *A Dual Life*, discusses the possibility that the Ashburnhams' ward, Nancy Rufford, is in fact an illegitimate daughter whom Edward fathered by Mrs Rufford, who subsequently committed suicide. 'It is only once one realizes that the truth verges on incest that the plot doesn't seem like romantic melodrama'.[10] Thus Edward's suicide would be spurred not by mere remorse at having embarked on yet another adulterous liaison, but by the discovery that he had done so, unwittingly, with his own natural daughter. That might also be taken to explain Nancy's subsequent decline into insanity. There are, it would seem, no incestuous relationships in *Betrayal*, but the question of paternity does certainly arise.

ROBERT
How long?
EMMA
Some time.
ROBERT
Yes, but how long exactly?
EMMA
Five years.
ROBERT
Five years.
Pause
Ned is one year old.
Pause
Did you hear what I said?
EMMA
Yes. He's your son. Jerry was in America. For two months.[11]

Finally, while the bulk of these suggested parallels put forward so far are to *The Good Soldier*, it is worth stressing that the reference in Pinter's text merely mentions Ford without specifying any particular work. Although the letter in Scene Five provides the occasion for the revelation of one of the betrayals in the play, another moment of betrayal is provided in Scene Six, where Jerry recounts returning home from an assignation with Emma, giving the excuse that he had been with one of his authors, called Spinks, only to be told by his wife Judith that Spinks had just rung to ask to speak to him, thereby blowing his alibi and rousing his wife's suspicions of his infidelity. In Ford's *A Call*, Dudley Leicester is put into a compromising position by answering a telephone when it rings in his ex-fiancée's house. Moreover this work, as does Pinter's *Betrayal*, involves the suspicion of a love rivalry between a husband and his closest friend (and best man) for the same woman.

Mention of *A Call* leads to possible evidence of further parallels with Ford elsewhere in Pinter's work. In *The Collection* (1961), a play originally written for television, and subsequently staged, Pinter also strays from the down-at-heel world of *The Room*, *The Birthday Party*, and *The Caretaker* – his cast comprises successful fashion designers and the settings include drawing-rooms with chic coffee tables and cocktail cabinets. The play involves two couples – James Horne, a jealous husband in his thirties and his wife Stella, who may or may not have slept with Bill Lloyd, a man 'in his late twenties' who lives (in what looks like a homosexual ménage) with Harry Kane, a fashion

designer in his forties, evidently successful enough to own a house in
Belgravia. The accusation of adultery arises following an initial
anonymous telephone call made, as in Part II Chapter 1 of *A Call*,
during the night (*The Collection*, Scene 1). This alone would not
constitute a conclusive link; however, a number of other coincidences,
when taken together, seem striking. In an exchange between the
jealous stalker James and the suspected adulterer Bill, the latter says
'I'm expecting guests in a minute. Cocktails. I'm standing for
Parliament next season',[12] while in *A Call* Ford describes Dudley
Leicester as

> At thirty-two, with a wife whom already people regarded as likely to be the
> making of him, a model land-lord, perfectly sure of a seat in the House,
> without a characteristic of any kind or an enemy in the world, there, gentle and
> exquisitely groomed, Dudley Leicester was a morning or so after his return to
> town.[13]

Further surprising parallels come to the surface when *A Call* and *The
Collection* are read side by side. At the end of Chapter II Part 1,
Dudley Leicester's imagination leaps to dire conclusions when he
unexpectedly receives a broken necklace in a letter from his wife:

> His wife's letter frightened him; when there fell from it a bracelet, he started
> as he had never in his life started at a stumble of his horse. He imagined that it
> was a sort of symbol, a sending back of his gifts. And even when he had read
> her large sparse words, and discovered that the curb chain of the bracelet was
> broken, and Pauline desired him to take it into the jeweller's to be repaired –
> even then the momentary relief gave way to a host of other fears. For Dudley
> Leicester had entered into a world of dread. (*Call* 50)

In *The Collection* Stella 'enters from a bedroom fixing a bracelet on
her wrist'.[14] This could of course be an entirely innocent, naturalistic
detail. However Stella has just committed (or it is suggested *may* have
committed) adultery. The bracelet as a symbol for infidelity is hardly
unique to Ford. It certainly features in this capacity in 'Beyond the
Pale' in Kipling's *Plain Tales From the Hills*,[15] and it may have its
origin in Maupassant, whom of course Ford revered (*La Parure*).
However, in context, together with the other details, the sense of *déjà
vu* when watching *The Collection* is strong. A final, apparently
naturalistic detail which provides a link between Ford and Pinter is the
attention given to animals in both texts. In *A Call* abnormal
prominence is given to Peter, a dachshund.[16] His role is quite versatile

for Ford's purposes. In a novel where it is suggested that humans conceal their motives behind inscrutability (very much a foreshadowing of *The Good Soldier*, which was to come five years later) the dog provides a clear contrast. 'Between his feet Peter was uttering little bubbles of dissatisfaction whenever Sir William spoke, as if his harsh voice caused the small dog the most acute nervous tension' (*Call* 115); and earlier, 'Between his feet Peter's mouth jerked twice and a little bubble of sound escaped. He was trying to tell his master that a bad man was coming up the stairs' (*Call* 114). The dog serves, in its muteness, as an ironic parallel to Dudley Leicester, rendered dumb by his paranoid breakdown following the intercepted telephone call.

> The little dog with the flapping ears was running wide on the turf, scenting the unaccustomed grasses.
> 'Oh, Peter's as near speaking as he ever can get', Grimshaw said.
> Katya laughed. 'That would be a solution', she said, 'if you took me on as Peter's nurse. But who's your dumb child now? I suppose it's your friend . . . ah! . . . Dudley Leicester.' (*Call* 134)

This makes an interesting comparison with Pinter's use of a cat in *The Collection*. Here a white Persian kitten is associated with the heroine Stella. Apart from being something of a stock symbol of sexuality (the cat in Manet's *Olympie* comes to mind) the kitten also surely stands, as Peter does in *A Call*, for dumbness. While humans have the capacity to articulate love through speech, they can also by the same means draw a veil over infidelity in a way that animals cannot. Moreover Pinter gives further stress to the comparison of humans with animals in regard to sexual attraction by having the aggrieved husband James say to his (possibly) errant wife:

> JAMES Mmm. Only thing ... he rather implied that you had led him on. Typical masculine thing to say, of course.
>
> STELLA That's a lie.
>
> JAMES You know what men are. I reminded him that you'd resisted, and you'd hated the whole thing, but that you'd been – how can we say – somehow hypnotized by him, it happens sometimes. He agreed it can happen sometimes. He told me he'd once been hypnotized by a cat. Wouldn't go into any more details, though.[17]

In *A Call* an animal, admittedly a dog rather than a cat, is used in a similar fashion to characterize some of the human cast and the relations between them. Just as Peter the dog follows his master Dudley about with 'complete docility'(*Call* 7) and can be prevailed upon to show similar obedience towards Robert Grimshaw, so Dudley at school was Grimshaw's obedient fag:

> Dudley Leicester, who, whatever he had, had no head for business, had been Robert Grimshaw's fag at school, and had been his almost daily companion at Oxford and ever since. (*Call* 19)

And:

> 'Dudley's the best fellow in the world: I know everything he's ever done and every thought he's ever thought for the last twenty years'. (*Call* 23)

Such parallels may strike the sceptical as coincidental rather than premeditated. But they point towards a more compelling case for putting the two writers in contact. For it is perhaps in another and more famous early play by Pinter that the most striking example of speechlessness is to be found. In Act II of *The Birthday Party* (1957) the rapid-fire question and answer pseudo-interrogation which Stanley Webber undergoes at the hands of McCann and Goldberg ('Who watered the wicket at Melbourne? ... Why did the chicken cross the road?'[18]) reduces him to a state of docility and literal aphasia. (The extent to which *The Birthday Party* arguably needs to be seen as an intertextual play may be gauged when the scene where Stanley's spectacles are smashed is viewed in the light of a similar episode in William Golding's seminal novel of 1954, *The Lord of the Flies*.[19]) Unlike Stanley, who seems destined for an institution, Dudley Leicester is restored from his paranoid breakdown to normal speech, his faithful wife and a happy family in *A Call*; but could this early novella of Ford's nevertheless have furnished a formative inspiration for what was to become one of the most signal moments in post-War British theatre? Or could it be *The Good Soldier* again that might have given Pinter his cue? For in that novel, Dowell tells how Ashburnham is driven to suicide after the double-act of relentless haranguing by his wife Leonora and their ward; and then how the ward, Nancy, is reduced to a near-speechless catatonia by the news of his death. Either way, what both authors share is that sense of the possibilities of aggression and danger in language.[20]

NOTES

1   Ford, *The Soul of London*, London: Alston Rivers, 1905, p. 12.
2   In fact Michael Billington in *The Life and Work of Harold Pinter*, London: Faber, 1996, p. 96 dates the beginnings of Pinter's interest in the bourgeois earlier still, to the radio play *A Slight Ache* of 1958.
3   *Betrayal*, London: Faber, 1978, pp. 82-3.
4   William Dohmen 'Pinter Plays with Disjunctive Chronologies' in *Harold Pinter: Critical Approaches* ed. Steven H. Gale, London/ Toronto: Associated University Presses, 1986, p. 198.
5   Anthony Roche, 'Pinter and Ireland' in *The Cambridge Companion to Harold Pinter*, ed. Peter Raby, Cambridge: Cambridge University Press, 2001, pp. 175-91.
6   Penelope Prentice, *The Pinter Ethic: The Erotic Aesthetic*, New York: Garland, 1994, p. 234.
7   Michael Billington, *The Life and Work of Harold Pinter*, p. 258.
8   Ford Madox Ford, *The Good Soldier*, New York and London: Norton, 1995 – henceforth *GS*; p. 5.
9   *Betrayal*, p. 87.
10 Max Saunders *Ford Madox Ford: A Dual Life*, Oxford: Oxford University Press, 1996, vol. 1, pp. 423-4.
11 *Betrayal*, pp. 85-86.
12 Harold Pinter *The Collection* in *Plays: 2*, London: Faber, 1996, p. 119.
13 Ford, *A Call* [1910], Manchester: Carcanet, 1984 – henceforth *Call*; p. 31.
14 *The Collection* in *Plays: 2*, p. 110.
15 Rudyard Kipling 'Beyond the Pale' in *Plain Tales From the Hills* [1889], Harmondsworth: Penguin, 1987, p. 163.
16 See Sara Haslam *Fragmenting Modernism: Ford Madox Ford, the Novel and the Great War*, Manchester: Manchester University Press, 2002, pp. 74-6, where the Freudian and phallic connotations of Peter the dachshund are explored in some detail.
17 *The Collection* in *Plays 2*, p. 131.
18 Harold Pinter, *The Birthday Party* in *Plays 1*, London: Faber, 1996, p. 45.
19 William Golding, *The Lord of the Flies*, London: Faber, 1954, pp. 75-6 and 186-8. The smashing of Piggy's spectacles is central both in the process of rendering him vulnerable and in the group's descent from social norms.
20 See Sondra J. Stang, 'A Reading of *The Good Soldier*', *Modern Language Quarterly*, 30:4 (1969), 545-63 (p. 547); and Saunders, vol. 1, p. 443.

THE GHOSTLY SURFACES OF THE PAST: A COMPARISON BETWEEN FORD'S WORKS AND A. S. BYATT'S *THE VIRGIN IN THE GARDEN*

Laura Colombino

'For Ford, the past – the English past, the European past, his own past – was an integral part of present experience and understanding'.[1] So writes A. S. Byatt in her 1984 'Introduction' to *The Fifth Queen*. The statement is almost a blueprint for her vision of literature later formulated in *On Histories and Stories: Selected Essays* (2000), where she shows her concern for the recognition of recent British fiction committed to the historical genre – from Ballard's *Empire of the Sun* to Tibor Fischer's *Under the Frog*. Rejecting the view of 'recent British writing' as essentially moribund under the weight of a lively post-colonial fiction, she claims the necessity to re-centre – or at least re-balance – the canon of post-war English literature to include 'purely "British" writers' as well as those, like 'Fischer and Ishiguro', who 'can look at British life from' both 'inside and outside'.[2] Then, as in her comment on Ford, she extends this map to include the European 'tradition', which here she identifies with 'the literary tale, or fairy tale'.[3] In relation to these issues, her piece on *The Fifth Queen* also foregrounds Ford's tendency to itemise, his penchant for the detailed reconstruction of the cultural furniture of bygone centuries. In this context she suggests Ford's (and, indirectly, her own) debt to Henry James's idea, expressed in 'The Art of Fiction' (1884), that '"[r]endering" tends to be concerned with evoking surfaces, especially visual surfaces'; these, she asserts, are conveyed by Ford with 'absolute minuteness' and 'solidity of specification'.[4]

What I will argue is that Byatt's late twentieth-century interest in these qualities of Ford's writing – features with which she feels perfectly in tune – can lead to the reassessment of some seemingly outdated aspects of Ford's fiction. Ford spanned several literary generations both biographically and creatively. Was this coexistence of past and present conducive to incoherence or to rich and fruitful juxtapositions? To what extent does his practice foreshadow the

postmodern appropriation of bygone centuries? This essay will try to
answer these questions, by analysing surprising links between Ford's
practice and Byatt's aesthetics. A comparison will be particularly
instructive in this respect: that between Ford's *Parade's End*
(particularly *Some Do Not . . .*) and Byatt's *The Virgin in the Garden*
written in 1978 but set in 1952, at the time of Queen Elizabeth II's
coronation. The latter work opens Byatt's own *roman fleuve* in four
volumes, which narrates the story of a gifted and eccentric Yorkshire
family and comprises also *Still Life* (1985), *Babel Tower* (1996), and *A
Whistling Woman* (2002). What I would like to broach here is the idea
that *Parade's End* and *The Virgin in the Garden* show a similar
interest in cultural identity and tradition at times of profound historical
change – when England emerged from the First and the Second World
War respectively – and that they often find similar strategies to
reconcile the old and the new. Extending the discussion also to other
works by Ford, namely *Hans Holbein* and *Vive Le Roy*, I will
investigate two forms of Ford and Byatt's interest in cultural and
individual history: the inventory and the portrait. These epitomise the
conception of visual surfaces as ghostly markings, flimsy traces of the
plenitude of the past whose retrieval is always uncertain and whose
evocation is poised between melancholy and parody. The theme of
memory will be explored in association with the issues of creation and
trauma.

Inventories

In *Some Do Not. . .* and *The Virgin in the Garden*, concerns about
tradition lead to a problematic appropriation of the past (Victorian for
both but also Elizabethan for the latter) conceived as a disappeared
world of organic knowledge. 'For the Victorians', Byatt argues,
'everything was part of one thing: science, religion, philosophy,
economics, politics, women, fiction, poetry. They didn't
compartmentalize'.[5] It is no accident that the motif of the cataloguing
mind is so obsessively recurrent in and central to both texts: it works
as a substitute for such organicism, this being viewed as irretrievably
lost – the object of an infinite desire for, and failed attempt at, total
repossession.

For Ford the war meant the end of the self-complacent
Victorian parade of such an integral and homogenous knowledge; a
self-satisfied exhibition in which the encyclopaedic Tietjens of *Some
Do Not . . .* still indulges. Welding countless items into formidable

wholes is one of his favourite pastimes: 'chaffinch, greenfinch, yellow-ammer', chimes his encyclopedic imagination during a walk in Valentine's company, '(*not*, my dear, hammer! *ammer* from the Middle High German for "finch"), garden warbler, Dartford warbler, pied-wagtail, known as "dishwasher". (These *charming* local dialect names)' (*PE* 105) and so on and so forth. '[I]t's the way' his 'mind works', thinks Valentine. 'It picks up useless facts as silver after you've polished it picks up sulphur vapour; and tarnishes! It arranges the useless facts in obsolescent patterns and makes Toryism out of them'.[6] As Saunders contends, therefore, *Parade's End* is 'a more thorough inventory of bric-à-brac – both people's material and mental furniture – than any of [Ford's] writings since *The Fifth Queen*'.[7] It is almost superfluous to notice that, as testified by Valentine's thoughts, a note of parody rings in Christopher's taxonomic endeavours. This suggests that his cataloguing obstinacy might have been inspired by *Bouvard et Pécuchet*, Flaubert's last, unfinished novel, which, in the mid-nineteenth century, systematically mocks the inconsistencies, irrelevances, and massive foolishness of received opinions. As Ford himself reminds us in *The March of Literature*, '[i]n the attempt to demonstrate the folly of accepted ideas to an indifferent world, Bouvard and Pécuchet had taken All Knowledge for their province, and [...] pursued each department of human folly with the determination of rats clinging to the jugular vein of terriers'.[8]

Hardly less prominent, in *The Virgin in the Garden*, are the inventorying and 'mathematical'[9] powers of Marcus's mind, which can provide just as painstaking, long catalogues of the world around. At its most synthetic, when the compositional order is simultaneously disclosed, his 'gaze' is like that 'of Argos, with a thousand foveae held motionless to a thousand points on the canvas'[10] of the world:

> He had played a game called spreading himself. This began with a deliberate extension of his field of vision, until by some sleight of perception he was looking out at once from the four-field corners, the high ends of the goal-posts, the running wire top of the fence. It was not any sense of containing the things he saw. Rather he surveyed them from no vantage point, or all at once. (*VG* 30)

Marcus is endowed with eidetic faculties, that is, the ability to perceive and recall a highly detailed image of a complex scene or pattern. The most convincing documentation of this ability is a case study conducted by Charles Stromeyer in 1970 and reported in *Psychology Today*.[11] The subject was a woman called Elizabeth who could memorise two separate grids of 1000 dots randomly placed, and then mentally merge them into a 3-D image that most people needed a stereoscopic viewer and both grids to see. In *The Virgin in the Garden*, the references to grids and Marcus's 'eidetic, stereoscopic visionary eye' (*VG* 211) testify to Byatt's knowledge of these experiments. But what is surprising is that, in *No More Parades*, Tietjens too is repeatedly credited with a similar capacity for an expanded field of mental vision: '[e]laborate problems' 'went before his eyes and ears', '[t]he whole map of the embattled world ran out in front of him – as large as a field' 'a ten-acre field of *papier mâché*' (*PE* 493).

Foucault was the first to describe the construction, in the so-called 'classical age' (roughly the eighteenth century), of disciplined and disciplinary spaces. According to him, the naturalist, the physician, and the economist are dazed by immensity, stunned by plurality, in that the numberless combinations resulting from the multiplicity of objects are too heavy a burden for them to carry. Their descriptions, prescriptions, organigrams are meant precisely to organise disquieting multiplicity and thwart chaos.[12] It is no accident that for Marcus the production of perfectly arranged mathematical visions amounts to a therapeutic technique 'for avoiding thought' (*VG* 74). This sounds close to Ford longing for states of 'profound lack of thought, of profound self-forgetfulness'[13] as well as reminding us, in *It Was the Nightingale*, that the creation of Tietjens owed much to Ford's close friend Marwood and his vision of arithmetic as soothing: '[w]hen he talked of Higher Mathematics it was as if he were listening to the voice of angels. I suppose [...] he saw resurrections when he thought of recurrent patterns in numbers'.[14] Yet, the more intractable the matter is, as Foucault describes it, the more its mastering involves psychosomatic strains; which is the reason why Tietjens and Marcus are often represented as deeply suffering in their efforts of omniscience. In *No More Parades*, Christopher's mind is plagued by the'[f]ragments of scenes of fighting, voices, names' which go 'before his eyes and ears' (*PE* 492-3) and become a form of torture.

Indeed, I think, we are not wide of the mark if we say that Tietjens foreshadows the role played in some postmodern novels by harassed, traumatised psyches on the verge of derangement and whose omniscient powers provide the only connecting principle of the narrative. I am thinking, for example, of Geoff Ryman's *The Child Garden* (1989) or Michael Moorcock's *Mother London* (1988). In the latter, the narration moves between WW2 and nowadays and enacts three traumatised psyches struggling to deal with the cacophony that is the life of the city; each of them spending time in hospitals and on medication because the city voices they hear telepathically are a painful perpetual presence. History and memory are conceived here as strongly marked by the experience of the individual and collective trauma of the Blitz.

But even more interesting is the fact that, for Byatt and Ford, the issue of memory is closely and similarly related to the act of creation. After all, was not *Mnemosyne* (the goddess of Memory) the mother of all the muses in Greek mythology? She represented the mental power which preserves and arranges the phenomena of experienced time, because, as Mitchell reminds us, '[t]he pictorial aspect of poetry is not simply its imagery but the patterns of order which allow its storage and retrieval in the mind'.[15] Sigmund Freud believed that in mental life nothing which has once been formed can perish. Everything you have ever experienced is there in the subconscious. The question is not whether you can retain memory, the question is whether you can retrieve it. If you wanted to mentally process the material and data collected from the smallest details of knowledge, you should develop the functions of eidetic memory and imaginative thinking. Rare or unlikely though these mnemonic powers may be, they are precisely what Ford claims to have used when writing *Parade's End*. Recalling the genesis of his tetralogy, he finds he still knows 'every "detail"' of military practices and incredibly every single feature of the landscapes he crossed during the war: 'I went over in my mind every contour of the road from Bailleul to Locre, Locre-Pont de Nieppe, Nieppe down to Armentières – and of all the by-roads from Nieppe to Ploegsteert, Westoutre, Dranoutre. And I found I could remember with astonishing vividness every house left, in September, 1916, along with the whole road, and almost every tree – and hundreds of shell-holes!' (*IWN* 205).

The Spectrality of the Veil
In this commitment to thoroughness, Ford admits,

> my mind is cluttered up with an amazing amount of useless detail. But to me it is not useless, for without it I should feel insecure. I may – and quite frequently do – plan out every scene, sometimes even every conversation, in a novel before I sit down to write it. But unless I know the history back to the remotest times of any place of which I am going to write, I cannot begin the work. And I must know –

> from personal observation, not reading – the shapes of windows, the nature of
> door-knobs, the aspects of kitchens, the material of which dresses are made, the
> leather used in shoes, the method used in manuring fields, the nature of bus
> tickets. I shall never use any of these things in the book. But unless I know what
> sort of door-knob his fingers closed on, how shall I – satisfactorily to myself – get
> my character out of doors? (*IWN* 204)

It is not just a matter of accurate documentation. A moving note of
anxiety resonates in these words, as if the attempt to regain the very
ontology of past existences and material circumstances were at stake.
This is doubly poignant, in that it implies both mental exertion and the
unexpressed awareness, or fear, that, as the pre-Socratic philosopher
Gorgias stated, even if something were ontologically knowable, it
would be neither expressible nor communicable. Ford is precariously
suspended between two uncertainties: the possibly unattainable being
into which he is delving and the ambitious attempt of its resurrection
in the reader's inner eye.

   This reminds me of the sketch by Hogarth which Ford repro-
duces in an essay on writing techniques to explain what Impressionism is. The 'drawing', which the painter 'made […] for a bet', represented a 'watchman with the pike over his shoulder and the dog at his
heels going in at a door, the whole being executed in four lines'.[16]

> Now, that is the high-watermark of Impressionism; since, if you look at those
> lines for long enough, you will begin to see the watchman with his slouch hat, the
> handle of the pike coming well down into the cobble-stones, the knee-breeches,
> the leathern garters strapped round his stocking, and the surly expression of the
> dog, which is bull-hound with a touch of mastiff in it. (*CW* 37)

The Impressionist writer's vocation is to 'make you see'[17] the being
behind and through the scanty traces left by words on the surface of
the page or behind the fugitive touch of the character's hand on the
door-knob. These ghostly markings should work as conductors to
revivify buried histories. But if Impressionism has to do with visual
evocation, what it conjures up is ghosts, not real beings; in Byatt's
own words, referring to the characters in *The Fifth Queen*, they are
'part solid, part emotion'.[18] Indeed, the term Impressionism could be
read also in this spectral light.

   In an interview Byatt refers to her novel *Possession* as 'a kind
of palimpsest or veil. It was going to be the images on the veil […]
through which my readers would guess that the shapes of the things
that were hidden behind the markings were not the same as the

markings'.[19] Here Byatt, who has always been deeply interested in painting, might be evoking the classical tale of the competition between the two Greek painters Zeuxis and Parrhasios (which, in any case, is worth mentioning, if only because it so exemplifies my point). Initially, 'Zeuxis has the advantage of having made grapes that attracted the birds'; 'his friend Parrhasios triumphs over him for having painted on the wall a veil, a veil so lifelike that Zeuxis, turning towards him said, *Well, and now show us what you have painted behind it*'.[20] At the same time, the reference to the palimpsest identifies Byatt's surfaces – painted surfaces, make-up (the whitening on Queen Elizabeth I's face), theatrical clothes, fabrics, all of them recurrent images in *The Virgin in the Garden*) – as the surface of a Freudian *Wunderblock*, or 'mystic writing pad', which, now and then, by adherence to the matrix below, retrieves the faint traces of the mnemonic, cultural reservoir beneath. It is symptomatic of this that, for Byatt, the 'ghostliness' 'of a biography' – which constitutes its inherent 'beauty'[21] – is the fact that the huge amount of facts it painstakingly collects are but the spectral tracings of the forever irretrievable personality behind the veil. Likewise, a plausible inter-pretation of her vision of *The Fifth Queen* is that the 'solid portraits' of Henry VIII are the real thing – ontologically – 'haunt[ing]' Ford and his reader not directly but through their spectral fictional project-ion: a 'phantasmagoria of almost featureless flesh', which is 'vague' in that, precisely, 'part solid, part emotion' (*PF* 17). As in Derrida's pun, ontology turns into hauntology, the paradoxical state of the spectre between being and non-being, alive and dead, presence and absence.[22] Unlike in George Eliot's *The Lifted Veil* (1859),[23] no curtain will be drawn. The work of art, for Byatt and Ford, is the curtain itself and the *ombres chinoises* projected on it.

According to the Derrida of *Specters of Marx*, ghosts are symptoms that insist their singular tale be retold and their wrongs acknowledged; the crime they suffered is their having been dispossessed of life, substance and full meaning. This is the reason why inventories can so easily turn into the void geometric grids of Marcus's vision: deprived of its contents, the space of the inventory – where every object falls into its compartment to celebrate the fiction of the whole – is nothing more that an empty pigeon-hole case. But one should consider also how Tietjens's solipsistic inventorying builds around him what Ford had earlier called a 'house of observations', which is itself ghostly, in that it is a pale phantom of nineteenth-century treatises of natural sciences. The naturalist, according to Ford, does not examine the rabbit, the weasel or the chaffinch to understand the outer world. Rather, '[h]e is building up his little house of observations; he is filling in the chinks of the wattle-wall that shuts out for him the monotony of his life'.[24] This process is not cognitive but aesthetic: it does not fathom the depths of reality, but cuts out its images and sets them in the crevices of the grill-work, putting together its reassuring, meaningless patchwork surface. Patterns are a substitute for meaning once it has flown away. As Marcus's visions, which order reality into modern geometric forms, Ford's inventories are at the junction between old taxonomies and modernist art. In 'A Day of Battle', for example, the enumeration of instructions which assemble the soldiers on the ground turns into a fantastic, as much as vacuous, pointillist dance: 'I myself seemed to have drifted there at the bidding of indifferently written characters on small scraps of paper' such as a 'WO telegram'; 'a yellow railway warrant; a white embarkation order; a pink movement order'.[25] Abstract textures intersect the taxonomies of the material world.

Similarly, in Byatt's *The Virgin in the Garden*, the cultural interconnections between the present and the past are like patterns drawn by intertwined threads: repeated, interrupted, taken up, altered, used and reused over the centuries and through social strata:

> In London thousands of small seed pearls and crystals were being sewn into a shimmering work on the Queen's coronation dress of white slipper satin. Emblems of Commonwealth and Empire were being embroidered in coloured silks, roses and thistles, maples and acorn, on the hem of this garment.
> Felicity Wells, co-ordinating the artistic efforts in Blesford, saw herself at the spinning centre of endless threads of culture, reknit, reknotted. (*VG* 137)

The projection of historical depths and cultural stratification onto the spatial plane of the patterned textile imaginatively conjoins two apparently opposing aspirations: on the one hand the pre- and post-modernist preoccupation with realism and history, on the other hand the two-dimensionality of modern abstract and decorative art.

The Portrait's Hauntology as Parody: Ford beyond Modernism

Inventories are not the only spectral surfaces for Byatt and Ford. Portraits, clothes and (for Byatt) even make-up, conceived as theatrical masks, play a similar role. In *Hans Holbein*, for example, Ford suggests that '[i]t is a common belief and possibly a very true belief that painters in painting figures exaggerate physical and mental traits so that the sitters assume some of their own peculiarities'; so '[o]ne might argue from the eyes of Holbein's pictures that the man himself was a good-humoured sceptic' (*Holbein* 43). The portrait points to something behind it: the original perception in which the surface is luminously bathed; but also, further behind, the juxtaposing body of the painter, the purest essence of all. Artists are, in Ford's words, 'mystical doubles' (*Holbein* 8), infinitely irretrievable and desirable because disclosed to our gaze only indirectly, through the infinite mediation of their sitters' physiognomies. The more these somehow replicate the original, the more they distance him from us, '[a]s some women', suggests Byatt, 'might desire unknown actors at first, and through them Benedick or Berowne or Hamlet, and through them a dead playwright' (*VG* 430). Past and present intersect and juxtapose their uncanny symmetries. In Ford's *Vive Le Roy*, Cassie 'descended the wooden steps, going down, a queen into her kingdom... As the King of here had once descended into the streets to walk among his faithful people'.[26] In *The Virgin in the Garden*, in the enactment of *Astrea*, a play on Queen Elizabeth I, Stephanie 'saw the symmetry of the' young actress 'spread-eagled on the grass in the warm sun, and the old woman [Queen Elizabeth I] laid out in the gathered dark as the ladies-in-waiting pulled the folds of her nightgown, after her death-struggle' (*VG* 479).

Physiognomies co-present *in absentia* reverberate all the way down to us through the centuries. '[T]he "here" of presence is taken from' their successive reincarnations 'since the' subject 'is not only this one, in this place, but the others in many other places' and times.[27] In *Holbein* Ford remarks: 'you will be astounded to see how exactly' the 'sketches at Windsor' 'resemble the faces you will pass in the Windsor streets' (*Holbein* 158). Likewise, at the beginning of Byatt's novel, visitors to the National Portrait Gallery in 1968 are 'the peripatetic folk with the new ancient faces'; the young women like 'several George Sands' and 'Mesdemoiselles Sacripant, in trousers' (*VG* 8). 'Under English macintoshes, English tweed, English cashmere, American tourists edged doggedly forward' (*VG* 89). The Jamesian and Fordian theme of the Europeanised and Anglicised American, as one may find in *Daisy Miller* (1878) or *The Good Soldier*, is revived here to show that surfaces can reveal but also, above all, mask, problematising individual and national identity. Consequently, even the real thing behind becomes suspect; or else

tinted, according to a typically postmodern practice, with parody.
'Turn' Elizabeth 'out of her kingdom in her petticoats and handy-
dandy, which is the actress, which is the queen?' (*VG* 14); strip the
royal persona (its imagined sacredness working as a sort of apotheosis
of the ontology of the human being) of his sumptuous clothes: which
is *le roi*, which is Leroy? Ford's *Vive Le Roy*, written in 1936, is a
novel on a king who is present only in other people's words and,
finally, in the actor impersonating him: Walter Leroy. Art itself is
represented in the novel as ghostly: always evoked but hardly ever
physically present. With World War Two looming large on the
horizon, art is more and more the hostage of a power depicted as
variously sinister, grotesque, and farcical.

The novel is Ford's last version of the theme – haunting him
throughout his career – of the royal effigy. But here parody is setting
up a trap. The display of mistaken identities, the dressing-up of Leroy
and Cassie as king and marquise, is, at heart, playful: it undoubtedly
prompts the reader to indulge in fantasies of royalty – '"[i]f I were the
king..."' is 'the question that every man sooner or later puts to
himself' (*VLR* 11) – and participate in the game. Clothes are powerful
conductors to prompt identification with fictional characters. Consider
the scenes preceding the meeting between Cassie and Walter, where,
through ludicrous disguises, great metamorphoses seem possible to
Cassie: Leroy will be the king, she his secret lover. The crescendo of
excitement and expectation is conveyed by the ever-changing,
dreamlike scenarios through which Cassie slides, in the infinitely
procrastinated approach to the fulfilment of her desire:

> They were in front of an illuminated cavern.... The vocables TU-LU-LU
> blazed.... They were in the hall of a theatre.... In vestibules where men stood
> about.... In a corridor papered with purple damascene... In the shadows of a box
> with before it a wall of light.... Seated in gilt chairs, out in the full light; lounging
> as if they had sat there all their lives. The Sergeant Carr, got up like a
> congressman, looked very gentlemanly for a congressman.... She herself was a
> Jewish maharanee.... What have you?... Feathered nudes down below....
> Posturing voluptuously out of time with the exciting music. (*VLR* 285)

These final scenes are interspersed with the strange, slightly irritating
echo of the crowd of Paris repeatedly 'whispering' (*VLR* 292) and
'laughing' (*VLR* 287, 293). Such flashes of people 'determined to
rejoice' (*VLR* 288), while Cassie's comic drama and sexual arousal is
going on, give us the unpleasant and embarrassing feeling that,

besides her, we ourselves, who have identified with her ambitions, are being laughed at. Enticed by the game of disguises promising the transfiguration of Leroy into the king, the readers are turned from spectators into protagonists. The writer may thus unmask *their own* desire, denude them of the wish in which they are clad and leave them metaphorically naked before a whispering and laughing crowd, as in Hans Andersen's fairy tale *The Emperor's New Clothes*. '[Biala] remembered [Ford]' in his late years, 'toying with' the idea of 'a detective novel in which the murderer was the reader' (Saunders, vol. 2, 493) – a project he would never realise. Yet what Ford does manage to turn the reader into here is, more playfully, the laughed-at co-protagonist of his detective farce.

Finally, it could be said that in *Vive Le Roy* Ford draws his conclusion about the theme of the past and royalty which has possessed him throughout his literary career, deciding that the final note to strike, when dealing with history, is parody. Such an emphasis foreshadows the postmodern appropriation of bygone centuries. For Ford as for Byatt, the past is the object of both a melancholic, ghostly reconstruction and a mocking re-enactment – a poetics which makes their works both realistic and experimental. Therefore, Ford's retrieval of the past and his juxtaposition of different times should be regarded not as a shortcoming but as an imaginative resource, as well as a technique akin to today's aesthetics. Our idea that poetry can ensue from the juxtaposition of the old and the new was, indeed, also his.

NOTES

1   A. S. Byatt, 'Introduction' to Ford Madox Ford, *The Fifth Queen*, London: Penguin, 1999, p. vii. The introduction first appeared in *The Fifth Queen* published by Oxford University Press in 1984.
2   A. S. Byatt, *On Histories and Stories: Selected Essays*, London: Chatto and Windus, 2000, pp. 3-4.
3   *Ibid*, p. 4.
4   A. S. Byatt, 'Introduction', pp. viii, xiv.
5   Mira Stout, 'What Possessed A. S. Byatt? A British Novelist's Breakthrough Surprises Everyone but the British Novelist', *New York Times Magazine*, 26 May 1991, p. 14.
6   Ford Madox Ford, *Some Do Not . . .* in *Parade's End*, Manchester: Carcanet, 1997 – henceforth *PE*; p. 135.

7   Max Saunders, *Ford Madox Ford: A Dual Life*, Oxford: Oxford University Press, 1996, vol. 2, p. 154.

8   Ford, *The March of Literature*, New York: Dial Press, 1938, p. 712.

9   A. S. Byatt, *The Virgin in the Garden*, London: Vintage, 2003 – henceforth *VG*; p. 74.

10 Norman Bryson, *Vision and Painting. The Logic of the Gaze*, London: Macmillan, 1983, p. 121. A fovea is an area consisting of a small depression in the retina where vision is most acute.

11 C. F. Stromeyer, 'Eidetikers', *Psychology Today*, 4 (November 1970), 76-80.

12 See Michel Foucault, *Surveiller et punir. Naissance de la prison*, Paris: Gallimard, 1975, p. 150.

13 Ford, *Hans Holbein the Younger: a Critical Monograph*, London: Duckworth, 1905 – henceforth *Holbein;* p. 152.

14 Ford, *It Was the Nightingale*, London: Heinemann, 1934 – henceforth *IWN;* p. 203.

15 W. J. T. Mitchell, 'Spatial Form in Literature: towards a General Theory', *Critical Enquiry*, 6:3 (Spring 1980), 558-9.

16 Ford, 'On Impressionism', in *Critical Writings of Ford Madox Ford*, ed. Frank MacShane, Lincoln: University of Nebraska Press, 1964 – henceforth *CW*; pp. 36-7.

17 'My task which I am trying to achieve is, by the power of the written word, to make you hear, to make you feel – it is, before all, to make you *see*'; Joseph Conrad, 'Preface' to *The Nigger of the 'Narcissus'*; *The Nigger of the 'Narcissus'/Typhoon and Other Stories*, Harmondsworth: Penguin, 1985, p. 13.

18 A. S. Byatt, *Portraits in Fiction*, London: Vintage, 2002 – henceforth *PF;* p. 17.

19 Margaret Reynolds and Jonathan Noakes, *A. S. Byatt: The Essential Guide*, London: Vintage, 2004, p. 17.

20 Jacques Lacan, *The Four Fundamental Concepts of Psychoanalysis. The Seminar of Jacques Lacan, Book XI*, New York and London: Norton, 1998, p. 103.

21 Reynolds and Noakes, *A. S. Byatt*, p. 20.

22 See Jacques Derrida, *Specters of Marx: The State of the Debt, the Work of Mourning and the New International*, London: Routledge, 1994.

23 Byatt's interest in George Eliot is well-known. She edited and introduced Eliot's *The Mill on the Floss* (1978) and co-edited, with Nicholas Warren, *George Eliot: Selected Essays, Poems and Other Writings* (1990), both for Penguin.

24 Ford, *The Heart of the Country*, London: Alston Rivers, 1906, p. 102.

25 Ford, 'A Day of Battle', in *War Prose*, ed. Max Saunders, Manchester: Carcanet, 1999, p. 38.

26 Ford, *Vive Le Roy*, Philadelphia: Lippincott, 1936 – henceforth *VLR*; p. 33.

27 Bryson, *Vision and Painting*, p. 122.

CONTRIBUTORS

CORWIN BADEN lives in the Vail Valley of Colorado's Rocky Mountains and speaks Mandarin Chinese. After graduating from Valparaiso University in 1992, Baden served as a teacher of English as a second language in Taiwan for three years before returning to the United States to teach high school literature. He currently teaches at Vail Christian High School and is completing his master's degree in the humanities through California State University, Dominguez Hills. His thesis explores 'Ford Madox Ford's Sea-change from the Fantastic to the Modern'.

BERNARD BERGONZI is Emeritus Professor of English at the University of Warwick, where he taught from 1966 to 1992. His most recent books are *War Poets and Other Subjects* (2000), *A Victorian Wanderer: the Life of Thomas Arnold the Younger* (2003), and *A Study in Greene* (2006).

LAURA COLOMBINO is Lecturer in English Literature at the University of Genoa, Italy. She is the author of *Ford Madox Ford. Visione/visualità e scrittura* (Naples: Edizioni Scientifiche Italiane, 2003). She has published articles on Thomas Hardy, Ford Madox Ford, J. G. Ballard, Iain Sinclair, Michael Moorcock, and Geoff Ryman. She is currently working on a book about London's architecture in contemporary British fiction.

JOHN COYLE is Head of the Department of English Literature at the University of Glasgow. His interests include modernist and post-modernist literature and culture from an international perspective and, specifically, Anglophone responses to Proust. He has published on a range of writers from Ruskin to Don DeLillo. His edition of Ford's *It Was the Nightingale* is published by Carcanet.

BRIAN IBBOTSON GROTH is Associate Professor in the Department of Communication, Culture and Languages at the Norwegian School of Management BI in Oslo. Here he teaches and does research on cross-cultural communication and negotiation with special emphasis on international negotiation and negotiation pedagogy. He wrote his master's thesis for the University of Oslo on the major female characters in Ford Madox Ford's *Parade's End* tetralogy and has published some of its major findings in 'The Dagger and the Sheath' in *Modernism and the Individual Talent* (Münster, Hamburg, London: Lit Verlag, 2002). Brian Ibbotson Groth contributed an article to *Ford Madox Ford and the City* published in 2005 in the fourth volume of *International Ford Madox Ford Studies*. The article looked at Ford's contrasting views of London as shown in two essays written in 1909 and 1936.

SARA HASLAM is Lecturer in Literature at the Open University, England. She is the author of *Fragmenting Modernism: Ford Madox Ford, the Novel and the Great War* (Manchester University Press, 2002), and editor of Ford's *England and the English* (Carcanet Press, 2003), as well as *Ford Madox Ford and the City*, the fourth volume of *International Ford Madox Ford Studies* (2005). She has published articles on Ford, Henry James, and modernism, most recently '*The Good Soldier*' in the *Blackwell Companion to Modernist Literature and Culture* (2006). Current projects include a book, *Victims of Time and Train: from Victorian Invention to Modernist Novel*. With pedagogy another of her interests, she has produced an interactive CD-ROM on the poetry of Thomas Hardy.

MONICA C. LEWIS received her Ph.D. in English and American Literature and Language from Harvard University in 2006. She is the Brown/Consortium for Faculty Diversity Fellow at Sewanee: The University of the South for the academic year 2006-2007. 'Trollope Re-Read' is excerpted from her current book project, tentatively titled *Anthony Trollope Among the Moderns: Reading Aloud in Britain 1850-1960*.

SUSAN LOWNDES MARQUES is a research student at King's College London, writing a dissertation entitled '"A Passing World": The Life and Times of Marie Belloc Lowndes'. She has lectured in twentieth century English Literature at the Universidade Nova in Lisbon, Portugal and has published articles on subjects surrounding her thesis. She has also worked as a primary teacher in London.

CHRISTOPHER MACGOWAN is Professor of English at the College of William and Mary. He has edited the poetry of William Carlos Williams (New Directions and Carcanet) and the correspondence of Williams and Denise Levertov. He has also published on Williams, Levertov, Sherwood Anderson, Nabokov, and Ford. His most recent book is *Twentieth Century American Poetry* (Blackwell, 2004).

SEAMUS O'MALLEY is a doctoral student at the Graduate Center of the City University of New York (CUNY). He received his Bachelors degree from New York University and his Masters from Hunter College, New York.

WILLIAM MILL is a fiction writer who divides his life between London, Norfolk and Ghana. He traces his ancestry back to John Stuart Mill, who had no children, and is currently working on a book which combines autobiography, philosophy and fiction.

MICHAEL PARASKOS studied English Literature and Art History at the University of Leeds and gained his doctorate on Herbert Read at the University of Nottingham in 2005. As well as curating exhibitions and organising conferences, he has written widely on contemporary and historic art and appeared on radio and television. He is the editor of a collection of essays on Herbert Read entitled *Re-Reading Read: New Critical Views on Herbert Read* (London: Freedom Press, 2007) and is currently writing a book on Read's sculpture criticism. He is the Henry Moore Fellow in Sculpture Studies at the University of Leeds School of Fine Art.

JÖRG W. RADEMACHER is currently Studienrat at Gymnasium i.E. Rhauderfehn, East Frisia, teaching English, French and Italian. He is the author of biographies of Victor Hugo, Oscar Wilde and James Joyce. He has also translated biographies of Michael Collins and Hitler, and works by Diderot, Hugo, Edgar Allan Poe, Wilde, Franz Hüffer and Ford himself. He is working on the English translation of his collection of 88 short biographies (including those of Hüffer, Ford, Violet Hunt and T. S. Eliot), entitled *Gelehrtes Münster und rundum* (2005) while preparing a revised and enlarged re-issue of his biography of James Joyce. His most recent book is an English translation of a travel guide, entitled *MünsterBook* (published by Daedalus Verlag).

STEPHEN ROGERS is currently a Research Fellow at the University of Nottingham, working for the A. H. R. C. funded Modernist Magazines Project. His interests include: Little Magazines and periodical literature in Great Britain, Ireland and the U. S. A. (1880-1960), Austin Osman Spare, Ford Madox Ford, Wyndham Lewis, Laura Riding and Robert Nye. He has recently written on Spare's magazines, *Form* (1916-22) and *The Golden Hind* (1922-24), and is now writing on Frank Harris and Guido Bruno and literary magazines in Greenwich Village, New York, during the First World War. He is a bibliophile with an interest in publication history.

MAX SAUNDERS is Professor of English at King's College London, where he teaches modern English, European, and American literature. He studied at the universities of Cambridge and Harvard, and was a Research Fellow and then College Lecturer at Selwyn College, Cambridge. He is the author of *Ford Madox Ford: A Dual Life*, 2 vols. (Oxford University Press, 1996), the editor of Ford's *Selected Poems, War Prose*, and (with Richard Stang) *Critical Essays* (Carcanet, 1997, 1999, 2002), and has published essays on Ford, Forster, Eliot, Joyce, Rosamond Lehmann, Richard Aldington, May Sinclair, Lawrence, Freud, Pound, Ruskin, and others.

PAUL SKINNER edited Ford Madox Ford's *No Enemy* for Carcanet Press (2002) and has published articles on Ford, Ezra Pound and Rudyard Kipling. He lives in Bristol, where he works in publishing, has recently completed a pocket guide to *Museums of London* (Westholme Publishing, 2007) and claims to be still writing a book about Ford Madox Ford.

HELEN SMITH is a lecturer at the University of East Anglia where she teaches courses in literary modernism and life-writing. Her doctoral thesis examined the influence of Edward Garnett on early twentieth century fiction, focusing on Garnett's relationships with Joseph Conrad, D. H. Lawrence and Sean O'Faolain. She is co-editor of *Women's Voices in Post-Communist Eastern Europe* (Bucharest: Editura Universit #i din Bucure$ti, 2005). She is currently writing a biography of Edward Garnett.

HELEN SOUTHWORTH is Assistant Professor of Literature at the Robert D. Clark Honors College at the University of Oregon. She is the author of *The Intersecting Realities and Fictions of Virginia Woolf and Colette* (Ohio State UP, 2004) and co-editor of *Woolf and the Art of Exploration: Selected Papers from the Fifteenth Annual International Virginia Woolf Conference* (Clemson University Press, 2006). She has written and presented work on a range of issues in the work of Woolf and Colette, and most recently on George Borrow and on Birmingham-born author John Hampson and the Hogarth Press. Her current research and teaching focuses on literary networks and literary publishing, on modernist geographies and Englishness and on immigrant fictions.

SUSAN SWARTZLANDER is Professor of English and Faculty Fellow in the Honors College at Grand Valley State University. She has a Ph.D. in English from Penn State University. Her publications include work on Joyce, Hemingway, Faulkner, Shaw, Hawthorne, Pynchon, Norah Hoult, and May Sarton, on whom she co-edited a volume of essays, *That Great Sanity* (Ann Arbor: University of Michigan Press, 1992). Writing about Ford's mentoring of Hemingway reminds her of two influences in her own career whom she would like to acknowledge gratefully: the late Philip Young, an extraordinary Hemingway scholar and teacher, and the late Forrest H. Armstrong, a Dean of Arts and Humanities who had a passion for Ford pilgrimages and whose interview of candidates for tenure track positions always began with a query about *The Good Soldier*.

ANAT VERNITSKI has published on Russian literature (especially turn-of-the-century), cinema and religion, and on Anglo-Russian relations. She has taught at the universities of Essex and Surrey, and at University College London. Her work on Russian revolutionary exiles in London is part of an ongoing project.

JOSEPH WIESENFARTH is Professor Emeritus at the University of Wisconsin-Madison. He has written extensively on Ford and on the English novel. His book *Gothic Manners and the Classic English Novel* (Madison, Wisconsin: University of Wisconsin Press, 1989) includes a chapter on *Parade's End*. He was guest editor for the special Ford issue of *Contemporary Literature*, 30:2 (Summer 1989), and editor of *History and Representation in Ford Madox Ford's Writings* (2004), volume 3 of *International Ford Madox Ford Studies*. His most recent book is *Ford Madox Ford and the Regiment of Women: Violet Hunt, Jean Rhys, Stella Bowen, and Janice Biala* (University of Wisconsin Press, 2005).

ANGUS WRENN teaches Literature and Society at the London School of Economics (University of London), a course which focuses on twentieth-century British literature in its social and political context. His particular scholarly interests are Henry James and Ford. He has published an essay on both these writers, together with Rebecca West and H. G. Wells: 'The Mad Woman We Love', in *Ford Madox Ford and the Republic of Letters*, ed. Vita Fortunati and Elena Lamberti (Bologna: CLUEB, 2002); as well as 'Henry, Hueffer, Holbein, History and Representation', in *History and Representation in Ford Madox Ford's Writings* (2004); and 'Angle of Elevation: Social Class, Transport and Perception of the City in *The Soul of London*' in *Ford Madox Ford and the City* (2005). He has recently completed a book on Henry James and the Second Empire and the contributions on James, Paul Bourget and Proust in *The Reception of Henry James in Europe*, ed. Annick Duperray (London: Continuum, 2007).

ABSTRACTS

CORWIN BADEN 'Richard Hughes: Ford's "Secret Sharer"'

Richard Hughes and Ford have been neglected by the wider public, and their work has not been compared. Yet the two men met in 1929, and stayed in touch until Ford's death a decade later. Their contacts, including Ford's praise of Hughes' novels, are assessed. Ford and Hughes are also connected by Conrad – Ford through collaboration and Hughes by association. Hughes's *A High Wind in Jamaica* and *In Hazard* essentially pick up where *Heart of Darkness* and *Typhoon* leave off. As writers of both children's stories and adult masterpieces (as identified by compilations such as The Modern Library's '100 Best Novels' of the twentieth century), Ford and Hughes journey as kindred spirits, probing the modern psyche, expressing the human need for psychological individuation, and exploring the unconscious in the individual and society.

BERNARD BERGONZI 'Ford and Graham Greene'

Greene always admired Ford's *The Good Soldier*, and early in his career he was delighted when Ford praised his *It's a Battlefield* (1934). The two men met when Ford visited England and exchanged mutual respects. Greene inserted favourable references to Ford in his literary journalism, and wrote a measured but admiring article on him when he died in 1939. Greene acknowledged that his treatment of first-person narrative in *The End of the Affair* (1951) was influenced by *The Good Soldier*, which he frequently reread. He paid a substantial tribute to Ford by editing *The Bodley Head Ford Madox Ford,* a selection from his writings originally in four volumes (1962-63).

LAURA COLOMBINO 'The Ghostly Surfaces of the Past: A Comparison between Ford's Fiction and A. S. Byatt's *The Virgin in the Garden*'

In her Introduction to *The Fifth Queen*, Byatt praises Ford's commitment to the representation of the past 'as an integral part of present experience and understanding' as well as his evocation of visual surfaces. Byatt's interest in these qualities of Ford's writing can lead to the reassessment of some seemingly outdated aspects of his fiction. This paper analyses surprising links between Ford's practice and Byatt's postmodern aesthetics through the comparison between *Some Do Not . . .* and *The Virgin in the Garden*. Extending the discussion also to other works by Ford, the essay analyses two forms of his and Byatt's interest in cultural and individual history: the portrait and the inventory. These epitomise the conception of visual surfaces as 'ghostly markings', flimsy traces of the plenitude of the past whose retrieval is always uncertain and whose evocation is poised between melancholy and parody. Finally, the theme of (cultural) memory is explored in association with the issues of creation and trauma.

JOHN COYLE, 'Mourning and Rumour in Ford and Proust'

In *It Was the Nightingale* Ford suggests that it was the death of Proust which prompted him to write *Parade's End*, while admitting that he had not to that date read any Proust. This gives rise to a discussion of mourning and rumour as aspects of memory distinct from the Proustian involuntary, which yet play important roles in *In Search Of Lost Time* as well as in Ford's work. The reconstruction of the self preoccupies both authors, with both presenting consciousness and reputation as under siege, but while Proust insists on the redemptive powers of memory, Ford confronts the destruction of memory and of the mind itself.

BRIAN IBBOTSON GROTH 'All at Sea with Petronella: A Ford Madox Ford Biographical Mystery'

If Shakespeare has his 'Dark Lady of the Sonnets', Ford now has his 'Lady from the Sea'. In other words each poet has written about a woman whose identity remains a mystery. In Ford's case it is 'Petronella' in his poem 'To Petronella at Sea' Long thought to be either fictional or a pseudonym for Jean Rhys, it now emerges that 'Petronella' was most probably someone else. This essay presents the evidence for this new view though is unable to solve what Max

Saunders has called a 'Ford Madox Ford biographical mystery': who was 'Petronella'?

SARA HASLAM 'The Prophet and the Sceptic: George Eliot and Ford Madox Ford'

Ford did not write very often, or very much, about George Eliot. His critical reflections on her writing occur on four occasions, in 1911, 1919, 1929 and 1931. This essay contends that, despite the lack of frequency in his critical comment, Eliot had a significant influence on the way in which he thought about, and practised, writing. Discussing each of his treatments of Eliot in detail, and also placing these reactions in context, this chapter concludes with an assessment of perhaps the most significant figure determining Ford's responses to Eliot: Henry James.

MONICA C. LEWIS 'Trollope Re-Read'

Ford Madox Ford read, reviewed, and admired the novels of Anthony Trollope throughout his literary career. This piece, taken from a longer article titled 'Telling the Gentleman's Story: Anthony Trollope and Ford Madox Ford', outlines Ford's critical assessments of Trollope's approach to storytelling as evidenced in early twentieth-century essays and reviews and briefly examines revealing parallels between Trollope's *Barchester Towers* (1857) and Ford's *The Good Soldier* (1915).

SUSAN LOWNDES MARQUES 'Marie Belloc Lowndes on Ford and Violet Hunt'

Marie Belloc Lowndes (1868-1947), prolific author and sister of Hilaire Belloc, knew Ford when he was involved with Violet Hunt. Published here for the first time is an edited transcript of the four-page typescript written towards the end of her life, giving her reminiscences of Ford and Hunt, and offering intriguing glimpses of how the couple were viewed as they attempted to secure Ford's divorce and their marriage.

CHRISTOPHER MACGOWAN 'Ford Madox Ford and William Carlos Williams: The Country Squire and Dr. Carlos'

The personal and literary relationship between Ford and William Carlos Williams covers more than five decades, from 1913, their first appearance in print together, to Williams' recollections and praise of Ford's work in the years following the older writer's death in 1939. This relationship moved in Williams' case from a somewhat distant hostility towards what he saw Ford representing, to an ambivalent respect, and finally to viewing Ford as engaged in much the same battle against an oppressive English tradition that Williams himself was fighting. In Ford's case he came to see Williams as an important writer whose neglect demonstrated much that was wrong with the worlds of publishing and academe. Taking up Williams' cause, Ford in the last months of his life made an appreciative but embarrassed Williams the center of a series of literary gatherings in New York City.

SEAMUS O'MALLEY '*The Return of the Soldier* and *Parade's End*: Ford's Reworking of West's Pastoral'

This essay argues that Rebecca West's *The Return of the Soldier* heavily influenced Ford Madox Ford's *Parade's End;* and that we can read *Parade's End* as a more complex and ultimately more optimistic rewriting of West's first novel. Both novels deal with shell-shock and amnesia; both depict the inseparability of the home front from the front line; both are written in a pastoral mode; and both use the offspring of the protagonists as a way of suggesting a future for society. Ford adapted many of West's techniques but his significant reworkings speak to the heart of his novel sequence.

WILLIAM MILL 'Hueffer/Ford and Wilson/Burgess'

Anthony Burgess (1917-94) was one of Ford's staunchest admirers. His references to Ford across a variety of works are assessed. In his 1970 *Encyclopaedia Britannica* essay on the novel he places Ford as a pioneer of technical innovation in the handling of time, space and fallible narration, helping Impressionism develop into interior monologue. He also values Ford's rendering of society and the power of sexuality. Ford's appearances in Burgess' autobiographies and novels tend towards the comedic, the comedy coming from plays upon Ford's change of names. This is related not only to Burgess' own use of pseudonyms, but to both men's sense of the fiction writer's existence between autobiography and fiction. The essay concludes with a discussion of *Earthly Powers*, a fictional autobiography narrated by a popular writer of Ford's era, sharing many of his contacts, and in which Ford himself appears as a character.

MICHAEL PARASKOS 'Herbert Read's Dilemma: Fatherly Advice from FMF'

For a brief period between 1918 and 1922 Ford Madox Ford and Herbert Read became good friends, with the latter often turning to Ford for advice on the writing of his planned novels. In some respects Ford operated as a surrogate father figure for Read, whose own father had died when Read was a child. Read's relationship with Ford appears to have been at its height in 1920 when Read was in a dilemma over whether to abandon novel writing or abandon his safe job in the British civil service. Ford's advice was to keep doing both, something that Read knew was impossible. Yet, if Ford had an enduring influence on Read it was his precisely in this advice to stay in the civil service, something that resulted in Read transferring to the government museums service and becoming ultimately one of the twentieth century's foremost writers on art and design.

JÖRG W. RADEMACHER 'Images of the First World War: Ford's "In October 1914" Read in the Context of Contemporary German Writers'

Reciting Ford Madox Ford's war poem 'In October 1914' in Münster/Westphalia in 2004 and 2006, helped shape the idea behind this essay which is to read Ford's seminal text through poetry and prose produced by some of his German contemporaries. For war writings by Hermann Löns, August Stramm, and Clara Ratzka read today as if they had been comparing notes with Ford Madox Ford, though there is no evidence for any contacts.

Ford, like Ratzka, survived the First World War, while Löns and Stramm were killed on the Western and Eastern Fronts respectively. While Ratzka sought to see German society as a whole, using a deceptively simple style of writing, her vision converges with Ford's in terms of foresight, whereas Löns and Stramm in their last months share the point of view Ford puts forward both from afar in 'In

October 1914' and in the *Parade's End* tetralogy based upon his own experience.

STEPHEN ROGERS '"A Royal Personage in Disguise": A Meeting between Ford and John Cowper Powys'

Ford Madox Ford and John Cowper Powys, who were of the same generation, and have both been treated more sympathetically in the U. S. A. than in their own country, actually met in New York City. This essay details the account of the brief meeting, as recorded by Powys, and contrasts their attitudes to literature, seeing their responses to Walt Whitman as a significant indication of such differences. It goes on to suggest that changing cultural paradigms were responsible for a shift in aesthetic strategies in novel writing during the 1930s, and this is related to the authors' careers. Ford's uneasy place alongside his contemporaries is noted, and the importance of integrating dominant accounts of modernism with more marginal figures (though not necessarily of lesser intrinsic importance) from the period is stressed.

MAX SAUNDERS 'Ford and Turgenev'

An early Ford manuscript fragment, 'Books for Exchange: II', is published here for the first time, and taken as a starting point for a consideration of Ford's evolving views of Turgenev, and for thinking about what 'literary contact' involved for him – not only his intimacy with other writers and their work, but friendships based on shared reading. The role of Turgenev as a talisman representing a supreme artistry is charted through Ford's criticism, in which the initial emphasis on the 'poetic' aspect of Turgenev's prose is supplemented by an admiration for him as exemplary novelist. Turgenev also increasingly preoccupies Ford as a test-case of his commitment to critical self-consciousness, as a writer whose pre-eminent technique he finds himself paradoxically unable to codify. Ford's way through this critical perplexity is to take Turgenev as exemplary of a series of further paradoxes embodying his Impressionist aesthetics: Turgenev's technical self-consciousness is founded on an empathetic selflessness, which in turn enables self-expression for the writer, self-discovery for the reader, and an effect of suspending the boundaries between the minds literature brings into contact.

HELEN SMITH 'Opposing Orbits: Ford, Edward Garnett and the Battle for Conrad'

This essay discusses the complex and ultimately troubled relationship between Ford and Edward Garnett, the publisher's reader, editor and critic, whom Ford had known since the days of his youth. Their initially close friendship deteriorated over time and the essay argues that many of the reasons for this can be discovered if a third figure is added to the picture – that of Joseph Conrad. Examining their relationship through Conrad highlights the aesthetic differences that existed between Garnett and Ford alongside the personal rivalries. Whilst Ford repeatedly emphasises the importance of French writing to Conrad, Garnett is determined to present the ex-mariner as a 'Slavic' writer in the line of the great Russians whose works Garnett tirelessly promoted. Their battle becomes particularly heated after Conrad's death as both men attempt to cast him according to their own aesthetic ideals and make their claims to lasting influence, not only over Conrad but in the wider world of the Republic of Letters.

HELEN SOUTHWORTH '"That Subtle and Difficult Thing: A National Spirit": Ford, Anglo-Saxondom and "the Gorgeously English" George Borrow'

Ford's references to the now largely overlooked Victorian British travel writer George Borrow (1803-1881), author of *Lavengro* and *The Bible in Spain,* whose work he devoured as a boy, are numerous. They include the Borrow-inspired poems, 'The Cuckoo and the Gipsy' and 'The Gipsy and the Townsman', mentions of Borrow in *Cinque Ports* and *Thus to Revisit*, echoes of Borrow in *England and the English* and a quite lengthy review of Clement Shorter's *George Borrow and his Circle*. In this essay, Ford is linked to Borrow in terms of Englishness and cosmopolitanism, both in a general sense and in terms of writing. Ford's Borrovian allusions are used to suggest that the idiosyncratic ideas about the mixedness of the English and about the landscape and inhabitants of the British Isles, as well as the unconventional literary style, of his eccentric predecessor, helped shape Ford's conception of 'Anglo-Saxondom' and his understanding of the relationship between the countryside and the city.

SUSAN SWARTZLANDER "'Thus to Revisit or Thus to Revise-It":
Ernest Hemingway, Defiant Disciple'

Ernest Hemingway arrived in Paris in 1924 eager to launch his literary
career and excited about working for Ford Madox Ford on *the
transatlantic review*. In short order, the literary disciple became a
detractor. Yet, in those early Paris years, Ford permeated
Hemingway's fiction. This essay details the ways in which
Hemingway worked quite deliberately to revisit and revise Ford's own
texts, playing on Ford's titles, repudiating Ford's idols, and writing
The Sun Also Rises as a challenge to Ford's poem 'Antwerp', which
asks about the Belgians in the Great War, 'Can any man so love his
land?' As Hemingway works out his own method 'to do the country',
in a way that does not romanticize the land, he parodies Ford's image
of himself as a country gentleman, countering with his own Jake
Barnes.

ANAT VERNITSKI 'The Complexity of Truth: Ford and the
Russians'

Ford had a long-standing association with Russian revolutionary
exiles, especially with David Soskice, who eventually became his
brother-in-law and collaborator in the *English Review*. Russian
revolutionary exiles were closely linked to the Rossettis and Garnetts;
Ford met a number of these revolutionaries and wrote about his
impressions. This essay looks at the role of Russians in Ford's life. It
also analyses the Russian references in Ford's writing, especially in
his memoirs and in the novel *The New Humpty-Dumpty*.

JOSEPH WIESENFARTH 'The Genius and the Donkey: The
Brothers Hueffer at Home and Abroad'

Ford's father called him a donkey and his grandfather called his
brother Oliver a genius. Both wrote books on England, France, and
New York. Ford's are still read along with his novels. Oliver's are not,
nor are his novels. They are accounts of his travels and of the people
he met in the places he visited. Ford's books were about 'Pure
Thought and the Arts' and how they fared in the places he wrote
about. Pure thought and the arts made cities like London, Paris, and
New York great because they established a culture and enabled a

civilized life to be lived there. And they were, unmistakably, the product of 'work', the 'original curse of mankind' and its 'original medicine'. Once 'we drop work our minds decay, our bodies atrophy, and it is all over with us in this world'. Oliver, unlike Ford, depended on his genius rather than work and produced ephemeral writing. Ford's embracing of work wholeheartedly made his books endure; indeed, made some of them classics.

ANGUS WRENN 'Long Letters about Ford Madox Ford'

Ford and Harold Pinter are not authors normally bracketed together, Ford belonging to the end of the nineteenth and early twentieth centuries, while Pinter, first performed in the 1950s, was still writing in the twenty-first. However, despite differences in terms of historical and class background, there are a number of remarkable affinities between certain of the two authors' works. Many illuminating parallels emerge between Ford's *A Call* and Pinter's *The Collection* and the *Birthday Party*, while in a play from the 1970s, *Betrayal*, Pinter alludes to Ford by name, signalling numerous points of comparison between the 'intricate tangle' which Ford sought to achieve in the plot of *The Good Soldier* and the radical reverse chronology of his own play.

ABBREVIATIONS

The following abbreviations have been used for works cited several times, whether in the text or in the notes. The list is divided into two alphabetical sections: works by Ford and by others. A full list of abbreviations to be used in future volumes can be found on the Ford Society website.

(i) Works by Ford

In most cases publication details given here are of first editions only. Contributors referring to a different edition have specified which one in the first endnote citing it.

AL	*Ancient Lights* (London: Chapman & Hall, 1911); published as *Memories and Impressions* (New York: Harper, 1911), see *MI*
CA	*The Critical Attitude* (London: Duckworth, 1911)
Call	*A Call* (London: Chatto & Windus, 1910)
CE	*Critical Essays*, ed. Max Saunders and Richard Stang (Manchester: Carcanet Press, 2002)
CP	*The Cinque Ports* (Edinburgh and London: William Blackwood and Sons, 1900)
CP1	*Collected Poems* (London: Max Goschen, 1913)
CP2	*Collected Poems* (New York: Oxford University Press, 1936 [published only in USA])
CW	*Critical Writings of Ford Madox Ford*, ed. Frank Mac-Shane (Lincoln: University of Nebraska Press, 1964)

EE   *England and the English* – collecting Ford's trilogy on Englishness, comprising: *Soul of London* (London: Alston Rivers, 1905); *The Heart of the Country* (Alston Rivers, 1906); and *The Spirit of the People* (London: Alston Rivers, 1907) – (New York: McClure, 1907); new edition, ed. Sara Haslam (Manchester: Carcanet, 2003)

EN   *The English Novel* (Philadelphia: J. B. Lippincott, 1929; London: Constable, 1930)

GS   *The Good Soldier* (London: John Lane, 1915); Oxford World's Classics edition, ed. Thomas C. Moser (Oxford: OUP, 1990); Norton Critical edition, ed. Martin Stannard (New York and London: Norton, 1995)

Holbein   *Hans Holbein* (London: Duckworth, 1905; New York: Dutton, 1905)

IWN   *It Was the Nightingale* (Philadelphia: J. B. Lippincott, 1933; London: William Heinemann, 1934)

JC   *Joseph Conrad* (London: Duckworth, 1924; Boston: Little, Brown, 1924)

LF   *Letters of Ford Madox Ford*, ed. Richard M. Ludwig (Princeton, NJ: Princeton University Press, 1965)

MF   *A Mirror to France* (London: Duckworth, 1926)

MI   *Memories and Impressions* (New York: Harper, 1911); US edition of *Ancient Lights* (London: Chapman & Hall, 1911)

ML   *The March of Literature* (New York: Dial Press, 1938; London: Allen & Unwin, 1939)

Mr. Clement Shorter   Ford, 'Literary Portraits – X.: Mr. Clement Shorter and "Borrow and His Circle"', *Outlook* (London) 32 (November 1913), 677-8

MS   *Mightier Than the Sword* (London: George Allen & Unwin, 1938 [first published as *Portraits from Life* [Boston: Houghton Mifflin, 1937]) – see *PL*

NE   *No Enemy* (New York: Macaulay, 1929) [written 1919, published only in USA in Ford's lifetime]; ed. Paul Skinner (Manchester: Carcanet, 2002)

NHD   *The New Humpty–Dumpty* [pseud. 'Daniel Chaucer'] (London and New York: John Lane, 1912)

NYE   *New York Essays* (New York: William Edwin Rudge, 1927)

NYNA   *New York is Not America* (London: Duckworth, 1927)

PE   *Parade's End* (one volume edition of all the Tietjens novels: *Some Do Not. . ., No More Parades, A Man Could Stand Up –,* and *Last Post*) (New York: Alfred A. Knopf, 1950); the same pagination is used by later Vintage, Penguin and Carcanet editions

PL   *Portraits from Life* (Boston: Houghton Mifflin, 1937; published in UK as *Mightier Than the Sword*, London: George Allen & Unwin, 1938)

RY   *Return to Yesterday* (London: Victor Gollancz, 1931)

Selected Poems   *Selected Poems,* ed. Max Saunders (Manchester: Carcanet, 1997)

SL   *The Soul of London* (London: Alston Rivers, 1905)

SLL   *The Simple Life Limited* [pseudonym: 'Daniel Chaucer'] (London: John Lane, 1911)

TR   *Thus to Revisit* (London: Chapman & Hall, 1921)

VLR   *Vive Le Roy* (Philadelphia: Lippincott, 1936; London: George Allen and Unwin, 1937)

WBTA   *When Blood is Their Argument* (New York & London: Hodder & Stoughton, 1915)

(ii) Works by Others

ABM   *Anthony Burgess and Modernity*, ed. Alan Roughley (Manchester: Manchester University Press, forthcoming, 2007)

Angier   Carole Angier, *Jean Rhys* (London: Penguin Books Ltd., 1992)

Annals   Herbert Read, A*nnals of Innocence and Experience* (London: Faber, 1940)

Ashton   Rosemary Ashton, *George Eliot: A Life* (London: Penguin, 1997)

Auto.   William Carlos Williams, *The Autobiography of William Carlos Williams* (New York: Random House, 1951)

Autobiography   John Cowper Powys, *Autobiography* [1934] (London: Macdonald, 1967)

Carroll   David Carroll, ed., *George Eliot: The Critical Heritage* (London: Routledge & Kegan Paul, 1971)

Collie   Michael Collie, *George Borrow: Eccentric* (Cambridge: Cambridge University Press, 1982)

CPW1   *The Collected Poems of William Carlos Williams: Volume I, 1909-1939* (New York: New Directions, 1986)

CPW2   *The Collected Poems of William Carlos Williams: Volume II, 1939-1962 (*New York: New Directions, 1988)

Dupke   Thomas Dupke, *Hermann Löns. Mythos und Wirklichkeit* (Hildesheim: Claassen, 1994)

EP   Anthony Burgess, *Earthly Powers* (Harmondsworth: Penguin, 1981)

FF   Oliver Madox Hueffer, *French France* (New York: D. Appleton, 1929)

GE   David Garnett, *The Golden Echo* (London: Chatto & Windus, 1953)

Goldring   Douglas Goldring, *Trained for Genius: The Life and Writings of Ford Madox Ford* (New York: E. P. Dutton, 1949)

Haight   Gordon S. Haight, ed. *A Century of George Eliot Criticism* (London: Methuen & Co., 1966)

Hollingsworth   Barry Hollingsworth, 'David Soskice in Russia in 1917', *European Studies Review* 6 (1976), 73 – 97

HSL   *Ernest Hemingway: Selected Letters, 1917-1961*, ed. Carlos Baker (New York: Charles Scribner's Sons, 1981)

IH   Richard Hughes, *In Hazard*, TIME Reading Program special edition (New York: Harper & Row, 1938; reprinted New York: TIME, 1966)

Imag.   William Carlos Williams, *Imaginations* (New York: New Directions, 1970)

Kenner   Hugh Kenner, 'The Poetics of Speech' in Richard Cassell, editor, *Ford Madox Ford: Modern Judgements* (London and Basingstoke: Macmillan, 1972)

LWBG   Anthony Burgess, *Little Wilson and Big God* (London: Heinemann, 1987)

Parrinder   Patrick Parrinder, "'All that is Solid Melts into Air": Ford and the Spirit of Edwardian England' in *History and Representation in Ford Madox Ford's Writing*, ed. Joseph Wiesenfarth (Amsterdam and London: Rodopi, 2004)

PF   A. S. Byatt, *Portraits in Fiction* (London: Vintage, 2002)

Presence   *The Presence of Ford Madox Ford*, ed. Sondra J. Stang (Philadelphia: University of Pennsylvania Press, 1981)

Rhys   Jean Rhys, *The Collected Short Stories* (New York : W. W. Norton & Company, 1987)

ROTS   Rebecca West, *The Return of the Soldier* (New York: Penguin, 1998)

SAR   Ernest Hemingway, *The Sun Also Rises* (New York: Scribner's Sons, 1926)

Saunders   Max Saunders, *Ford Madox Ford: A Dual Life*, 2 volumes (Oxford: Oxford University Press, 1996)

SE   Oliver Madox Hueffer, *Some of the English: A Study towards a Study* (New York: D. Appleton, 1930)

Sketches   Ivan Turgenev, *Sketches from a Hunter's Album*, trans. and ed., Richard Freeborn (Harmondsworth: Penguin, 1985)

Soskice   Juliet Soskice, *Chapters from Childhood: Reminiscences of an Artist's Granddaughter* (London: Turtle Point Press, 1994)

Stramm I   August Stramm, *Gedichte, Dramen, Prosa, Briefe*, ed. Jörg Drews (Stuttgart: Reclam, 1997)

Stramm II   August Stramm, *Dramen und Gedichte*, selection and afterword by René Radrizzani (Stuttgart: Reclam, 1979)

VG   A. S. Byatt, *The Virgin in the Garden* (London: Vintage, 2003)

VNY   Oliver Madox Hueffer, *A Vagabond in New York* (London: John Lane The Bodley Head, 1913)

Other volumes in the series:

THE
FORD
MADOX
FORD
SOCIETY

Ford c. 1915   ©Alfred Cohen, 2000   Registered Charity No. 1084040

This international society was founded in 1997 to promote knowledge of and interest in Ford. Honorary Members include Julian Barnes, A. S. Byatt, Hans-Magnus Enzensberger, Samuel Hynes, Alan Judd, Sir Frank Kermode, Ruth Rendell, Michael Schmidt, John Sutherland, and Gore Vidal. There are currently over one hundred members altogether, from more than ten countries. The Society continues to organize an active programme of events. Besides regular meetings in Britain, we have held conferences in Italy, Germany, and the U.S.A. Since 2002 we have published this annual series, International Ford Madox Ford Studies, distributed free to members. *Ford Madox Ford: A Reappraisal* (2002), *Ford Madox Ford's Modernity* (2003), *History and Representation in Ford Madox Ford's Writings* (2004), *Ford Madox Ford and the City* (2005), and *Ford Madox Ford and Englishness* (2006) are all still available. Future issues are planned on Ford's involvements with cultural transformations and literary networks; and on Ford as an editor. If you are an admirer, an enthusiast, a reader, a scholar, or a student of anything Fordian, then this Society wants to hear from you, and welcomes your participation in its activities.

The Society normally organises events and publishes Newsletters each year. A celebratory day on 'Ford Madox Ford: Writing and Painting', was staged in 1998. In 1999 we participated in two conferences: one on Ford and Modernism held in Germany; the other in Kent on Ford, Conrad and James. For 1999-2000 we held a day conference in London on 'Ford and the City' and a Ford panel at the 2000 MLA convention in Washington. There were sizeable conferences at the Universities of Bologna in 2001 and Madison-Wisconsin in 2002. December 2004 saw a conference in Manchester on 'Ford and Englishness'. Future meetings are planned in Birmingham, Genoa, and Turku, Finland. The Society has also inaugurated a series of Ford Lectures, which have been given by Martin Stannard, Alan Judd, David Crane, Sergio Perosa, Oliver Soskice, Nicholas Delbanco, and Zinovy Zinik. To join, please see the website for details; or send your name and address (including an e-mail address if possible), and a cheque made payable to 'The Ford Madox Ford Society', to: Sara Haslam, Dept of Literature, Open University, Walton Hall, Milton Keynes, MK7 6AA.

Annual rates: **Sterling:** Individuals: £12 (by standing order); Concessions £6; Member Organisations £17.50
             US Dollars: Any category: $25

For further information, either contact Sara Haslam (Treasurer) at the above address, or Max Saunders (Chairman) by e-mail at: max.saunders@kcl.ac.uk
The Society's Website is at: **www.rialto.com/fordmadoxford_society**